The Principles of
Practical
Cost-benefit
Analysis

ROBERT SUGDEN

AND

ALAN WILLIAMS

OXFORD UNIVERSITY PRESS

Oxford University Press, Walton Street, Oxford OX2 6DP

OXFORD LONDON GLASGOW NEW YORK
TORONTO MELBOURNE WELLINGTON CAPE TOWN
NAIROBI DAR ES SALAAM KUALA LUMPUR
SINGAPORE JAKARTA HONG KONG TOKYO
DELHI BOMBAY CALCUTTA MADRAS KARACHI

First published 1978
Reprinted 1979

British Library Cataloguing in Publication Data

Sugden, Robert
    The principles of practical cost-benefit analysis.
    1. Cost effectiveness
    I. Title   II. Williams, Alan, b.1927
    339.4'1   HD47   77-30571

    ISBN 0-19-877040-5
    ISBN 0-19-877041-3 Pbk

Typeset by Hope Services, Wantage
Printed in Great Britain
by J.W. Arrowsmith Ltd., Bristol

Preface

Some explanation is perhaps required of authors who offer to the public 'another book on cost-benefit analysis'.

The distinguishing features of this book are implicit in its somewhat paradoxical title. Our aim is to offer a basic understanding of the *practice* of cost-benefit analysis. By this we do not mean that we have written a book of rules for decision-making; since the precise set of issues raised by any two decisions are seldom the same, any such exhaustive cook-book would inevitably be both extremely cumbersome and intellectually unsatisfactory. Nor are we presenting a description of the institutional framework within which public decisions are taken. Cost-benefit analysis is a way of organizing thought, a way of reasoning about decision-making. The structure of a book on the subject must be grounded in the logic of rational choice. But the cost-benefit analyst needs more than a firm grasp of a relatively few basic and extremely fruitful economic principles. He or she also needs the ability to apply these principles creatively to tackle practical problems. It is for this reason that we make constant use of illustrative examples and offer the reader a large number of problems to work through. Believing that a working understanding of cost-benefit analysis can be gained without venturing very far into the intricacies of theoretical welfare economics, we have resisted the temptation to explore the intellectual attractions of this territory. We believe that by limiting ourselves to the discussion of those economic principles that are directly relevant to the practice of cost-benefit analysis we have written a book that is accessible to people without formal training in economics, but with a working interest in the subject.

This book is composed of five interwoven strands:

1. *The central text* This forms the core of the book (and is set in larger type than the rest). This core provides a self-contained exposition of the fundamental principles of cost-benefit analysis. The simpler and more familiar concepts of financial appraisal are used as a starting-point; from this beginning the additional problems of cost-benefit analysis are introduced progressively. Although the level of difficulty increases as the book progresses, at no point do we use any but the most elementary mathematics nor do we assume familiarity with economic theory. Wherever possible, examples are used to aid the exposition. Particular attention is given to those issues that are of

central importance to practical cost-benefit analysis; the use of shadow prices, the use of consumers' surplus measurements, and the problems of valuing goods that do not have market prices, all receive extensive treatment. In contrast we avoid protracted discussion of the finer points of theoretical welfare economics when these do not have immediate practical relevance. We also have little to say about the problems of finding and interpreting the statistical data on which any cost-benefit analysis must rest. Our emphasis is on the process of economic reasoning that lies at the heart of a cost-benefit analysis.

2. *Examples* Interspersed among sections of the central text are sections devoted to the discussion of particular applications of the basic principles of financial appraisal and cost-benefit analysis. These examples illustrate some of the ways in which theory can be put into practice.

3. *Problems* At the end of many of the chapters are problems for the reader to tackle for himself or herself. These problems require the application of the principles expounded in the preceding chapters. Typically, something more is called for than mechanical manipulation of numbers according to closely defined 'rules'; some degree of creative thinking is necessary too. (It should perhaps be said of both the problems and the examples that, where numerical information is given, this is designed so that the conceptual issues being illustrated emerge as clearly as possible. Consequently this 'information' should not be taken to be more than, at most, a highly stylized representation of reality; it is the *issues* raised that are realistic.) Suggested solutions to the problems are given in Appendix 2 at the end of the book. The reader is advised to read the 'Notes on the Problems' in that appendix before tackling the problems.

4. *Appendices to chapters* The exposition in the central text is designed to be accessible to those without a formal training in economics. This means that it is not possible to relate very explicitly the principles of cost-benefit analysis to the more general principles of economics from which they derive. To fill this gap we have included a number of more 'technical' appendices. These do not introduce important additional principles, but rather give a more formal and general treatment of ideas already expounded informally. We believe that these will be useful to economics-trained readers, but other readers will lose little of practical significance by omitting them.

5. *Guides to further reading* At the end of each chapter (except the first) is a brief guide to further reading. References are made both to practical applications of the principles discussed in the

chapter and to technical literature dealing with particular points of theory in more detail. The former references should be of interest to all readers; the latter, for the most part, are likely to prove impenetrable for the non-economist.

Acknowledgements

I should like to take this opportunity to acknowledge my great debts to all those who have been my teachers, from my school-days onwards. I owe a special debt of this kind to my co-author Alan Williams, since it was he who, when I was one of his under-graduate students, first aroused and encouraged my interest in cost-benefit analysis. I should like also to thank all those colleagues and students at York, other friends and my family, in arguments with whom many of the ideas which appear in this book were developed.

Particular thanks are due to Gordon DeWolf, David Henderson and Charles Normand, each of whom read through complete drafts of this book and suggested improvements, and to Rita Harrison for her typing.

Robert Sugden

This book arose out of an idea which I discussed several times with Robert Sugden, and which he was happy to take up, develop, and put into effect in a lucid, rigorous and dedicated manner which I cannot fail to admire. He used me as a sounding board as the work grew, and reacted sensitively and responsively when my points seemed to him sensible, and charitably ignored the others. He therefore considers that I should be regarded as the joint author of the book, even though he has written it.

Alan Williams

Contents

Part I: The Framework

1. The Framework

1.1. Project appraisal

This book is about the appraisal of projects. A *project*, broadly defined, is a way of using resources; a decision between undertaking and not undertaking a project is a choice between alternative ways of using resources. *Project appraisal* is a process of investigation and reasoning designed to assist a decision-maker to reach an informed and rational choice.

In this book we shall be concerned mainly with *public* choices. That is, we shall be concerned with choices that are made within organizations that are expected to act in the public interest. Such organizations we shall call *public agencies* or sometimes simply *the government*. Any person or group that is entrusted with a choice about the activities of a public agency will, for simplicity in exposition, be called *the decision-maker*. This noun is singular (and male) only for convenience; it is to be read as including the possibility that choices may be made by groups of individuals acting collectively in committees.

In the course of this book we shall discuss a wide range of choice problems of the kinds typically faced by public decision-makers. Where should a new hospital be located? Should a branch-line railway service be closed? Should more places be provided for workers to be retrained at the taxpayers' expense? And so on. The choices that we shall discuss are all, to a lesser or greater extent, complex. Even if the decision-maker is completely clear in his own mind about the ends that he should pursue—that is, he has an explicit *objective*—and even if he is well-informed about the courses of action between which he is to choose, it is assumed that it is still not immediately obvious which course of action he should select. Only by a process of reasoning can he work out which option is most consistent with his objective. It is this process of reasoning that forms the main subject-matter of this book.

We shall find it convenient to talk as if the act of taking a decision has been separated from the the task of reasoning which course of action is most consistent with the decision-maker's objective. We shall talk as if the latter task has been assigned to someone called *the analyst*. We shall adopt the convention of making the analyst singular and male and a different person from the decision-maker. The analayst's role is that of 'technical' or 'professional' adviser to the decision-maker. This book will be primarily concerned with the role

of the analyst. But it should always be remembered that this stylization of the roles of decision-maker and analyst is a matter of convenience in exposition, and nothing more. The task of advising a public
decision-maker might in practice be given to a group of people rather
than to a single individual. Or the decision-maker might not call for
advice at all, but reason through a problem for himself—in which case
he would be acting as his own analyst. Or someone with the technical
skills of our analyst might be asked to take on some of the functions
of the decision-maker—for example, by making a recommendation
based on his own judgements of what objective his agency ought to
pursue. Finally, it should be said that the analyst need not be a full-
time professional economist; an engineer, for example, might simultaneously give advice both on the feasibility of a project and on its
consistency with the decision-maker's objectives. Much more could be
said about the relationships between the roles of decision-maker and
analyst, but at this stage it would be premature. We shall return to
this subject in Chapter 16 when some of these relationships will be
discussed further.

Although interesting and relevant, it is not our purpose to *describe*
the organizational structures within which public decisions are taken.
We address ourselves instead to the intellectual and analytical dimension of choice. The analytical problems of choosing from a set of
alternatives by reference to a stated objective are in many important
ways independent of the institution within which the chooser works.
The problems that we shall pass on to our analyst are problems that
must be faced, in some way or another, by some person or other,
whenever complex public decisions have to be taken.

1.2. Objectives

The starting-point for project appraisal must be a statement of the
objective that is being pursued by the decision-maker. Rational
choice is impossible unless the chooser knows what he is trying to
achieve. This objective must be formulated in a way that is specific
enough to allow it to be used as the basis of analysis. That is, the task
of identifying which of the set of alternative courses of action is
most consistent with the objective should, as far as possible, be a
purely technical problem. To take an example, a public agency might
claim that its objective was to pursue the public interest. But this
does not advance matters very far, for there are many conflicting
ways of interpreting 'the public interest' and beyond testing them for
internal consistency no amount of analysis can show which of these
rival interpretations ought to be preferred.

In some cases public decision-makers are given little discretion to
set their agencies' objectives; the ends that they are to pursue are

clearly laid down, and the problem of selecting an objective for project appraisal is quite simple. In other instances, agencies are only given as guidance rather imprecise forms of words—such as 'public interest'. Then the decision-maker has to choose how to interpret his instructions. In this book we shall consider a range of alternative objectives that a decision-maker might choose, or to be instructed, to pursue.

We shall begin (in Part II) by considering the most straightforward case, that of a financial objective. A financial objective is one that is formulated solely in terms of entities in an agency's financial accounts. This type of objective is familiar in the context of the privately owned corporate firm, where the firm's managers are paid to pursue the interests of its owners, the shareholders. Managers are expected to seek to maximize the flow of money income received over time by shareholders from the firm. (An alternative formulation is that the total value of the shares—that is, the shareholders' wealth invested in the firm—should be maximized.)

There are many circumstances in which public agencies are expected to behave according to 'business' or 'commercial' principles —that is, to model their behaviour on that of private firms. The model of the private firm is applicable to public agencies only in relation to certain restricted types of decision; and the extent to which the model is applicable varies greatly between agencies. At one end of the spectrum are publicly owned corporations, like the British nationalized industries, which produce goods and services for sale. Such corporations have many similarities to privately owned firms. Although typically they are subject to various constraints imposed by the government in the public interest, they are generally expected to use commercial criteria for a wide range of decisions. At the other end of the spectrum are those agencies, such as police forces, which produce services that cannot be sold to consumers. Decisions about the level of provision of such services are necessarily taken on criteria other than the narrowly financial. But even such agencies as police forces take some decisions for which financial appraisal would be considered normal. A police force, for example, might have to choose between alternative methods of construction for its headquarters. Since (we may assume) the quality of the services provided by the police would not be directly affected by a decision between, say, brick and concrete construction, the decision might well be taken on the criterion of minimizing the financial costs, over time, of providing a particular quantity and quality of office space.

If we are to use the idea of 'commercial criteria' as the basis for project appraisal we must specify this idea more clearly. If the public agency is to model its behaviour on that of a private firm, the obvious analogue to the shareholders of the private firm is the body of tax-payers. The analogue to the shareholders' dividend income from the firm is the net flow of funds between the public agency and the tax-payer in the form of financial surpluses paid out by the agency or, conversely, grants and subsidies of public money received by the agency. For the present it is sufficient to interpret the concept of 'using commercial criteria' as implying the objective of maximizing a public agency's net financial surplus over time. This of course is precisely equivalent to the objective of minimizing its net require-ment over time of grant or subsidy from public funds. Again, in more limited cases such as that of the choice of construction methods for the police headquarters, this objective is equivalent to that of minimizing the financial costs over time of providing some given level of service. (The point of this example is that although the agency in question obviously has objectives other than that of minimizing its grant requirement, only the financial objective is deemed to be relevant to the particular decision under consideration at the time). All of these equivalent formulations of 'commercial criteria' will be called *the financial objective*. Project appraisal carried out by refer-ence to such an objective is *financial appraisal*.

Some readers may be tempted to argue immediately that a financial objective is far too limited to represent the complexity of the public interest in the activities of public agencies. The authors of a book on cost-benefit analysis have a natural inclination to share such a view and we are discussing financial objectives primarily as a convenient point of entry into more complex formulations. But it should also be remembered that objectives have a purpose beyond that of communicating to a decision-maker how his ultimate em-ployers, the public, would wish him to behave. They also provide a means of monitoring the performance of the decision-maker, of checking that he does in fact act as the public wish. While a very simple and clearly defined objective may not capture all the dim-ensions of the public interest, it has the countervailing advantage of making it relatively easy to monitor the decision-maker's success in pursuing the public interest in those dimensions that it does capture.

Another possible criticism of our formulation of the financial objective may be answered by following through the argument about the need to monitor decision-makers. Some writers have argued strongly that the activities of large privately owned firms are not, in fact, particularly well explained by the hypothesis that managers act in the interests of shareholders; managers have, and use, some degree of discretion to operate firms in their personal interest.[1] Similarly, the decision-makers of public agencies might be expected to act in ways that were not always consistent with the interests of the public.[2]

These arguments have force as *descriptive* statements about how decision-makers behave in fact. But we are not writing a descriptive book. If in fact decision-makers always acted precisely in accordance with the objectives that they were expected to pursue, there would be no purpose in writing a book to suggest ways of ensuring that objectives and choices were consistent. One of the main merits of formal and explicit analysis as part of the public decision-making process is that it increases the accountability of the decision-maker to the public (a point which will be discussed in some detail in Chapter 16).

Nevertheless, a financial objective can, at best, be used only in relation to a restricted class of decision problems. Where projects are designed to produce services which will not be sold—for example, the construction of a public road whose use is not to be subject to a toll—financial appraisal would not carry us very far nor be very helpful. Even where financial appraisal might, at first sight, seem to be much more relevant, it may still turn out to be of limited usefulness. For example, consider a health authority choosing between two alternative locations for a hospital, when, on purely medical grounds, the two locations are equally satisfactory. (Such a choice will be the subject of a problem in Chapter 3.) If the health authority were concerned solely with the quantity and quality of its product—health care—and about the *financial* costs of producing it, financial appraisal would clearly be appropriate. But suppose that one of the locations is much more accessible than the other for patients and their visitors. This would affect the financial accounts of the health authority to some extent if, for example, the health authority were responsible for the financial costs of ambulance services, which would be greater if the less accessible site were chosen. But choosing the less accessible site would impose many more costs than these—costs which would not be registered in the authority's financial accounts. It would impose costs on patients and visitors by making travelling to and from the hospital more difficult. These people are taxpayers and voters. There is a strong argument that a public decision about the location of a hospital should take account of such costs, just as much as of costs that are registered in financial accounts.

In many cases, then, public decision-makers will wish to follow objectives that are broader in scope than the financial objective. Such objectives are considered in Part III of this book.

It is far from easy to formulate an objective which is broad enough to take account of all of the effects of a project which are relevant to a decision-maker while being precise enough to allow analysis to be based on it. For the present we may say that a 'broad' or 'social' objective ought to take account of all of the effects of a project on members of the public, irrespective of who is affected and of whether or not the effect is captured in a financial account. An appraisal based on such an objective is a *cost-benefit analysis*.

But this statement of what a social objective should be leaves many questions unanswered. If *all* of the effects of a project, even those which are not registered in financial accounts, are relevant to a cost-benefit analysis, how are these effects to be measured and valued? With financial appraisal, there is always an external standard— however arbitrary—of measurement and value. This standard is provided by the accounting conventions used by the agency making the appraisal. These conventions define the agency's financial surplus (or deficit), which is the entity to be maximized (or minimized). It may be said that in cost-benefit analysis the objective is to maximize social welfare, but this takes us no further, for 'social welfare' cannot be defined by reference to any widely used external yardstick.

The closest we can come to this is to begin our discussion of cost-benefit analysis by considering a relatively simple social objective, the 'potential Pareto improvement criterion'. This criterion will be discussed in more detail in Chapter 7. Essentially, it says that a project should be undertaken if, and only if, the gainers from the project *could* (but not necessarily actually do) fully compensate the losers from the project without themselves becoming net losers. This amounts to saying that the effects of a project should be evaluated by reference to the 'willingness to pay' of the individuals affected. That is, a favourable effect is evaluated by the maximum sum of money that the beneficiaries would be willing to pay to have it, and an unfavourable effect is evaluated by the minimum sum of money that the sufferers would be willing to accept as compensation for putting up with it.

It is clear that this objective is much wider in scope than the financial objective. To return to the example of choosing a location for a hospital, we have already said that costs incurred by patients and visitors travelling to and from the hospital would not be taken account of in a financial appraisal. But, presumably, these individuals would be willing to pay some amount of money to ensure that the hospital was located in a place more, rather than less, accessible for them. If so, a cost-benefit analysis based on the potential Pareto improvement criterion would take account of the relative accessibility of different sites.

Nevertheless, some decision-makers may feel that the potential Pareto improvement criterion does not go far enough in taking project appraisal away from the confines of financial accounting. To use willingness to pay as the source of all valuations is to retain a 'market' concept of value. Decision-makers may, on occasion, wish to reject this concept. For example, the willingness-to-pay principle attaches equal weight to an extra pound's worth of consumption, whoever is the consumer, while for various reasons a decision-maker might prefer to use different weights for different groups of people. In the later chapters of Part III (from Chapter 13 onwards) we shall consider the implications of using 'decision-makers' valuations' of the effects of projects in place of valuations based on individuals' willingness to pay. It should perhaps be said here that whether decision-makers' valuations may properly be included in a cost-benefit analysis is itself a matter of dispute among economists; we shall return to this issue in Chapter 7 and again in Chapter 16.

To sum up, our strategy is to consider a number of possible objectives, ranging progressively from the relatively straightforward to the extremely complex. Although the simplest objective we consider, the financial objective, is of interest in its own right, its main significance here is that it can be regarded as a convenient point of entry into the territory of cost-benefit analysis. Almost all of the issues considered in Part II will be picked up again in the discussion of cost-benefit analysis in Part III.

Notes

[1] Much has been written on this subject. Wildsmith (1973) offers a clear introduction to the literature.

[2] This issue has been explored by, for example, Breton (1974) and Niskanen (1971).

Part II: Financial Appraisal

2. Time

2.1. Time preference

Most important decisions about whether or not to undertake projects are not simply decisions about the use of resources at one point in time. They involve some commitment of resources or promise of returns in the future as well as in the present. Very often decisions have to be made about whether to incur costs in the present in return for benefits in the future; every investment project, from building a lamp standard to building an international airport, requires a decision of this kind. Alternatively, a decision may have to be taken about whether to accept a commitment to future costs in return for present benefits, as would be the case if a firm chose to sell some of its stock of capital.

In such cases it is not enough to state the financial objective of a public agency as being to maximize its net financial surplus (or minimize its net requirement of grant or subsidy). Equally, it is not enough to state the objective of a private firm as being to maximize its payments to shareholders. Such objectives say nothing, for example, about how far it is worth reducing an agency's financial surplus in one period so as to be able to increase it in another. In other words, they say nothing about time preference.

A good starting-point for tackling the problems of the time dimension in project appraisal is to consider the preferences of individuals between consumption at different points in time.

Consider an individual at a particular point in time, the present, who can look forward to consuming goods not only in the present year but also in future years. He will not necessarily be indifferent to the choice between the prospect of £1 worth of additional consumption now and that of £1 worth of additional consumption next year, even if all prices are expected to remain constant (as we shall suppose, for the moment, in the interests of simplicity). Consumption in one time period is a different good from consumption in another, just as apples and oranges are different goods.

An individual is said to have *time preference* between consumption in different periods. This is measured by his *marginal time preference rate* (MTPR for short). If he is indifferent between the prospect of £1 extra consumption in one year and the prospect of £1·10 extra consumption in the following year he is said to have a marginal time preference rate of 0·10 or 10 per cent per year. ('Per year' is often omitted for the sake of brevity.)

The word 'marginal' is used because a MTPR measures an individual's preferences between small increments of consumption in different periods. This presupposes that the individual has some expectations about the amount of consumption he will enjoy in different periods; these expectations form the datum from which small changes can be appraised. His MTPR will vary according to the datum. We should expect, other things being equal, that a person would have a higher MTPR the more he expects to be able to consume in the future relative to his present consumption. To take an extreme example, a prisoner who is due to be released in one year's time would probably expect to consume far more next year than this. He would be willing to sacrifice a relatively large amount of next year's consumption in return for a relatively small increase in consumption this year. That is, he would have a high MTPR between one year and the next. Of course he probably is not *able* to trade consumption between these two years—this is one reason why his MTPR is high. This underlines a very important point: time preference is about *preferences* and exists independently of any system by which trade might take place. MTPRs should not be confused with interest rates, which are phenomena of particular systems of economic organization.

Now consider an individual who has the opportunity to undertake an investment project which would require him to give up £9 consumption in one year (year 0) but which would enable him to enjoy £11 extra consumption the following year (year 1). If we know his MTPR we can calculate the amount of extra consumption that, if enjoyed in year 0, he would regard as being of equal value to the prospect of £11 extra consumption in year 1. If his MTPR is 10 per cent per year he regards £10 in year 0 as having the same value as the prospect of £11 in year 1. That is, this prospect has a *present value* to him of £10 in year 0. Since the project involves his incurring a cost of £9 in year 0, he will regard the opportunity to undertake the project as being of equal value to £1 consumption in year 0. That is, the present value of the net stream of consumption resulting from undertaking the project—or, more simply, the *net present value of the project*—is £1 in year 0. Clearly, if the net present value of a project to an individual is positive, that individual prefers the consumption pattern achieved by his undertaking the project to the pattern achieved by his not undertaking it. If the net present value of a project is negative, the converse is true.

More generally, suppose that an individual has a MTPR of r per period (expressed as a decimal and not as a percentage). Thus he is indifferent between the prosect of 1 unit of extra consumption in period 0 and that of $1 + r$ units of extra consumption in period 1. Similarly, he is indifferent between either of these prospects and that of $(1 + r)^2$ units of extra consumption in period 2. Conversely, one extra unit enjoyed in period 1 has a present value of $1/(1 + r)$ units in period 0; one extra unit enjoyed in period 2 has a present value of $1/(1 + r)^2$ units in period 0, and so on. The arithmetic process of calculating present values is known as *discounting*. The rate—r in this example—at which future returns are discounted to present values can be called the *discount rate*. (This term, unlike the term 'maginal time preference rate', implies no interpretation of the rate it refers to; a discount rate is simply a number which is used in an arithmetic manipulation.)

Now suppose that our individual is faced with the opportunity to undertake a project which would cause his consumption in the periods 0, 1, 2, . . ., n to change by the small increments C_0, C_1, C_2, . . ., C_n. (A positive value indicates an increase, a negative value a decrease). The net present value of the project in period 0 is

$$C_0 + \frac{C_1}{1 + r} + \frac{C_2}{(1 + r)^2} + \ldots + \frac{C_n}{(1 + r)^n}. \qquad 2.1$$

If this value is positive, our individual is better off if he undertakes the project than if he does not. If it is negative, he is better off not to undertake it.

So far nothing has been said about interest rates—that is, about the possibility of individuals being able to borrow and lend money. This omission has been deliberate, since the concept of time preference is completely independent of the possibility of borrowing and lending. Even Robinson Crusoe would have had a MTPR. The existence of a market interest rate does, however, greatly simplify the problem of *identifying* the MTPRs of individuals.

To discuss borrowing and lending we must consider at least two individuals, for the ideas would have no meaning in a Robinson Crusoe economy. Suppose, for the moment, that there are two individuals, Mr. A and Mr. B, that each has a stock of claims on consumption both in the present year (year 0) and in the next year (year 1). Suppose that, with their initial sets of claims, Mr. A has a MTPR of 8 per cent while Mr. B's is 10 per cent. They will not be content to remain in this situation, for they can make deals which make both of them better off. A might offer to lend £10 to B in year 0, in return for a promise by B to repay £10·9 in year 1—that is, A offers to lend B at an interest rate of 9 per cent per year. The changes in A's consumption implied by this plan have a positive present value to him; so do the changes in B's consumption to B. Both would be better off by making the transaction. If, after the deal, B's MTPR is still higher than A's, they can both become still better off by agreeing to a further deal of a similar kind. As long as their MTPRs differ, they can make such mutually beneficial transactions.

The limit on such trade is that an individual's MTPR varies according to the relative size of his claims on present and future consumption. As A lends more to B, his claims on consumption in period 0 decrease while his claims on consumption in period 1 increase. This will tend to increase his preference for extra consumption now relative to extra consumption later; in other words, his MTPR will tend to increase. For similar, exactly opposite reasons, B's MTPR will tend to fall. Ultimately they will reach a situation where their MTPRs are equal (say 9 per cent) and then there will be no opportunity for further mutually satisfactory borrowing and lending.

In a market economy, each individual typically does not choose how much to borrow or lend by considering possible deals with particular individuals, as in the example above. Instead, each chooses in relation to interest rates offered to him by banks and similar institutions. But the principle is the same. Suppose that it is possible for any individual to borrow and lend without limit at some interest rate, say 9 per cent per year. If, with his initial set of claims on present and future consumption, an individual's MTPR is greater than 9 per cent, he will borrow; if it is less than 9 per cent he will lend. In either case he will borrow or lend until his MTPR is equal to the market interest rate. (The magnitude of the market interest rate is itself determined by the necessity for transactions to have both a borrower and a lender. The market rate is that rate that ensures that the total amount that people wish to lend equals the total amount that people wish to borrow.)

So if an individual can borrow and lend freely at a given interest rate, his attempts to make himself as well off as possible will ensure that this rate is a measure of his MTPR. If everyone in a community can borrow and lend at the same interest rate, they will all share a common MTPR.

A more formal treatment of the content of this section is given in an appendix to this chapter.

2.2.   The discount rate for a public agency: a preliminary treatment

So far we have been considering choices made by individuals. This is convenient, for the idea of an individual having preferences is an easy one to grasp. But almost all the projects to be considered in this book are undertaken by organizations, not by individuals. The preferences of more than one person are relevant to such decisions.

Let us begin by considering the case of a firm privately owned by a number of shareholders. This is a convenient starting-point since, as noted in Chapter 1, financial appraisal in public agencies may be regarded as an attempt to model public decision-making on the practice of private firms. Each shareholder in a private firm will want the firm to be run in his own interest; that is, he will want the present value of his money income from the firm to be maximized. (It is assumed here that the activities of the firm do not significantly affect the shareholder in any other role than as the recipient of dividends.)

Suppose that, if the firm undertakes a particular project, the total income received by all shareholders taken together will change by $x_0, x_1, \ldots, x_n$ in periods $0, 1, \ldots, n$. (A positive value corresponds to an increase in income and a negative value to a decrease.) Then if one particular shareholder receives a proportionate share, s, of the receipts of all shareholders, his receipts will change by $sx_0, sx_1, \ldots, sx_n$. If his MTPR is r he will want the firm to undertake the project if and only if

$$sx_0 + \frac{sx_1}{1+r} + \frac{sx_2}{(1+r)^2} + \ldots + \frac{sx_n}{(1+r)^n} > 0. \qquad 2.2$$

Dividing throughout by s, this can be rewritten as

$$x_0 + \frac{x_1}{1+r} + \frac{x_2}{(1+r)^2} + \ldots + \frac{x_n}{(1+r)^n} > 0. \qquad 2.3$$

In words, he will want the firm to undertake the project if and only if the changes in the receipts of all shareholders taken together have a positive present value when they are discounted as *his* MTPR.

If an individual can borrow and lend freely at a single market rate of interest, his MTPR will equal that rate. So if all shareholders have access to the same market interest rate, all will have the same MTPR. In these circumstances all will agree on the criterion that should be used in the firm for choosing whether or not to undertake projects. A project should be undertaken if and only if the changes it implies for the total receipts of shareholders have a positive present value when discounted at the market interest rate.

This analysis can be reinterpreted to refer to a public agency using commercial criteria. If all members of the community (the agency's 'shareholders') have access to the same market rate of interest, then this rate should be used as the agency's discount rate. A project should be undertaken if and only if its net financial returns—that is, its contributions to reducing the agency's subsidy requirement—are positive when discounted at the market rate of interest.

For the present we shall not pursue this question further. We shall simply take it as given that there is such a market interest rate. In Chapter 4 we shall go on to explore some of the problems that arise when there is no single market interest rate.

2.3.   Two examples

An open-cast mining project

A publicly owned mining undertaking is considering a plan to mine coal by open-cast working at a certain site. The effects of this plan on the net financial surplus of the undertaking in the relevant years are summarized in Table 2.1. If the market interest rate is 10 per cent, the present value of the project in year 0 (in £m) is

$$-1 \cdot 0 + \frac{0 \cdot 4}{1 \cdot 1} + \frac{0 \cdot 4}{(1 \cdot 1)^2} + \frac{0 \cdot 4}{(1 \cdot 1)^3} + \frac{0 \cdot 4}{(1 \cdot 1)^4} - \frac{0 \cdot 2}{(1 \cdot 1)^5}.$$

Table 2.1
Financial costs and returns of mining project

Net increase in financial surplus of undertaking (£m) in year:

	0	1	2	3	4	5
Buying and equipping site	−1·0					
Revenue from sale of coal *minus* recurrent costs of labour, maintenance etc.		+0·4	+0·4	+0·4	+0·4	
Reclamation of site						−0·3
Sale of site						+0·1
Total	−1·0	+0·4	+0·4	+0·4	+0·4	−0·2

Such calculations can be tedious. Fortunately, however, they can be carried out quite simply by using tables of *discount factors* and *annuity factors*. (The notation introduced here will be used throughout this book.)

The discount factor $v_{t,r}$ is the present value in period 0 of a sum of one unit accruing in period t, if the discount rate is r. Arithmetically,

$$v_{t,r} = \frac{1}{(1 + r)^t}. \qquad 2.4$$

The annuity factor $a_{n,r}$ is the present value in period 0 of an income stream consisting of one unit accruing in each of the periods 1 to n, if the discount rate is r. Arithmetically,

$$a_{n,r} = \frac{1}{1 + r} + \frac{1}{(1 + r)^2} + \ldots + \frac{1}{(1 + r)^n} \qquad 2.5$$

or in terms of discount factors,

$$a_{n,r} = v_{1,r} + v_{2,r} + \ldots + v_{n,r}. \qquad 2.6$$

Tables of discount and annuity factors for various vaues of r are given in Appendix 1 (pp. 243-246).

We can now write the present value of the project, PV, as

$$PV = -1 \cdot 0 + 0 \cdot 4 a_{4, 0 \cdot 10} - 0 \cdot 2 v_{5, 0 \cdot 10}. \qquad 2.7$$

Substituting the numerical values of the two factors,

$$PV = -1 \cdot 0 + (0 \cdot 4 \times 3 \cdot 1699) - (0 \cdot 2 \times 0 \cdot 6209) = 0 \cdot 1438 \qquad 2.8$$

The project has a positive present value and thus is worth undertaking. To be more precise, the opportunity to undertake it is worth £143 800 in year 0.

New buildings or conversions of old ones?

A university plans to provide additional accommodation for students from year 2 onwards. New buildings could be constructed during years 0 and 1, at a cost of £200 000 (divided equally between the two years). An alternative policy is to buy existing, relatively old, houses and convert them to provide accommodation for the students. This would involve a cost of £180 000, borne in year 1.

To set against their lower initial costs, conversions have two disadvantages:

1. The costs of maintaining converted buildings are higher than those for new buildings. (These costs are borne by the univeristy.) Maintenance costs for the conversions would be £5000 per year; for new buildings these costs would be £2000 per year for the first 25 years and £5000 per year thereafter.

2. New buildings are expected to have a life of 50 years, compared with 25 years for converted buildings.

If the market interest rate is 10 per cent, which policy is to be preferred according to the criteria of financial appraisal?

Provided that the university is confident that accommodation of this type will be required for the next 50 years, it is appropriate to compare the costs of providing 50 years of accommodation by each of the two policies. We shall assume that, if conversions are chosen, it will be possible to replace the original conversions when their life is over by converting further old houses at costs exactly equal to those of the first generation of conversions. The second generation of conversions would need to be made in year 26. We shall also assume that any financial returns that can be had by disposing of buildings at the ends of their lives are negligible. On these assumptions, the financial costs that are relevant to this decision are those listed in Table 2.2.

These costs may be compared in either of two formally identical ways. We could calculate the present value of the costs for each of the two alternative policies; the policy with the lowest present value

Table 2.2
Financial costs of student accommodation

Costs incurred (£'000) *in year(s):*

	0	1	2–26	26	27–51
Conversions	—	180	5 *per year*	180	5 *per year*
New buildings	100	100	2 *per year*	—	5 *per year*
Net saving from choosing new buildings	−100	80	3 *per year*	180	—

of costs would be preferred. Or we could consider the policy of 'choosing new buildings instead of conversions' as an investment project, incurring initial costs (the higher initial costs of new buildings) in return for future benefits (saving in maintenance costs, and the avoidance of the obligation to provide replacement accommodation in year 26). At a discount rate of 10 per cent, this investment project has a present value of

$$-100 + 80\, v_{1,0.10} + 3a_{25,0.10}\, v_{1,0.10} + 180v_{26,0.10} = 12 \cdot 586 \text{ thousand} \atop \text{pounds}$$

By choosing new buildings rather than conversions the university makes net savings over the whole period that are equivalent in value to approximately £13 000 saved in year 0.

2.4. The internal rate of return

Obviously, the outcome of any project appraisal is sensitive to the value of the discount rate. Since the process of discounting at a positive rate is that of giving greater weights to costs and returns the earlier they occur, high discount rates tend to favour those alternatives with costs occurring relatively late and benefits occurring relatively early.

In the example of the open-cast mining project (given in Section 2.3), with a market interest rate of 10 per cent, the project was worth undertaking. If instead the market interest rate had been, say, 20 per cent, the project would have had a negative present value and would not have been worth undertaking. Similarly, in the choice between new buildings and conversions (also given in Section 2.3), with an interest rate of 10 per cent, new buildings were preferred. If instead the interest rate had been as high as 15 per cent, conversions would have been preferred.

For each of these choices between two alternative courses of action there is a *critical value* of the interest rate which would lead to the result that the two alternatives were equally preferred. (This critical value is between 17 and 18 per cent for the choice between undertaking and not undertaking the mining project and is between 12 and 13 per cent for the choice between new buildings and conversions.)

When we are dealing with a straightforward investment project, in which early costs are followed by later returns, the interpretation of the critical value of the interest rate is also straightforward. The project will be acceptable if and only if the critical value of the interest rate—that is, the rate at which the project has a zero net present value—is greater than the actual value of the interest rate. This can be used as a decision rule, and is equivalent to the 'net present value rule' we have used so far. The critical value of the interest rate is often called the *internal rate of return* or *yield* of the project. If the internal rate of return of an invement project is greater than the interest rate, the project should be undertaken.

In this simple form, however, the 'internal rate of return rule' is of limited application. It is applicable only to investment projects—that is, to projects with early costs followed by later returns. But disinvestment projects—projects with early returns followed by later costs—are also quite conceivable. The higher the interest rate the *more* favourably is a disinvestment project regarded. Thus the critical value of the interest rate for a disinvestment project must be interpreted as the lowest value of the interest rate that would justify undertaking it. In other words, a disinvestment project should be undertaken only if the true value of the interest rate is *greater than* the critical value.

To make things more complicated, some projects are neither pure investment nor pure disinvestment. The open-cast mining project, for instance, had early costs followed by later returns followed by still later costs. In such a case it is not immediately obvious how to interpret the critical value of the interest rate. (For the mining project, the critical value is in fact the highest value of interest rate that would justify undertaking the project.) It is not even obvious in such cases that there will be only one critical value.

In this book we shall continue to use the concept of present value because of its simplicity, its generality, and its intuitive appeal. Further discussion of the limitations of the 'internal rate of return rule' and of ways of revising the rule so as to overcome some of its limitations can be found in other works. (See the 'Further Reading' suggested at the end of this chapter.)

2.5. Choosing between three or more alternative courses of action

So far we have considered only choices between two alternative courses of action. Choices often have to be made between more than two such courses.

Consider, for example, the choice between new buildings and conversions discussed in Section 2.3 above. It was assumed that the university had already decided that some form of accommodation had to be provided; the choice was simply between alternative ways of doing this. But suppose instead that it is quite feasible for students to find their own accommodation if none is provided by the university, and that *how much* accommodation the university provides is itself a matter for decision. Suppose that the financial return from letting either of the two forms of accommodation is £29 700 per year. (This is the university's income from the rents paid by students, less all financial costs borne by the university other than those of building and maintenance.)

There are now three alternative courses of action: constructing new buildings, making conversions, and doing nothing. Or, to put this another way, constructing new buildings and making conversions are two *mutually exclusive projects.* That is, each is a project which requires a decision to 'undertake' or 'not undertake', but the possibility of undertaking both is not to be considered.

We have taken our objective to be that of minimizing the university's net subsidy requirement. This clearly implies that neither project should be undertaken unless it has a positive present value, and that if both satisfy this criterion, the project with the greater present value should be undertaken. If the market interest rate is 10 per cent, the present value of the project of constructing and letting new buildings is approximately £56 500 and that of the other project is approximately £43 900. The best course of action is to construct the new buildings. (It should be clear that this procedure can be generalized to apply to any number of mutually exclusive projects.)

That new buildings are preferable to conversions when both are viewed as projects with financial returns as well as costs is, of course, entirely consistent with the analysis made in Section 2.3. This showed that the present value of the costs of new buildings was less than the present value of the costs of conversions; and the financial returns of the two projects are identical.

It can however be shown that the internal rate of return of the 'new buildings' project is slightly less than 13 per cent and that the internal rate of return of the 'conversions' project is slightly more than 13 per cent. At first sight this is confusing, for it seems to imply that the second project is more profitable than the first. But there is no justification for this conclusion. There is nothing in the definition of the internal rate of return that implies that a project with a higher internal rate of return is necessarily preferable to one with a lower rate. The correct conclusion to draw from the information given is that *if* the market interest rate were 13 per cent, the 'new buildings' project would not be worth undertaking and the 'conversions' project would be worth undertaking. But since the market interest rate in fact is 10 per cent (we have assumed), this conclusion is of little relevance to decision-making.

Mutually exclusive projects are commonly encountered in project appraisal. One common type of mutually exclusive project is represented by the previous example—a choice between alternative methods of producing a particular output (in the example, accommodation for students).

Another common and related type of problem concerns the timing of projects. Whenever a project cannot be duplicated exactly, alternative timings constitute mutually exclusive courses of action. For example, building a dam on a particular site this year pre-empts the alternative of building a dam on the same site in five years' time. It may be that a project which has a positive present value if started in one year would have a considerably greater present value if started in some other year; that is, changing the project's starting date may produce net gains. (A notable example of this was discovered by the Roskill Commission which investigated the problem of choosing a site for a third London airport. It was found that very great savings could be made by deferring the starting date for the project beyond the date that previously had been proposed.)[1]

Project appraisal can be particularly complex when there is *interdependence* between projects. Two projects are interdependent if the present value of one is affected by whether or not the other is undertaken. Consider, for example, a passenger transport authority with the opportunity to undertake two projects. One project, project A, would increase the speed of rail services between a suburban area and the city centre. The other, project B, would increase the frequency of bus services to and from the suburban railway stations. The present value of each of these projects would presumably be greater if it were undertaken in conjunction with the other project than if it were undertaken alone. This is yet another example of mutually exclusive projects, for this problem may be considered as involving *three* projects: project A alone, project B alone, and the combination of projects A and B. A decision to 'undertake' or 'not undertake' has to be made for each of these three projects; and it is logically impossible to undertake more than one. The three projects are mutually exclusive.

2.6. Mutually exclusive projects: an example

A government agency in a developing country is considering sites in a river valley for dams to generate hydro-electric power. There is already one dam in the valley, at site B. This is owned by a private firm, and is used to generate power for a smelting works also owned by the firm. Two sites are available for additional dams: site A, upstream of B, and site C, downstream of B.

The purpose of dams is to store water during rainy periods to release in dry periods. Thus a dam helps to even out the flow of the river downstream of it and so increases the electricity-generating capacity of any downstream dams. The generating capacities of the three dams—the one existing dam and the two proposed ones—are summed up in Table 2.3. (Thus, for example, if B is the only dam on the river, it generates electricity worth $1·2 m per year. If dam A is built, B's output increases in value by $0·4 m per year; and if dam C is built, the existence of B contributes $0·3 m to the output of that dam.) The price of electricity is taken to be constant over time and independent of how many dams are built; all output can be sold at this price.

Table 2.3
Value of electricity generated at three dams

Electrcity resulting from existence of dam at:

		A	B	C
Electricity generated at:	A	1·0	—	—
	B	0·4	1·2	—
	C	0·15	0·3	1·1

Figures measure the value, in $m of local currency, of electricity generated per year.

The cost of building a dam and generating station at A is $19·0 m, to be paid the year before the dam comes into use (year 0). The equivalent cost for *C* is $20·5 m. The market interest rate is 6 per cent.

There are four alternative courses of action for the agency: to build only at A, to build only at C, to build at both, and to build at neither. The costs and returns of the first three alternatives, measured relative to the fourth alternative of doing nothing, are summarized in Table 2.4. (It is assumed that each of the proposed dams would have a life of 50 years, that the existing, privately owned dam would remain in use throughout that period, and that if dams were built both at A and C they would come into use simultaneously.) The figures in the third column of this table show the present values of the net financial returns to

Table 2.4
Financial costs and returns of projects to government agency and to private firm

Dam(s) at	Construction cost (year 0)	Annual return to agency (years 1—50)	Present value in year 0 of project to agency	Annual gain to firm (years 1—50)	Present value in year 0 of gains to firm
A	19·0	1·0	−3·238	0·4	6·305
C	20·5	1·4	1·567	—	—
A and C	39·5	2·55	0·693	0·4	6·305

All figures in $m.

the agency from adopting each of the three alternatives. It emerges that the project of building a dam only at A has a negative present value; it would be better for the agency to do nothing at all. The other two alternatives both have positive present values, but that of building only at C has the higher present value. According to the criteria of financial appraisal, this is the best policy for the agency to adopt.

One interesting possibility remains. In calculating the financial returns of the projects to the public agency it was assumed that the agency was not able to charge the private firm for the benefits that the latter would receive if a dam were built at A. Financial appraisal then produces the conclusion that it is not in the interests of the agency to build a dam there. There remains, however, an opportunity for the firm and the agency to come to a mutually satisfactory arrangement by which dams would be built at both A and C. For the agency to build both dams, rather than only the one at C, is for it to incur financial losses with a present value of $0·874 m (the difference between $1·567 m and $0·693 m). But the existence of the dam at A confers benefits on the firm by increasing the output of the firm's own dam. These benefits have a present value of $6·305 m. It would thus be in the interests of both parties to agree that the agency build both at A and C in return for payments by the private firm with a present value in the range $0·874 m to $6·305 m. In later chapters it will emerge that the theoretical possibility of such deals is of some significance for cost-benefit analysis.

Appendix: Time preference--a more formal treatment

The arguments of Section 2.1 can be presented more formally and concisely by using the economic theory of consumer choice.

To allow a diagrammatic presentation we shall consider the simplest form of decision involving time, and define only two time periods, period 0 (present) and period 1 (future). Further we shall consider an economy with only one good, 'consumption'.

We can represent the preference ordering of any given individual over alternative combinations of present and future conumption in the form of an indifference map as in Figure 2.1. (Any point on the diagram corresponds to some conceivable combination of present and future consumption by our individual. An 'indifference curve', such as I_1 or I_2, is a line joining combinations between which he is indifferent. Points to the north-east of an indifference curve are preferred to points on it, and these in turn are preferred to points south-west of it.)

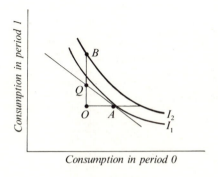

Fig. 2.1

The slope of the indifference curve passing through any point is a measure of the individual's marginal time preference at this point. For example, at point A in Figure 2.1 the slope of the indifference curve I_1 is $-OQ/OA$. This implies that if our individual initially had the set of claims on present and future consumption that point A represents, he would consider a loss of one unit of present consumption to be exactly compensated for by a gain of OQ/OA units of future consumption. His MTPR, r, is given by

$$r = \frac{OQ}{OA} - 1.$$

Now suppose that our individual is initially at point A, but has the opportunity to undertake a project which would require him to give up OA present consumption in return for OB future consumption. Thus his choice is between staying at point A and moving to point B. B is on a higher indifference curve than A and so he is better off if he undertakes the project.

In practice it is difficult to proceed beyond this formal statement of the problem without making a further simplification. This is to assume that the indifference curves in the area around points A and B can be approximated by parallel straight lines. This amounts to assuming that the individual's MTPR is unaffected by changes in present and future consumption of the magnitude involved in the decision between undertaking the project and not undertaking it. As an approximation, this is satisfactory if the changes in present and future consumption being considered are small in relation to the individual's total consumption in each period. With this approximation, Figure 2.1 can be redrawn as Figure 2.2.

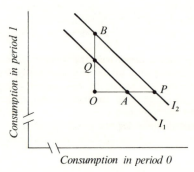

Fig. 2.2

The present value of a project to an individual is the amount of extra present consumption whose value to him is equal to that of the net consumption stream resulting from his undertaking the project. In Figure 2.2, since the individual is indifferent between B and P (both being on indifference curve I_2) the present value of the project is AP. The MTPR, r, is related to the slope of the indifference curves by the equation

$$r = \frac{OB}{OA + AP} - 1$$

which can be rearranged in the form

$$AP = -OA + \frac{OB}{1 + r}.$$

This is the equation for calculating the present value of the project; it is equivalent to Equation 2.1 which was derived in Section 2.1 above.

Now consider the possibility of borrowing and lending at a market interest rate. Suppose that Mr. *A* has the initial endowment of claims on present and future consumption represented by point P_A in Figure 2.3a, and that he is able

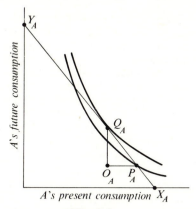

Fig. 2.3a

to borrow and lend freely at the interest rate i. This means that he can move from point P_A to any point on the 'consumption possibility frontier' $X_A Y_A$ through P_A, whose gradient is given by the interest rate:

$$i = \frac{O_A Q_A}{O_A P_A} - 1.$$

At this initial position, P_A, his MTPR is less than the interest rate (the indifference curve through P_A slopes downwards less steeply than the line $X_A Y_A$.) The best position he can reach is Q_A, where the line $X_A Y_A$ is tangent to the highest attainable indifference curve—in other words, where the MTPR and interest rate are equal. He reaches this point by lending $O_A P_A$ in the present in return for $O_A Q_A$ in the future.

An alternative possibility is represented in Figure 2.3b, where Mr. *B* also faces an interest rate of i. His initial endowment is P_B but by borrowing or

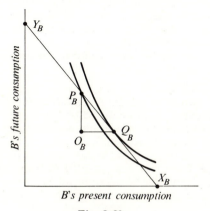

Fig. 2.3b

lending he can reach any point on the line $X_B Y_B$. At P_B his MTPR is greater than i. He reaches the best attainable position, Q_B, by borrowing $O_B Q_B$ in the present in return for a promise to repay $O_B P_B$ in the future. Having made this transaction, he, like Mr. A, has a MTPR equal to the interest rate.

Problems

1. A railway undertaking (a public agency) is carrying out a programme of modernizing level crossings. Unmodernized level crossings which carry railways across minor roads are operated manually by crossing-keepers, who are usually retired railway workers receiving a small income for doing this work. To install automatic barriers at such a crossing costs £20 200 (in year 0), and results in subsequent cost savings (from year 1 onwards) of £1900 per year. The useful life of a set of automatic barriers and associated equipment is estimated to be 20 years, after which it must be replaced. Should the programme of modernization be continued? The market interest rate is 8 per cent. Is this conclusion altered if the market interest rate is 6 per cent?

2. A bridge carrying a main road over a river is in need of major repairs. The road currently has only a single carriageway. To rebuild the bridge to carry the existing width of road would cost £300 000 (in year 0). It is planned, however, to widen the road to dual carriageways during year 8. If the river bridge were only wide enough for the old road, it would have to be widened at a further cost of £240 000 in that year. An apparently more far-sighted policy would be to build at the outset a bridge wide enough to carry the dual-carriageway road when it is built. The cost of such a bridge would be £420 000 in year 0. Would such 'far-sightedness' be in the interests of the taxpayers who bear the costs of roadworks? The market interest rate is 10 per cent.

3. It is planned to increase the number of beds in a certain hospital. This increase will take place in stages from year 1 to year 5. Meals in the hospital are prepared in a single kitchen. If no improvements are made to this kitchen, the cost of preparing meals will be £48 000 in year 1, £52 000 in year 2, £58 000 in year 3, £62 000 in year 4, and £66 000 in year 5 and in each year following. Some improvements could be made to the kitchen to make it more suited to producing larger numbers of meals per day. These improvements would reduce the cost of preparing meals to £40 000 in year 1, £42 000 in year 2, £46 000 in year 3, £48 000 in year 4, and £50 000 in year 5 and in each year following. To carry out the improvements would cost £110 000, to be paid the year before the improvements come into use. It is expected that the whole kitchen will be replaced after the end of year 19, and so the improvements being considered will not produce any cost savings after this year.

Should the improvements be made, and if so, when? The market interest rate is 10 per cent.

4. A company was set up four years ago (year −4) to exploit an oil field. The company is entirely owned by private shareholders and owns exclusive rights to the oil field. The shareholders subscribed £10·0 m in year −4, which was spent on buying these rights and on buying and installing capital equipment. So far (that is, up to year 0), no dividends have been paid and no oil has been produced. It is expected that oil will be produced from year 1, and that dividends of £2·95 m per year will be paid from year 1 to year 30 inclusive. (Beyond this date it is expected that no dividends will be paid, the oil field being exhausted.) It can be calculated that, if these dividends were paid, the internal rate of return on the

shareholders' original investment would be approximately 16 per cent. This is well in excess of the market interest rate of 8 per cent, reflecting the fact that the potential yield of the oil field has proved to be much greater than was expected in year —4.

The government wishes to acquire a 50 per cent holding in the company. That is, by paying in year 0 a sum of money to existing shareholders it will acquire the right to one half of the company's dividends in each year following. The government will use statutory powers to do this. The payment made by the government in year 0 will thus be determined, not by bargaining between buyer and sellers, but unilaterally by the government. The government, however, says that it intends that shareholders should be fully compensated—that is, shareholders should not be made worse off as a result of the government's action.

The government proposes to pay £9·1 m as compensation. This implies that the shareholders will have invested £10·0 m in year —4, and will receive in return £9·1 m in year 0 followed by £1·475 m (50 per cent of the total dividend) in each of years 1 to 30. This stream of outlays and returns has an internal rate of return of approximately 16 per cent. The government has thus allowed shareholders to achieve the same rate of return on their original investment as they would have enjoyed had the government not intervened.

Should shareholders consider themselves exactly compensated? If not, what payment by the government *would* exactly compensate them?

Notes
[1] See Abelson and Flowerdew (1972).

Further reading
The economic analysis on which this chapter is based derives from the classic work of Fisher (1930). Fisher's analysis is clearly expounded and developed by Hirshleifer (1958).

The appraisal of projects by private firms is discussed in the present book primarily because of the analogies that can sometimes be drawn between private firms and public agencies. Much fuller treatments of the subject matter of this chapter can be found in Bierman and Smidt (1975), Chapters 1—4, and in Merrett and Sykes (1973), Chapters 1, 2 and 5. Both these books are directly concerned with the appraisal of projects by private firms. Merrett and Sykes's Chapter 5 presents a method (the extended yield method) for overcoming some of the problems associated with the use of internal rates of return to decide whether or not to undertake projects.

For a detailed discussion of the economic issues involved in choosing between new buildings and improvements to old buildings, see Needleman (1969). For a detailed discussion of the appraisal of river development projects, see Krutilla and Eckstein (1958).

3. Costs and Returns in Financial Appraisal

3.1. Opportunity cost

Since project appraisal concerns choices between alternative courses of action, the value of one course can be determined only relative to that of some alternative course. Thus the costs of a project that are relevant for project appraisal are those that would be incurred if the project were undertaken but that would not be incurred if it were not. We are interested in what is forgone as a result of undertaking a project—that is, in the *opportunity cost* of the project. Similarly, the revenue of a project is the extra amount that would be earned if the project were undertaken rather than not undertaken.

The important point is that in project appraisal, costs and returns (values) relate to *courses of action*. This is a different concept of cost from that used in most financial accounting. In financial accounting it is normal for values to be related to concrete things, such as buildings or machines or man years of labour. Values attached to things in this way can be added and subtracted, which is often convenient. The value of a firm, for example, can be treated as the sum of the values of the things it owns; the value of a machine can be broken down into the values of individual hours of machine use. But despite its convenience, this way of treating values is not appropriate for project appraisal. Various reasons why this is so are considered below.

3.2. Depreciation

Financial accounting uses the concept of 'depreciation'. This is a way of breaking down the capital cost of an asset—say, a house or a machine—into the notional costs of using it in the various years of its life. The traditional method of 'historic cost' depreciation derives these notional costs (or depreciation allowances) by dividing the amount actually paid for an asset over the years of its life. For many purposes, this procedure is useful. It is often used, amongst other things, as a basis for calculating the tax liabilities of firms. But in itself a depreciation allowance is no more than a book-keeping convention. It does not reflect directly any opportunity cost.

Consider, for example, a proposal to close a rail service. One of the financial benefits of this proposal is that the railway undertaking is relieved of the costs of running trains. In so far as these are the costs of labour and fuel, working out the opportunity cost of running trains is probably fairly straightforward. But what of the costs of the trains themselves?

The trains that are used on the service will have been paid for at some time in the past, and from this historic cost a depreciation allowance per train per year can be calculated by conventional accounting methods. But this figure is of no direct relevance to the choice between closing and not closing the service. The opportunity cost of using the trains on this particular service is their value to the railway company in their best alternative use.

It may be that by closing the service the company can use the trains elsewhere and so postpone buying (or manufacturing) new ones. Postponing buying a new train has a financial benefit to the company, and this benefit is a measure of the opportunity cost of using the old trains on the original service. If the cost of buying trains has increased since the old ones were bought, then the opportunity cost of using them will be greater than the notional cost measured by depreciation allowances.

Alternatively, it may be that the company already has as many trains as it will need for many years to come and that if the service is closed the trains will simply be scrapped. In this case the opportunity cost of using the trains is the forgone scrap value. Almost certainly this will be less than the cost as measured by depreciation allowances.

So the opportunity cost of using an asset may be different from the relevant depreciation allowances. Similarly, the total opportunity cost of using an asset over its whole life, when discounted back to a present value in the year the asset was bought, may be different from the payment actually made for it in that year. Such differences are likely to arise whenever the initial decision to buy an asset is based on expectations about the future that are not fulfilled—or when these expectations are being called into question by a decision to be taken.

Take, for example, our case of the trains which will be scrapped if the service on which they run is closed. When they were originally bought, we may presume, it was not expected that they would be scrapped so early. Depreciation allowances would have been calculated on the basis of the trains' expected lives. This expectation is being called into question by the proposal to close the service. With the benefit of hindsight, we may be able to say that the initial decision to buy the trains was a mistaken one. But in project appraisal, bygones are bygones. It would be irrational for the railway undertaking to make less use of the trains it owns on the grounds that it ought never to have bought them in the first place.

A similar but opposite argument applies when initial expectations were too pessimistic. An asset, for example, may turn out to have a much longer useful life than was expected when it was bought. The time comes when, according to financial accounts, it is 'fully depreciated': the whole of its historic cost has been 'paid off' in notional depreciation allowances. But if it still is capable of being put to alternative uses, its use has an opportunity cost.

3.3.   Marginal cost

Costs of goods and services are functions of quantities. That is, the cost of producing a good depends on how much is produced. Projects very commonly require decisions not about whether to produce at all but about whether to produce a little more or a little less. For such decisions we need to know how much more it costs to produce an extra unit of output (or how much less it costs to produce one unit less). This is the *marginal cost* of the output.

Traditional financial accounting has been mainly concerned with *average* costs. Average costs are much easier to identify than marginal costs; one needs only to know the total quantity produced and the total cost incurred and then to divide the latter by the former. Average costs also are convenient for book-keeping because of the way they can be manipulated in an accounting system. If one answers the question 'what does this cost?' by giving the average cost per unit, this figure then has the useful attribute that when one multiplies it by the actual total number of units produced one gets the actual total cost. But, as was pointed out above, project appraisal is not concerned with apportioning actual total costs between actual units of output. It is concerned with identifying the future opportunity costs of alternative future courses of action, to which average historic costs may be a very poor guide.

To return once again to the example of the railway closure, consider a railway line on which both a passenger service and a goods service are run. The existence of the track, maintained to a certain standard, is necessary for both services. If we were concerned with book-keeping, we should have to decide how to apportion between the two services the costs of keeping the track in existence. We might, for instance, decide notionally to divide the cost equally between trains, and 'charge' each service with a sum equal to the average cost per train multiplied by the number of trains. But this, or any similar procedure, is completely arbitrary and has no relevance for project appraisal.

Suppose that it is proposed to close the passenger service but to keep the goods service. Then we need to know the *extra* costs of maintaining the line for both services rather than just for goods.

Similarly, if instead it is proposed to close the goods service and keep the passenger one, we need to know the extra costs of maintaining the line for both services rather than just for passengers. These two opportunity costs will no doubt come to less than the total cost of maintaining the track. But there is nothing wrong or unsatisfactory about that. Each opportunity cost was worked out in relation to a different decision problem. If a decision had to be made about whether to close the line altogether—yet another problem—the total cost of maintaining the track would be relevant.

Identifying marginal costs can be quite difficult. Information about costs usually has to be obtained from financial accounts, since no other sources are to hand. Financial accounts usually provide information only about total and average costs. The analyst has to find some way of inferring marginal costs from this. There are two main ways of proceeding.

Components of costs

One method is to try to extract as much information as possible from the breakdowns of costs that are used in financial accounts, and then to reassemble this information in a way which allows marginal costs to be identified.

As an example, consider the problem of working out the marginal cost of producing meals in a hospital. (Such information would be useful in an appraisal of a proposal to expand an existing hospital.) A typical set of financial accounts would show the total cost of producing meals in recent years, and the numbers produced. Costs would be broken down into such components as 'maintenance', 'fuel', 'food', 'labour' and so on. With a knowledge of the technology and system of organization of food preparation in hospitals, an analyst might be able to classify each of these components as fixed or variable costs. It might be that expenditure on maintenance was determined by the design of a kitchen rather than by the number of meals prepared in it, and so if no change in the kitchen design were planned these would be fixed costs. Other costs might be regarded as being directly proportionate to output. Expenditure on unprepared food might come into this category. Dividing labour costs between fixed and variable components would probably be more difficult, but estimates could be made. (It might be that some categories of labour costs increase more than in proportion with output.) All this information could then be reassembled as a *cost function*, giving the total costs of different hypothetical levels of output. From this function, marginal costs could be calculated.

Statistical estimation

An alternative approach is to infer the extra costs of increasing the output of one firm or plant from a set of observations of the total costs incurred by firms or plant producing different levels of output. (These observations can be in cross-section—that is, observations of different firms at one point in time—, or in time series—that is, observations of the same firm at different points in time.)

To return to the hospital example, the analyst might collect information about the total costs of preparing meals at the hospital in different years in the recent past, and then seek to explain statistically differences in total cost between years. One key variable would be the number of meals prepared each year. (Others would include indices of food prices and of wage rates—of which more will be said shortly.) The aim would be to estimate statistically the cost function.

3.4.   An example: The costs of operating bus services

Until recently it was common for British public transport undertakings to express the costs of operating bus services only as an average cost per bus mile (or bus kilometre). In its simplest form, this method is simply to calculate the average cost by dividing the total cost of operating a fleet of buses in a particular period of time by the total distance travelled by the fleet during that period. (The costs of buying buses and other forms of capital are included in the total costs by using depreciation allowances.)

Knowledge of such average costs is, unfortunately, of little use in choosing between alternative transport policies. The opportunity cost to a bus undertaking of running, say, 100 additional bus kilometers a week on a particular service may be very different from 100 times the average cost per bus kilometre.

One problem with the use of these average costs in policy making stems from the use of depreciation allowances in the calculation of average costs—a problem discussed in Section 3.2. A further drawback is that average rather than marginal costs are being measured. If a decision is required about whether to operate an additional bus service, what is needed is a measure of marginal cost. There are a number of reasons for expecting average and marginal costs to be different.

Some of the costs of operating buses are overheads in the sense that they relate to items required by a bus fleet as a whole—for example, garaging and administration. It may be that these costs increase less than in proportion to the number of buses in the fleet or to the number of kilometres run. If this is so, marginal cost will tend to be less than average cost. Other costs are overheads in a different sense; they relate to *buses* rather than *bus kilometres*. The costs of buying buses, and some of the costs of garaging and maintaining them, can most usefully be expressed as costs per bus.

And it is not self-evident that bus kilometres provide the best dimension along which to measure variable (as opposed to overhead) costs. Some costs—costs of fuel, for example—are likely to be closely related to the distance travelled by the buses of a fleet. But other items of expenditure vary with the length of time that buses are on the road. Expenditure on drivers' wages will clearly vary in this way. Some maintenance costs may also be determined by the length of time that buses are in use; and even fuel costs may be determined partly by this, for at lower speeds fuel consumption may be higher.

These distinctions between costs per bus, costs per bus kilometre and costs per bus hour are important because different kinds of service will require extra buses, extra bus kilometres and extra bus hours in different proportions.

One way of trying to identify the marginal costs of operating particular kinds of service is to use the approach of statistical estimation (see Section 3.3).

Suppose that a study is made of the total costs reported by a large number of bus fleets in a particular year. The object is to explain differences between the costs of different fleets. An obvious problem in interpreting such reported costs is that expenditure on buying pieces of capital is normally recorded in accounts by use of depreciation allowances. The major item of capital expenditure that is relevant to decisions about whether to operate additional bus services is expenditure on buying buses. Thus one way of side-stepping this problem is to subtract from the total costs recorded in the accounts of bus undertakings all costs related to the buying of buses. This item of expenditure can then be treated separately.

Suppose that it is found that the differences between the costs reported by different bus fleets can be explained quite well by the equation

$$C = 250\,000 + 1500b + 3{\cdot}80h + 0{\cdot}06k$$

where C is the total cost (in £ per year) of running a fleet of buses, b is the number of buses in the fleet, h is the number of bus hours run each year and k is the number of bus kilometres run each year. C excludes all expenditure on buying buses. Buses cost £24 000 each and have a life of 15 years. (The useful life of a bus can be assumed to be determined by the fact that, as time goes on, its design becomes increasingly obsolete. Thus its life is independent of the number of kilometres it travels and of the number of hours it is on the road.)

Now consider a typical bus fleet with, say, 300 buses, each of which travels an average of 48 000 kilometres per year and is on the road for an average of 3000 hours per year. The total costs of such a fleet, excluding the costs of buying buses, would be in the region of £4·984 m per year. (This is the cost that would be predicted by the equation give above.) Assuming a market interest rate of 8 per cent, an expenditure of £24 000 on buying a bus in any year 0 is equal in value to the prospect of expenditures of £2804 per year in each of years 1 to 15. One might therefore assign for accounting purposes a notional cost (or depreciation allowance) of £2804 per bus per year. Multiplying by the 300 buses in the fleet gives a total of £0·841 m per year. Adding this to the £4·984 m costs already calculated gives a total accounting cost of £5·825 m per year. We might expect our typical bus fleet to report such a 'total cost' in its accounts. Dividing by the total number of bus kilometres travelled by the fleet's buses in a year gives an average cost of £0·40 per bus kilometre.

Now consider two proposals to introduce new bus services. One service, service A, is designed to attract commuters to use public transport instead of cars. It will run only during peak hours on the five working days of the week, and because it is run at the times when roads are most congested, its average speed is very low. The other service, service B, is to run for a large part of the day on seven days a week, between two towns connected by a fast road. The average speed of buses will be relatively high. Details of the two services are given in Table 3.1. It is assumed that the existing bus fleet is fully used during peak hours and so additional buses would have to be bought if it were decided to operate either of the two services. (The number of additional buses needed to run a service is slightly greater than the number that is required to be on the road at any time, since a bus can be expected to break down occasionally and to need periodic maintenance.)

In Table 3.2 the costs of running each of these services for a period of 15 years is set out. (Fifteen years is chosen for convenience, since this is the life of a bus.) The accounting costs of the services are calculated using the average cost of £0·40 per bus kilometre. Since the services require the same number of bus

Table 3.1
Characteristics of two bus services

	Bus km per week	Hours of service per week	Average speed (km per hour)	Additional buses required
Service A	4000	20	14	16
Service B	4000	96	25	2

Table 3.2
Accounting and opportunity costs of two bus services

	Cost incurred in year(s) 0	1—15	Present value in year 0
Accounting costs			
Service A	—	83·2 *per year*	712·2
Service B	—	83·2 *per year*	712·2
Opportunity costs			
Service A	384·0	92·9 *per year*	1179·5
Service B	48·0	47·1 *per year*	451·1

All costs in £'000. Present value calculated by using a discount rate of 8 per cent.

kilometres per week, the accounting costs of the two services are equal (equivalent to a present value of £712 200 in year 0). The opportunity costs of the two services are calculated from the equation given above. (Each additional bus implies additional costs of £1500 per year, each additional bus hour implies £3·80 in additional costs, and each additional bus kilometer implies £0·06 in additional costs). Over and above these recurrent costs, each additional bus costs £24 000 which must be paid in year 0. It emerges that the opportunity costs of service A (equivalent to a present value of £1 179 500) are much greater than the accounting costs, while the opportunity costs of service B (equivalent to a present value of £451 100) are much less than the corresponding accounting costs. If decisions about whether or not to run services were taken by reference to the accounting concept of average costs per bus kilometre, there would be a tendency to run too many services with characteristics like those of service A and too few services like service B.

3.5. Price changes

So far we have assumed, for the sake of simplicity, that all prices are expected to remain constant over the life of a project. Such an assumption is, to put it mildly, unrealistic. Fortunately, however, it is not particularly difficult when appraising a project to make allowance for expected price changes.

In discussing price changes an important distinction must be drawn between changes in the general level of prices and changes in relative prices.

Changes in the general level of prices

Suppose that at some point in time an individual feels certain that in the future all prices will increase at a steady rate of f per year; thus any bundle of goods that costs £1 in one year will cost £$1(1 + f)$ in the next. Suppose also that our individual has a marginal time preference rate of r per year expressed *in real terms*. That is, he is indifferent between the prospect of having an extra £1 to spend on consumption in year 0 and that of having an extra £$(1 + r)(1 + f)$ to spend in year 1. Similarly he is indifferent between either and the prospect of having £$(1 + r)^2 (1 + f)^2$ to spend in year 2, and so on. We may define a *nominal* MTPR—that is, a time preference rate applicable to units of consumption measured in 'nominal' or money terms—such that

$$1 + R = (1 + r)(1 + f) \qquad\qquad 3.1$$

where R is the nominal MTPR. Provided that r and f are small, we may approximate[1] and write

$$R \simeq r + f. \qquad\qquad 3.2$$

That is, the nominal MTPR is the sum of the real MTPR and the expected rate of price increase.

Now consider a project that would require a firm to buy q_0, q_1, . . ., q_n extra units of some good in years 0, 1, . . ., n. Suppose that the price per unit of this good is p_0 in year 0. Since all prices are expected to rise at the rate f per year, the price of this particular good will be $p_0(1 + f)$ in year 1, $p_0(1 + f)^2$ in year 2, and so on. Thus the *money* costs to be imposed on shareholders in successive years are $p_0 q_0$, $p_0(1 + f)q_1$, $p_0(1 + f)^2 q_2$, . . ., $p_0(1 + f)^n q_n$. To convert these money costs to a present value, we must use a nominal MTPR. If all the firm's shareholders have the same real MTPR, r, their common nominal MTPR, R, will be given by Equation 3.1. The present value of this stream of costs is thus given by

present value =

$$p_0 q_0 + \frac{p_0(1 + f)q_1}{(1 + r)(1 + f)} + \frac{p_0(1 + f)^2 q_2}{(1 + r)^2 (1 + f)^2} + \ldots + \frac{p_0(1 + f)^n q_n}{(1 + r)^n (1 + f)^n}$$

$$= p_0 q_0 + \frac{p_0 q_1}{1 + r} + \frac{p_0 q_2}{(1 + r)^2} + \ldots + \frac{p_0 q_n}{(1 + r)^n}. \qquad 3.3$$

The term f has been eliminated from the expression. The present value of this stream of costs is expressed in terms of the quantities of the good bought in the various years, the price of the good in year 0, and the *real* MTPR. Thus, provided that *relative* prices are expected to remain unchanged, increments of expenditure or revenue in future time periods may be valued by using present prices and a real MTPR.

If then the real MTPR is known, there is no need to predict future rates of increase in the general price level.

There is, however, a problem here. Market interest rates, which are observable phenomena, are usually expressed in nominal terms. This means that it is people's nominal MTPRs that can be inferred directly from observations of market interest rates. To be able to deduce what their real MTPRs are, we need to know what rate of increase of prices they expect. Expectations in themselves are unobservable, and the kinds of market—insurance markets—in which people might 'reveal' their expectations for the most part do not exist. The analyst must make some assumptions about how people form their expectations. For example, one might assume that people expect that the rate of inflation in future years will be the same as the rate they experienced in the previous year. (If the analyst is not confident about the correctness of any one method of inferring expectations, he will be uncertain about what discount rate to use. How uncertainty can be taken account of in project appraisal is the subject of Chapter 5 below.)

Changes in relative prices

If relative prices are expected to change, things are a little more complex.

Suppose, as an initial simplification, that the prices of all goods except one are expected to increase at the rate of f per year, and that the odd good takes up only a very small part of anyone's total spending. Thus if someone is indifferent to the choice between the prospect of having an extra £1 to spend on consumption in one year and that of having an extra $£(1 + r)(1 + f)$ to spend the next year we can regard r as his real MTPR.

Consider a project that requires a firm to buy $q_0, q_1, \ldots, q_n$ additional units of some good in years $0, 1, \ldots, n$. The price of units of this good will be, in money terms, $p_0, p_1, \ldots, p_n$ in the respective years. If all shareholders have the same real MTPR, r, the present value of this stream of costs is

$$p_0 q_0 + \frac{p_1 q_1}{(1 + r)(1 + f)} + \frac{p_2 q_2}{(1 + r)^2 (1 + f)^2} + \ldots + \frac{p_n q_n}{(1 + r)^n (1 + f)^n}. \qquad 3.4$$

Now suppose that the good that the firm buys is the odd one whose price does not increase at the rate of f per year. Instead its price increases at the rate of f' per year. We may then rewrite the present value of the stream of costs as

$$p_0 q_0 + \frac{p_0 \left[\frac{1 + f'}{1 + f}\right] q_1}{1 + r} + \frac{p_0 \left[\frac{1 + f'}{1 + f}\right]^2 q_2}{(1 + r)^2} + \ldots + \frac{p_0 \left[\frac{1 + f'}{1 + f}\right]^n q_n}{(1 + r)^n}. \qquad 3.5$$

In words, we may still discount at the *real* MTPR but units of consumption of a particular good in the future may not be valued simply at the good's present price. Instead, this price must be adjusted to take account of expected changes in its value *relative to the general price level*. (For ease of calculation, it is often convenient in practice to use the approximations given in Note 1 and rewrite Equation 3.5 as

$$p_0 q_0 + \frac{p_0 q_1}{1 + r - (f' - f)} + \frac{p_0 q_2}{[1 + r - (f' - f)]^2} + \ldots + \frac{p_0 q_n}{[1 + r - (f' - f)]^n} \qquad 3.6$$

since the numerical values of terms such as $1/[1 + r - (f' - f)]$ can be found from tables of discount factors. In effect, one is discounting costs or returns expressed in present prices at the rate $r - (f' - f)$, where r is the real MTPR and $(f' - f)$ is the annual rate of increase of the price of the good concerned relative to the general price level.)

In reality, of course, prices of different goods change at different rates over time. The assumption that the prices of all goods but one increase at the same rate is not realistic. But it is possible to construct indices of the rate of change of the general level of prices for consumption goods, and such indices are frequently published by governments and independent research organizations. We need merely to reinterpret f as the expected rate of increase in the general price level for consumption goods.

That we should be concerned with the prices of *consumption* goods is important. We have asserted that firms and public agencies ultimately are concerned about the effects of their activities on the incomes of individual shareholders and taxpayers. These people will value increments of money income according to the amount of extra consumption goods they can buy with the money. Other indices, such as indices of wholesale prices of manufactured goods, might *seem* to be more relevant to the activities of firms; but here we are concerned not directly with the activities of the firm but with the preferences of its shareholders.

Problems

1. A certain highway authority is responsible for 2400 lane kilometres of major road. Roads may be built either of concrete or of asphalt. Concrete is more costly in the first instance but is more durable. Currently the whole of the authority's road network is built of asphalt. The authority's chief engineer, however, proposes that as it becomes necessary to reconstruct roads, asphalt roads should be replaced by concrete ones. He argues:

An asphalt road can be expected to have a life of 20 years, after which it must be reconstructed completely. The cost of reconstructing a road in asphalt is £30 000 per lane kilometre. A concrete road has a life of 40 years and it costs £38 000 per lane kilometre to reconstruct a road in concrete. The costs of routine maintenance are the same for the two types of road.

With our current policy of building roads of asphalt we incur costs of £3·60 m per year. This is the annual depreciation of our investment in the road network. In other words, we must spend £3·60 m per year to prevent the average age of our roads from increasing (and hence to prevent the average quality from declining). This is done by our having a rolling programme of reconstruction of roads, one-twentieth of the road network being reconstructed each year. £3·60 m is the cost of reconstructing 120 lane kilometres of road.

If instead our policy were to build roads of concrete, the annual depreciation cost would be only £2·28 m. (A rolling programme of reconstruction would involve only one-fortieth of the road network—that is, 60 lane kilometres—each year.)

It is clear from this that concrete roads are, in the long run, significantly cheaper than asphalt roads.

Is this conclusion the correct one to draw from the information presented? Note that the argument makes no reference to interest rates or to time preference. (The market interest rate is 10 per cent.)

2. Reconsider Problem 1 of Chapter 2 (p. 28). This concerns a proposal to modernize a railway level crossing. The cost of modernizing the crossing is £20 200, to be paid in year 0. According to the original statement of the problem, the annual saving in costs as a result of the modernization would be £1900 per year, enjoyed in years 1 to 20 inclusive.

Suppose that both these figures—the £20 200 cost of modernization and the £1900 per year cost saving—are measured according to the prices current in year 0. It is generally expected that over the next 20 years the price level for consumption goods will increase by 5 per cent per year. The annual cost savings as a result of modernizing the crossing are savings on expenditure on labour; it is expected that the price of labour will increase by 7 per cent per year over the same period. The market rate of interest, measured in terms of money (that is, the nominal interest rate) is 13 per cent. Is the modernizing of the crossing justified according to the criteria of financial appraisal?

3. A health authority plans to build a new hospital. It owns a site of 12 hectares at A, which it bought in readiness 8 years ago (year −8). (Plans for building the hospital have been postponed several times.) Unfortunately, since this site was bought it has become increasingly subject to noise nuisance from air traffic, a problem which was not forseen when the land was bought. It is now clear that a hospital on this site would need to be sound-proofed, which in turn would require it to be air-conditioned. This would mean a substantial increase on the costs of building a conventional hospital. The health authority has investigated the possibility of building the hospital on another and quieter site, and has selected site B as the best available alternative to A.

The main points of comparison between the two sites are the following:

(*i*) Land is more expensive at B than at A. The 12 hectare site at A cost £300 000 in year −8. Between that year and year 0, land prices in general increased by 75 per cent, while the prices of consumption goods increased by 50 per cent. The current market value of the site at A is, however, only £415 000; the increasing noise nuisance has ensured that the money value of land at A has increased much less quickly than that of land in general. At B, land now costs £70 000 per hectare. If the hospital is to be built at B that site must be bought now (that is, in year 0).

(*ii*) Although a 12-hectare site is large enough to accommodate the hospital that is currently being planned, it is now thought preferable to have a larger site of 18 hectares. This is because a larger site would reduce the costs of building extensions, should these be required in the future. Site A is surrounded by houses and so cannot be increased in size. There are no difficulties in buying 18 hectares at B. Should site B be selected, then 18 hectares will be bought at a cost of £1 260 000 and the surplus land will be left unused until and unless an extension to the hospital is required. (If this surplus land is not bought now it will be sold for housebuilding and so buying it now is the only way of ensuring its availability in the future.)

(*iii*) The extra costs of building and maintaining a sound-proofed, air-conditioned hospital of the type necessary at A, rather than a conventional hospital of the type that would be suitable at B, have present value of £920 000 when discounted to year 0. (The market rate of interest is 10 per cent. Building work would take place in years 1 to 4 and it is assumed that a hospital would have a 50-year life.)

(*iv*) Site B is further than A from the main population centres of the area that the hospital will serve. B would thus be a less convenient site for patients and their visitors to travel to and from. For the most part, the cost of travelling to and from hospital are borne by the travellers themselves and do not affect the grant requirement of the health authority. When patients travel by ambulance, however, the costs of operating the ambulances is borne by the health authority. Around 12 per cent of all journeys to hospital for treatment are by ambulance, and ambulances are costly vehicles to operate. It is estimated that the present value in year 0 of the additional costs of running ambulances to and from a hospital at B, rather than to and from one at A, is £105 000.

(*v*) In the opinion of medical experts, a sound-proofed hospital at A and a conventional hospital at B would be equally effective medically.

The health authority wishes to use the criteria of financial appraisal—that is, to minimize the present value of its grant requirements. If you were asked to advise the authority on its decision between the two sites, what advice would you give?

Notes

[1] If x and y are two small fractions,

$$(1 + x)(1 + y) = 1 + x + y + xy \simeq 1 + x + y$$

and
$$\frac{(1 + x)}{(1 + y)} \simeq 1 + x - y \simeq \frac{1}{1 + y - x}.$$

These approximations are extremely useful in practice, since they allow many calculations to be carried out by using discount and annuity factors.

Further reading

In this book no attempt is made to introduce the reader to the statistical techniques that must be used to produce the data on which project appraisal rests. Introductory texts on statistical method abound. The interested reader might consult, for example, Hey (1974), Kane (1968) or Thomas (1973).

The general point that the notion of cost must be related to a decision taken in a particular context is the theme of the various contributions in Buchanan and Thirlby (1973) of which Chapter 6 (Thirlby, 'The subjective theory of value and accounting "cost"') is particularly relevant here. A simpler statement, closer to orthodox accountancy, is provided by Chapter 6 of Bierman and Smidt (1975), and the implications for cost analysis are explored in Hart (1973) and in Chapter 10 of Merewitz and Sosnick (1971).

4. The Discount Rate in Financial Appraisal

4.1. 'Perfect' capital markets

Our discussion of the treatment of time in financial appraisal has been greatly simplified by our assumption that there is a single, easily-observed 'market rate of interest', at which anyone can borrow or lend freely. In technical terms, a 'perfect capital market' has been assumed.

If such an interest rate exists, it is easy to infer the marginal time preference rate of any individual. (If interest rates are expressed in nominal terms and price increases are expected, things are not quite so simple—as was shown in Section 3.5 above.) And all individuals share the same MTPR. So there is no problem in choosing a discount rate for appraising projects whose costs and returns are shared by a number of individuals.

A further convenience is that there is no need to distinguish between an individual's *income* and his *consumption.* So far we have not made this distinction very clearly. We have said that time preference is about the timing of *consumption*, yet in appraising projects we have applied MTPRs to the *income* received by shareholders or taxpayers from firms or public agencies. Implicitly we have assumed that income is consumed as soon as it is received: none is saved to be consumed later.

There is, however, no need to make this assumption if each shareholder or taxpayer can borrow and lend freely at a market interest rate. This is because the present value of the extra consumption that is made available to him by a project is independent of the period in which he chooses to enjoy it; all that matters is the period in which income is received.

Suppose, for example, that someone is to receive £10 next year (year 1). If the rate of interest is 10%, so is his MTPR. If he chooses to use this income to buy £10 worth of consumption in year 1, its present value in year 0 is £9·09 (discounted at his MTPR). Instead, he might plan to consume none of this extra income in year 1, but to save it all to consume in year 2. He would save by lending for a year at the market interest rate of 10%, thus being able to consume £1·10 in year 2. Discounted at his MTPR of 10%, this again has a present value of £9·09. Or again, he might decide not to wait even until year

1 for his promised increase in consumption. He could borrow £9·09 in year 0 and spend it on immediate consumption. His extra income of £10 in year 1 would just repay the loan with interest.

In the foregoing discussion, the changes in our individual's income were taken to be small ones. But this is not necessary either. Suppose that a project involves him in an outlay of £1000 in year 0 for a return of £1200 in year 1. If his income, without the project, is £2000 a year, these changes are significant ones. Given that he expects to consume £2000 in each of the two years, he might have a MTPR of 10%. Even though the project has an internal rate of return of 20%, it is quite possible that he would prefer the prospect of £2000 worth of consumption in each year to that of £1000 worth in year 0 and £3200 worth in year 1. In other words, if the changes in his income were to cause equal changes in his consumption, they would be sufficiently large to affect his MTPR. However, if there is a perfect capital market and an interest rate of 10% he can become better off by undertaking the project than by not. Suppose he borrows £1091 in year 0. Of this he can spend £1000 on financing the project and the remaining £91 on extra consumption. In year 1 his income from the project, £1200, will just repay the loan with interest.

So long as the present value of a project, when costs and returns are discounted at the market interest rate, is positive, such an opportunity is open. The size of this present value (£91 in the example) is a measure of the extra consumption that can be enjoyed in the present, without any sacrifices later, if undertaking the project is combined with appropriate borrowing or lending transactions.

So, if this present value is positive, a project is worth undertaking: it provides the individual with a way to make himself better off. He may in fact not choose this particular way of taking all the benefits of the project in the present; he may prefer other ways of allocating his consumption over time. But the important point is that the fact that the present value is positive implies that he can make himself better off by undertaking the project. Conversely, if the present value is negative, he cannot make himself as well off by undertaking it as he can by not.

(A more formal presentation of these arguments is given in an appendix to this chapter.)

4.2.   Differences in MTPRs between individuals

In practice things are not so simple as we have been assuming. There is no single 'market interest rate' to be observed, and there are strong reasons for believing that different individuals have different MTPRs.

So far we have carefully avoided raising the problem of *uncertainty*. (This will be discussed in Chapter 5.) But transactions that involve someone sacrificing income in the present in return for a promise of more income in the future are inherently risky. The lender faces the risk that the person who borrows from him will not repay, or will do so only after the lender has been put to the expense of using some form of coercion. The protection given to borrowers by the laws of bankruptcy and by the concept of limited liability increases the risks to lenders. The interest rate promised by the borrower may not represent solely a payment to compensate the lender for postponing consumption; it may also represent compensation for the lender's bearing the risk that the borrower may default.

When appraising projects whose costs and returns are not in themselves uncertain, we are interested in individuals' MTPRs pure and simple—that is, in their preferences between *certain* claims on consumption in different periods. (It will be argued in Chapter 5 that, even when projects have uncertain costs and returns, it still usually is convenient to separate the concept of time preference from that of uncertainty.) In principle, therefore, we require observations of interest rates at which people can borrow and lend without risk.

The 'gilt-edged' markets in which individuals lend to governments at fixed interest rates seem at first sight to be ones that allow risk-free lending. The main problem here is that interest rates are usually specified in nominal rather than real terms. The difficulties that this raises, and the way that these can be tackled, were briefly discussed in Section 3.5 above.

A further problem in inferring individuals' MTPRs from observations of the interest rates at which they lend arises from the tax system. Under many tax systems, income from interest is taxable. If additional income from interest accruing to a particular individual is taxed at the rate t, and if the nominal interest rate is i per year, he will receive after tax only $£i(1 - t)$ per year for each additional £1 that he lends. This after-tax rate is the true measure of the rate at which he can trade present for future consumption and so it is with this that his MTPR will be brought into equality. Thus if different individuals are taxed at the margin at different rates, their MTPRs will be different even if there is a single market interest rate.

An attempt to infer from market interest rates the MTPRs of people who are borrowing runs into problems of a different kind. Here the risks are borne not by the borrowers but by those from whom they borrow.

It is difficult to think of a market in which private individuals borrow but which lenders regard as risk-free. (Borrowing by firms and public organizations will be considered shortly.) The degree of risk is believed to be related to various characteristics of the borrower, such as his income, wealth, occupation and social status. Consequently borrowing rates differ according to the borrower's chracteristics. Further, the process of collecting information about the reliability of a borrower is costly. These costs typically are incurred by institutions such as banks and building societies which play an intermediary role between borrowers and lenders. To cover these transaction costs they must offer lenders a lower interest rate than they demand from borrowers.

All this implies that borrowers will have higher MTPRs than lenders and that borrowers who are conventionally thought to be less reliable will have higher MTPRs than those thought to be more reliable. A study undertaken in the 1950s in the U.S.A. provided empirical support for these deductions. The average MTPR for lenders with low incomes was 3%; for low-income households borrowing by hire purchase the average MTPR was 12%.[1]

If MTPRs differ between individuals it becomes difficult to select a discount rate for appraising projects whose costs and returns are shared by a number of individuals. As was shown in Section 2.2, in such a case each shareholder will want projects to be appraised by using *his* MTPR. If different shareholders have different MTPRs they will disagree about how projects should be appraised. Selecting a discount rate involves resolving in some way a conflict of interest between shareholders.

For a private firm, this difficulty is not as great as it looks. The shareholders of a firm are a self-selecting group; each is free to sell his shares at any time. Suppose, for example, that a particular shareholder has a MTPR of 15% (let us say, because he is heavily in debt and is borrowing at a high marginal interest rate) while the firm whose shares he holds appraises its projects by using a discount rate of 5%. In his view the firm will be over-investing. The obvious response is for him to sell his shares to someone else who has a lower MTPR. (The lower is one's MTPR, the higher is the present value of a claim on a given stream of future consumption. Thus the value of a share to a man with a low MTPR is greater than its value to a man with a high MTPR.) We should expect, therefore, that the MTPRs of shareholders would tend to be clustered around the discount rate that the firm uses.

Unfortunately this argument cannot be extended to the case of public agencies. The people we have chosen to treat as the shareholders of public agencies are the taxpayers; and taxpayers usually are not thought of as a self-selecting group. There are good reasons for expecting that different taxpayers will have different MTPRs; and there is evidence that this is so.[2]

4.3.   The 'cost of capital' approach

In the previous section our arguments were centred on individuals' time preferences and the interest rates faced by individuals.

An alternative approach is to focus on the interest rate at which the firm or public agency can borrow and lend. In certain circumstances this approach allows the difficult problems raised by differences in MTPRs to be side-stepped. If a firm is able to borrow and lend freely at a given rate of interest, it is in the shareholders' interests that this rate (or 'cost of capital') should be used as the firm's discount rate for appraising projects. This conclusion holds whatever the MTPRs of individual shareholders happen to be.

Suppose that a firm can borrow and lend at an interest rate of 10%, while two of its shareholders, Messrs. A and B, have MTPRs of 6% and 20% respectively. The firm has the opportunity to invest £1000 in year 0, which will earn a return of £120 per year, in perpetuity, from year 1. Suppose that the firm finances this project by reducing its dividends in year 0 by £1000 and so is able to increase its dividends in all subsequent years by £120. Suppose that A and B are each entitled to a one-thousandth share of the firm's dividends. Then to A, who has a MTPR of 6%, this project has a positive present value of £1. To B, whose MTPR is 20%, the project has a negative present value: *minus* £0·4. The two shareholders will disagree as to whether the project should be undertaken, given that it is to be financed in this particular way.

Now consider the project in relation to the interest rate at which the firm can borrow and lend. Discounted at this rate (10%), the project has a present value of £200. What is the significance of this result for our two shareholders? It means that, by combining the undertaking of the project with appropriate borrowing or lending, the firm could increase its dividends by £200 in year 0 without reducing them in any other year. (The firm must borrow £1200 in year 0. The £120 per year interest on this loan would be paid out of the project's returns, while the project's costs—£1000 in year 0—would be financed by the loan, leaving a surplus of £200 in year 0.) A and B would both prefer this strategy to that of not undertaking the project at all, since they would each receive an extra £0·2 in year 0 if the strategy were followed.

In general, if a project has a positive present value when its costs and returns are discounted at the rate at which a firm can borrow and lend, it is possible to make all shareholders better off by undertaking the project if it is financed appropriately. Conversely, if a project has a negative present value when this discount rate is used, the project should not be undertaken. For every time stream of dividends that can be attained by undertaking the project, there is an alternative time stream, which can be attained by not undertaking the project, that would be preferred by all shareholders.

The 'cost of capital' approach can identify projects which have the *potential* to make all shareholders better off. It does not, however, give any guidance as to how projects ought to be financed. To return to the original example, we considered two alternative ways of financing our firm's project. The first method was to finance it entirely at the expense of dividends in year 0; the second method was to finance it entirely from a loan. The second method, unlike the first, made both A and B better off than they would have been if the project had not been undertaken. But A would prefer the project to be financed by the first method—which gave him net gains with a present value of £1—rather than by the second—which gave gains worth only £0·2. If shareholders have different MTPRs they will disagree about how projects ought to be financed.

(Analytically, this argument is very similar to the argument presented in Section 4.1 above, that if an individual can borrow and lend freely at a given interest rate, he will seek to maximize the present value of his income, discounted at this interest rate, irrespective of the pattern of his preferences about the timing of his consumption. A more formal presentation of both these arguments is given in an appendix to this chapter.)

Limitations of a simple cost of capital approach: private firms

The approach suggested above, as it stands, is applicable only if a firm can borrow and lend freely at a single, given rate of interest.

Unfortunately for the analyst, however, it may be no easier for a firm to borrow at a risk-free rate of interest that it is for a private individual—and for the same reasons. Lending to a firm is risky. Lenders require compensation for bearing this risk and for bearing the costs of gathering information about the borrower. Thus the rate at which a firm can borrow is likely to be higher than the rate at which it can lend. Further, the more heavily indebted a firm is, the greater the risks to lenders will be thought to be, and so the greater will be the cost of borrowing. Thus the rate at which the firm can, at the margin, transform present dividends into future ones (and vice versa) is not constant.

This need not create insuperable difficulties, however. If a firm currently is lending, the rate at which it lends is the marginal rate at which it can transform present dividends into future ones. This rate is also the marginal rate at which it can transform future dividends into present ones, by lending less. Provided that a project is sufficiently small that financing it does not affect the firm's status as a lender, nor the rate at which it lends, the original arguments of this Section apply. The lending rate is the appropriate discount rate for the firm to use in appraising the project.

If a firm currently is borrowing, there is a marginal borrowing rate which measures the cost to the firm (in forgone future dividends) of securing additional present income in the form of loans. This same rate also measures the rate at which present dividends can be transformed into future ones (by repaying loans). Again, the original arguments can be reinterpreted. Provided that a project is sufficiently small that financing it does not affect the marginal borrowing rate, this rate is the appropriate discount rate to use in appraising the project.

The most difficult problems arise if a firm is neither borrowing nor lending. The 'cost of capital' approach then may break down, for the marginal rate at which present dividends can be transformed (by lending) into future ones may not be the same as the marginal rate at which future dividends can be transformed (by borrowing) into present ones. In these circumstances, the 'cost of capital' approach cannot show whether projects should be appraised by discounting at the lending rate, at the borrowing rate, or at some intermediate rate. A choice can be made only by reference to the time preferences of shareholders—which is to return to the difficulties of Section 4.2.

The cost of capital approach and public agencies

The analysis of the 'cost of capital' approach in relation to the private firm could be pursued much further, as it has been in the literature of business finance. For our purposes, however, this is unnecessary. In the main, we are concerned with private firms only insofar as useful analogies can be drawn between their behaviour and that of public agencies.

If a public agency is able to borrow and lend freely at a given interest rate, then the 'cost of capital' approach is appropriate for a financial appraisal of the agency's projects. But the opportunities for public agencies to borrow and lend are often far more limited than those open to private firms. In the U.K., the borrowing and lending activities of most public agencies are closely supervised and constrained by the central government. Finance for investment projects is often provided in the form of direct grants from government funds. An agency that receives all of its finance in this way and that has no contact with borrowing and lending markets cannot take its discount rate from any cost of capital: there is none. Other public agencies receive finance for projects in the form of loans, at interest, from government funds. But such loans usually are not available freely, on request; they are rationed by the central government. This gives rise to the problems of appraising projects under a regime of 'capital rationing'. (These problems will be discussed in Chapter 6.)

4.4. Conclusion

In many ways, then, the conclusions of this chapter are negative ones. At crucial points the analogy between the private firm and the public agency breaks down. The injunction that a public agency should use 'commercial criteria' is insufficiently clear to direct the agency to a 'correct' discount rate.

In the U.K. this problem is dealt with by the central government setting, as an act of policy, a 'test rate of discount' to be used by public agencies when appraising projects.[3] Since at this stage we are considering decisions taken at the level of the agency, we may take such a discount rate as given as part of the objectives of any public agency. That is, the objective is to minimize the present value of an agency's net subsidy requirements over time, discounted at a government-determined discount rate. In Part II of this book we shall consider the criteria that might be used by a central government when choosing a test rate of discount or 'social discount rate'. (See Chapter 15.)

Appendix: Perfect capital markets and the 'cost of capital' approach— a more formal treatment

This appendix presents more formally the arguments of Sections 4.1 and 4.3.

For convenience of exposition, consider the two-period one-good model of individual choice that was introduced in the appendix to Chapter 2. An individual chooses between alternative 'bundles' of two goods, 'present consumption' (c_0) and 'claims on future consumption' (c_1). His preferences between such bundles are represented by a family of indifference curves, such as I_1 and I_2 in Figure 4.1.

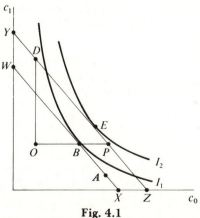

Fig. 4.1

Suppose that our individual initially has the combination of claims on present and future consumption represented by point A. Suppose, too, that he is able to borrow and lend freely at a market rate of interest, and so can reach any point on the consumption possibility frontier WX. B, being the most-preferred point, will be chosen.

Now suppose that the individual has the opportunity to undertake a project which requires an outlay of OB in the present in return for a gain of OD in the future. He thus has the opportunity to move to point D. This combination of claims on present and future consumption is itself less preferred than the original point B. (D lies below and to the left of the indifference curve I_1.) However, by combining undertaking the project with appropriate borrowing and lending at the market interest rate he can reach any point on the consumption possibility frontier YZ (parallel to WX and passing through D). The best attainable position is E, which is preferred to B. By undertaking the project, then, our individual provides himself with an opportunity to make himself better off.

Provided that the post-project consumption possibility frontier, YZ, lies to the right of the pre-project frontier, WX, there must be some point (such as E) on the post-project frontier which is preferred to B. Conversely, if the post-project frontier lies to the left of the pre-project one, no such preferred point can exist. So to judge whether it is in our individual's interest to undertake the project, we do not need to know which point on the post-project frontier is the most preferred. All that we need to know is which frontier lies to the right of the other. A simple way of expressing this is in terms of present values. Discounted at the market rate of interest, the present value of our project is BP. (For a demonstration that this is so, see the appendix to Chapter 2.) The statement that the present value of the project is positive is exactly equivalent to the statement that the post-project frontier lies to the right of the pre-project frontier. Conversely, if the present value is negative this order is reversed.

To demonstrate the case for the 'cost of capital' approach in the appraisal of projects of private firms, all that is necessary is to reinterpret the above analysis. Consider a case in which the shareholders of a firm must choose how much dividend should be distributed in each of two periods; c_0 represents 'present dividends' and c_1 'future dividends'. Suppose that point A in Figure 4.1 represents a combination of present and future dividend that the firm is initially in a position to distribute. Now suppose that the firm can borrow and lend freely at a given interest rate (the 'cost of capital'). This allows the firm to reach any combination of present and future dividends that is on the 'dividend possibility frontier' WX. If we know nothing about the time preferences of shareholders we do not know which point on this line will be chosen; and if different shareholders have different MTPRs they will disagree about which point will be chosen. But some point, say B, will—by one means or another—be chosen. (The indifference curves I_1 and I_2 have no significance in the present discussion.)

Now suppose that the firm has the opportunity to undertake an investment project which costs OB in the present and provides a return of OD in the future. If (as in the case illustrated in the diagram) the dividend possibility frontier associated with point D—that is, the line YZ—lies to the right of the pre-project dividend possibility frontier, it is possible, by combining the project with appropriate borrowing or lending, for the firm to distribute more dividend in the present than it would have done in the absence of the project, while distributing no less dividend in the future. That is, a point like P, to the right of B, can be reached. No matter what his MTPR, every shareholder would regard this as an improvement on the initial position. There is, then, a strong case that all shareholders would wish that the project be undertaken. Conversely, if the magnitudes of OB and OD were such that the dividend possibility frontier through D lay to the left of the pre-project frontier, there would be, for every point on the post-project frontier, a clearly preferable (or dominating) point on the pre-project frontier. That is, for every combination of present and future dividends that could be attained by undertaking the project there would be an unambiguously preferable combination that could be attained without undertaking the project. In this case, presumably, shareholders would agree that the project should not be undertaken.

The rule that the project should be undertaken if and only if the post-project dividend possibility frontier lies to the right of the pre-project frontier can be re-expressed as the rule that the project should be undertaken if and only if the present value of the project, when costs and returns are discounted at the firm's cost of capital, is positive.

Notes

[1] See Krutilla and Eckstein (1958), Table 7, p. 98.

[2] See Note 1.

[3] This policy was first formulated in a White Paper published by the British Government in 1967. See H.M.S.O. (1967).

Further reading

This chapter, like Chapter 2, rests on the theoretical foundations laid down by Fisher (1930) and Hirshleifer (1958).

For a fuller treatment of the subject matter of this chapter in relation to project appraisal by private firms, see Merrett and Sykes (1973), Chapters 3 and 4.

5. Uncertainty

5.1. States and outcomes

Acquiring information is costly. We should not therefore expect people making choices to be fully informed about the consequences of their taking each of the courses of action open to them. And, of course, it is not always *possible* to be fully informed. Some information—such as whether it will rain in central London on 26 August next year—is beyond the ingenuity of anyone to suppy at any price. Project appraisal typically takes place in an environment of uncertainty.

So far in this book we have been careful to side-step this problem. We have always assumed that the outcome of each course of action being considered can be known with certainty. For the purpose of project appraisal, the *outcome* of a course of action is its effect on whatever entity the decision-maker is seeking to maximize (or minimize)—that is, its contribution to the achievement of the decision-maker's objective. In an environment of certainty the analyst's task is simply to identify the outcome of each of the alternative courses of action being considered.

But when there is uncertainty things are rather more difficult. To say that uncertainty exists in the world is to say that there is a set of (more than one) possible *events* or *states of the world*, each of which could occur or exist but only one of which will. To say that a decision problem is affected by uncertainty is to say that the outcome of at least one of the courses of action being considered is different according to which state of the world occurs. For example, consider the problem of choosing whether or not to drill for oil at a particular site. To put things at their simplest, there are two states of the world, *either* that there is oil beneath the site *or* that there is not. Typically there will be no way of knowing with certainty which of these states of the world actually exists, other than by drilling; thus the outcome of drilling is necessarily uncertain at the time the decision between drilling and not drilling is made.

This way of looking at the problem suggests a way of summarizing what is known about a decision problem. A list should be made of all the states of the world that are regarded as possible. For each state it should then be shown what the outcome would be, if that state occurred, of taking each of the available alternative courses of action. Since we have defined outcomes in relation to objectives, each outcome in the list could be calculated only by a process of analysis of the kind suggested in previous chapters. This system of presenting information is known, rather grandly, as *sensitivity analysis.*

For each possible state of the world there will be a course of action that would be best, were it known with certainty that that particular state would occur. It is conceivable that one course of action will *dominate* the alternatives—that is, whichever state of the world is to occur, the same course of action is the best. Clearly, in this case there is no further problem; the decision is 'not sensitive' to the uncertainty that has been considered. If, however, one course of action does not dominate the others, the problem remains of choosing which course to take.

Intuitively one can recognize that there are ways of judging the wisdom of choices made under uncertainty of this kind. Consider, for example, a householder choosing whether to take out insurance against fire. If the state of the world 'house burns down' occurs, the outcome of insuring will be a large financial saving (relative to not insuring). Conversely, if the state 'house does not burn down' occurs, the outcome of insuring will be a financial loss (the insurance premium). Neither of the two available courses of action dominates the others. Yet one might still assert that the householder would be wise to take out an insurance policy on particular terms.

A sound choice, it would seem, is made by weighing in some way the likelihoods of the different states of the world and their respective implications for the outcomes of different courses of action. The simplest approach is to leave the matter here and to say that it is the decision-maker's job to weigh these factors in whatever way he believes to be most appropriate. The task of the analyst goes no further than supplying the decision-maker with the findings of a sensitivity analysis.

5.2. The use of subjective probabilities: cumulative probability distributions

If the analyst goes no further than making a sensitivity analysis, and if this does not reveal that one course of action dominates the available alternatives, the task of weighing the various possible outcomes falls to the decision-maker. The analyst can, however, go further. The weighing of possible outcomes may itself be subjected to analysis. This requires there to be criteria for identifying rational choices made under uncertainty. While the nature of the problem is such that an element of judgement cannot be avoided, it is possible to confine judgement to the areas where it is strictly necessary. Expanding the area to be covered by explicit analysis makes the decision-maker more accountable to his ultimate employers and reduces the likelihood of inconsistent decision-making.

One starting-point is to assert that rational choice under uncertainty should be based on judgements about the relative likelihoods or probabilities of particular states of the world occurring. This seems intuitively reasonable. The more likely is a particular state of the world (say, one's house catching fire), the more account should be taken of the implications of this state when making decisions (say, about fire insurance).

Here we need the formal mathematical language of probability, which can be summarized very briefly in two sentences. For any conceivable state of the world there is a probability that the state will occur, and by convention this probability is represented by a number not less than 0 and not greater than 1. If there are a number of states, one and only one of which must occur, then the probabilities of these states must sum to 1.

Mathematics, of course, cannot tell us what 'probability' means and philosophically, probability is a very difficult concept. We shall adopt the 'subjective' or 'Bayesian'[1] interpretation of probability and say that the probability of an event is a measure of some person's degree of belief that this event will occur. Thus, for example, if a hospital administrator feels the same degree of belief that a particular hospital extension will be built in the next 20 years as that he could cut a well-shuffled pack of cards and draw the ace of spades, then in his judgement the probability of the extenstion being built is 1/52 or about 0·019.

This provides a way by which anyone can assign probabilities to any events. Obviously the amount of knowledge that a person has about the forces affecting an event will influence his judgement about its probability; and a third party may believe that one person's judgement is better than another's. But knowledge is not a precondition for being able to assign *some* probability to an event. Probability numbers are merely a language in which judgements of a particular kind can be expressed.

In a decision problem that involves uncertainty, probabilities can be assigned to those states of the world that are uncertain and that affect the outcome of the decision; these probabilities can then be used as data for analysis. An important problem arises here, however: who is to make the judgements of probabilities? Since statements of probabilities are subjective, the formation of probability judgements cannot be regarded as a purely technical task. Consider, for example, the problem of choosing whether or not to drill for oil (discussed in Section 5.1 above). The greater is the probability that oil exists below the drilling site, the stronger is the case for drilling. But suppose that, after considering the same evidence, one expert believes that the probability that there is oil is 0·6 while another believes it to be only 0·4. Each maintains his own judgement despite knowing that the other disagrees. There is no objective way of determining which—if either—of the experts is 'right'. Even if a hole is drilled and (let us say) no oil is found, each expert may maintain that his own judgement was sound at the time it was made, given the evidence then available. Thus under uncertainty, unless sensitivity analysis shows one course of action to dominate the others, a decision must inevitably be based upon subjective judgements. In our stylization of the decision-making process, the decision-maker is ultimately responsible for choosing. If the purpose of appraisal is to assist him in this task it should use judgements to which he subscribes. Where it is not clear what probabilities should be used in an appraisal, or who should be delegated the work of supplying probability judgements, the proper person to resolve the question is the decision-maker.

One might object to this position by arguing that the decision-maker is merely the agent of the general public (in the case of a public agency) or of the shareholders (in the case of a private firm). Should not the decision-maker use the probability judgements of those people for whom he is the agent? Our view is that the decision-maker's ultimate employers inevitably are not well-informed about the possible consequences of most of the decisions that have to be taken on their behalf. They expect the decision-maker to make himself better-informed and then to act in the light of this information. That is, they expect him to react to uncertainty by using his own judgement. Consequently, we shall treat probability judgements that have been made by, or sanctioned by, the decision-maker as if they were shared by each of the people on whose behalf he acts.

When numerical probabilities have been attached to states of the world, the possible outcomes of a project can be expressed as a *probability distribution.* In some circumstances it is possible, simply by comparing the probability distibutions associated with alternative courses of action, to infer which of these courses is to be preferred.

For concreteness, consider some individual who must choose whether or not to undertake one of three mutually exclusive projects, A, B and C. The outcomes of these projects depend on which of four possible states of the world (i, ii, iii, and iv) occurs. The relevant information is summarized in Table 5.1. We shall assume that, if none of the projects were undertaken, our individual's wealth would be the same whichever state occurred. (This datum level of wealth may be denoted by $\overline{W}$.)

Without any consideration of the probabilities of the four states, it can be deduced that B is preferable to A. Whichever state occurs, the present value of B is at least as great as that of A, and in three of these states B has a higher present value. That is, a sensitivity analysis shows that B dominates A. But, seen from this viewpoint, C neither dominates nor is dominated by either A or B.

Table 5.1

State	Probability	Present value of project (£'000)		
		A	B	C
i	0·3	3·0	4·0	2·0
ii	0·3	−2·0	0·0	4·0
iii	0·2	1·0	1·0	−4·0
iv	0·2	−5·0	−4·0	0·0

Table 5.2

x (£'000)	Probability that wealth $\geqslant W + x$ course of action:			
	A	B	C	O
5·0	0·0	0·0	0·0	0·0
4·0	0·0	0·3	0·3	0·0
3·0	0·3	0·3	0·3	0·0
2·0	0·3	0·3	0·6	0·0
1·0	0·5	0·5	0·6	0·0
0·0	0·5	0·8	0·8	1·0
−1·0	0·5	0·8	0·8	1·0
−2·0	0·8	0·8	0·8	1·0
−3·0	0·8	0·8	0·8	1·0
−4·0	0·8	1·0	1·0	1·0
−5·0	1·0	1·0	1·0	1·0

Now suppose that our individual attaches to the four states of the world the probabilities that are listed in Table 5.1. It is now possible to make a further deduction: that C is preferable to either A or B. Table 5.2 gives a *cumulative probability distribution* of outcomes for each of the four available courses of action—undertaking each of the three projects, and doing nothing. ('Doing nothing' is denoted by O in the table.) For each of a range of possible outcomes—possible values of the individual's wealth—the table shows the probability that the actual outcome will be *at least as* favourable as this, given that he takes a particular course of action. (For example, if he undertakes project A there is a probability of 0·5 that his wealth will be at least as great as $\overline{W}$ + £1000.) It emerges that the probability distribution for the course of action C dominates those for A and B. That is, for every possible level of wealth, the probability that this will be achieved by undertaking project C is at least as great as the equivalent probabilities for the other two projects; and for some levels of wealth the probability for C is higher. Not surprisingly, given our earlier deduction, B also dominates A in the same way. It is not possible, however, to use this approach to deduce whether it is preferable to undertake project C or to do nothing; the probability distribution for C neither dominates nor is dominated by that for O.

(As a technical aside, it should perhaps be noted that the foregoing argument requires the assumption that the relationship between wealth and utility is the same in all states of the world. A very brief discussion of utility theory is given in an appendix to this chapter.)

5.3. The expected value criterion

The rule that one course of action should be preferred to another if the cumulative probability distribution of outcomes for the first action dominates that for the second often is insufficiently strong to produce a clear conclusion as to which action should be preferred. One way to proceed is to use the *expected value criterion*.

This decision rule is based on the concept of *mathematical expectation*. Formally, suppose that there are n states of the world, one and only one of which must occur, and that the probability that each state will occur is $p_1, p_2, \ldots, p_n$. Let the outcome of each state be a net gain of $x_1, x_2, \ldots, x_n$. Then the mathematical expectation, or expected value, of net gain is

$$p_1 x_1 + p_2 x_2 + \ldots + p_n x_n.$$

In words, it is a weighted average of the possible outcomes, with each being weighted by its probability. The expected value criterion is that, where there is uncertainty, project appraisal should use the mathematical expectation of the outcome of a project as if it were *the* outcome, known with certainty. (In the example presented in the preceding section, it can be calculated from the information given in Table 5.1 that the expected value of the present value of project A—the 'expected present value' of A—is *minus* £500. The expected present value of B is £600 and that of C is £1000. According to the expected value criterion, then, not only is it better to undertake C than either of the other two projects; it is also better to undertake C than to do nothing.)

One way of trying to justify the use of the expected value criterion is to think in terms of risks that can be repeated many times, each repeat being independent of the others. Consider, for example, a project which has two possible outcomes, 'success' which implies a gain of £10 000 and 'failure' which implies a loss of £8000. Suppose that a decision-maker judges that success and failure are equally probable; the project thus has an expected value of £1000. In judging the probability of success to be 0·5, the decision-maker is declaring that he believes the project is as likely to succeed as (say) a fair coin is likely to fall 'heads' when tossed. Thus, in his judgement, accepting the project is equivalent to accepting a gamble on the toss of a coin, in which 'heads' means a gain of £10 000 and 'tails' a loss of £8000. Now this is a gamble that can be repeated many times. If it were repeated a very large number of times, one can be confident that the average gain per gamble would be close to £1000—the expected value of the outcome of a single gamble. In this sense, an expected value is an average outcome. To say that the project—which itself is not repeatable—has an expected value of £1000 is to say that it is equivalent to a single gamble, of a 'repeatable' kind, whose average outcome is a gain of £1000.

This *suggests* that the expected value criterion might be an appropriate one for firms and public agencies to use. It does not, however, show definitely that the criterion should be used.

To explore this issue further, we must consider the interests of the shareholders of a private firm or of taxpayers in relation to public agencies. It is these interests which should dictate the criteria to be used for financial appraisal.

Consider a firm and one of its shareholders. (As usual, for 'firm' and 'shareholder', 'public agency' and 'taxpayer' may be substituted.) If the firm undertakes a project whose outcome is uncertain, the shareholder's future income from the firm is thereby made uncertain. Take, for example, the project discussed above, with a 0·5 probability of a gain of £10 000 and a 0·5 probability of a loss of £8000. A man who holds a 1/1000 share in a firm undertaking a project with these characteristics has a 0·5 probability of a gain of £10 and a 0·5 probability of a loss of £8. If he regards this prospect as equivalent to that of a certain gain of £1 (which is its expected value), then he will want the firm to behave as if the project as a whole were worth £1000. That is, he will want the firm to use the expected value criterion for project appraisal.

So the expected value criterion is appropriate for the firm if, when a project implies that individual shareholders have uncertain prospects of changes in their incomes, each shareholder values his prospect at its expected value. In other words, the *certainty equivalent* of the uncertain prospect is equal to its expected value. (The certainty equivalent of an uncertain prospect to a particular individual is the sum of money such that the individual is indifferent between, on the one hand, receiving this sum—or paying it, if the certainty equivalent is negative—, and on the other, the prospect itself.)

Introspection suggests that certainty equivalent and expected value are approximately equal, given two conditions.

The first condition is that only small changes in wealth should be at risk. Thus, it is asserted, a gamble involving a gain of 10p if a coin falls 'heads' and a loss of 10p if it falls 'tails' has, for most people, a certainty equivalent very close to zero. However, a similar gamble with a stake of £10 000 rather than 10p would have, for most people, a certainty equivalent considerably less than zero. (The state of assigning to uncertain prospects of changes in wealth, certainty equivalents which are less than expected values is known technically as *risk aversion*. It is usual to assume that individuals will show risk aversion where large changes in their wealth are at risk.)

The second condition is that risks should be independent. Suppose that a project will have different outcomes according to which of two states, A and B, occurs. The risk that this project imposes on an individual is 'independent' if, in the absence of the project, that individual's wealth would be the same whichever of the two states occurred. As an example of a non-independent risk, consider a project which consists of using additional fertilizers in the growing of a particular crop. The return on this investment to the farmer who undertakes the project is the additional value of the crop that results from the use of fertilizers. This additional value will depend upon the climate during the growing season, a factor which is uncertain at the time the investment is made. Let us suppose that the return will be greater if there is 'high rainfall' (state A) than if there is 'low rainfall' (state B). If the farmer's main source of income is from the sale of his crops, it is quite probable that, irrespective of whether or not he invests in fertilizers, his income would be substantially different according to which state occurred. If high rainfall is associated with high income, even if the investment is not made, then the investment produces high returns in a state in which the investor is relatively rich and low returns in a state in which he is relatively poor. If he is risk-averse, we should expect him to attach a certainty equivalent value to the returns of the project that is lower than their expected value. Conversely, if high rainfall is associated with low income, undertaking the project is a form of insurance. We should then expect the certainty equivalent value of the project to be greater than its expected value.

(In an appendix to this chapter it is shown that the arguments presented above are consistent with a particular set of assumptions about individuals' preferences between uncertain prospects.)

The kinds of risk involved in the projects of firms and public agencies commonly satisfy both of the conditions that are necessary for the expected value criterion to be appropriate.

Both the shareholder-owned firm and the public agency are institutions that permit the 'spreading' of risks. That is, the costs and returns of risky projects can be shared amongst a large number of individuals.

If a firm has many shareholders, none of whom holds more than a small proportion of its shares, only a very large change in the firm's profits would have significant effects on the wealth of individual shareholders. And there are good reasons to expect this state of affairs to be the general rule. If individuals are risk-averse we should not expect them to choose to put all their eggs in one basket by holding a large proportion of their wealth in the form of shares in a single firm. (There are countervailing factors, however. Large blocks of shares may be held as a means by which the shareholder can have power over the affairs of a firm. They may be held as a way of economizing on the 'transaction costs' of buying and selling shares. If different individuals have different judgements about probabilities, the ownership of a firm's shares may be concentrated in the hands of a few people who are particularly optimistic about the firm's prospects.)

The public agency, at least insofar as financial appraisal is conccerned, is a risk-spreading institution. A change in the grant requirement of a public agency would have to be very large indeed before the tax changes that it brought about had significant effects on the wealth of individual taxpayers.

Whether the second condition, of 'independent risk', is met in a particular case is a matter for judgement. But cases where it is met sufficiently closely for practical purposes are very common.

5.4.   The risk premium on the discount rate

A common device for taking account of uncertainty in project appraisal is the addition of a 'risk premium' to the discount rate. There are a number of different arguments that can be made for this procedure. Here we shall consider two of them.

Probability of failure

Consider a project, undertaken by a private firm, to manufacture and market a new product. The capital cost of the project, c, will be borne in year 0; sales will begin in year 1. Market research shows that the current demand for the product is such that the project's net revenue would be x per year. This research, however, is based upon knowledge of the state of the market in year 0. There is much uncertainty about market conditions in future years, since new competitors may enter the market, and innovation might make the product obsolete. It would, therefore, be unwise to expect the present demand to continue indefinitely.

Suppose that, as a rough approximation, the decision-maker expresses his judgements about this uncertainty in the following way. There is some probability, p, that the project will fail in year 0. If it fails, no revenue will be earned. If it does not fail in year 0, it will earn x in year 1. Again, however, there is a probability p that the project will fail in this year, and that no subsequent revenue will be earned. In each year of the project's life, given that it is has survived so far, there is a probability p that it will fail.

Applying the expected value criterion, the expected value of revenue in period 1 is $(1 - p)x$, the expected value of revenue in period 2 is $(1 - p)^2 x$, and so on. The expected present value of the project is thus

$$-c + \frac{(1 - p)x}{1 + r} + \frac{(1 - p)^2 x}{(1 + r)^2} + \ldots \qquad 5.1$$

where r is the MTPR of shareholders.

Using the approximation introduced in Chapter 3 (Note 1), this expected present value can be rewritten as

$$-c + \frac{x}{1 + r + p} + \frac{x}{(1 + r + p)^2} + \ldots \qquad 5.2$$

So calculating the expected present value of the project, using a discount rate of r, is, in this case, equivalent to calculating the present value of the stream of returns that would be earned if the project did not fail and using a discount rate of $r + p$. p is a *risk premium*.

There are probably many projects whose uncertainties can conveniently and not too unrealistically be expressed as a constant probability of failure per year. In these cases the risk premium method is formally correct.

The danger in the risk premium method is that it adds together two numbers that conceptually are quite distinct—a probability and a time preference rate. As a means of calculating expected present values by using discount tables, the method undoubtedly is convenient. But it is also an invitation to confused thinking, for the synthetic discount rate produced by adding r and p has no clear intuitive meaning. In thinking about a problem, and in presenting conclusions, it is far sounder to keep probabilities and time preference rates separate. The objective underlying project appraisal—in this case, maximizing the expected present value of shareholders' incomes, using a MTPR of r—should always be explicit. So should the judgements being made about the probabilities of different outcomes—in this case, the 'probability of failure'.

Risk aversion

The risk premium method can also be used as a means of incorporating risk aversion into project appraisal. This interpretation makes the use of a risk premium different in principle from the use of the expected value criterion.

With this approach, the costs or returns of a risky project in each period of its life are represented by a single estimate. Often it is not clearly spelled out what this estimate really is, but it probably is best to interpret it as an expected value of costs or returns. The present value of this stream of costs and returns is then calculated by discounting at a rate arrived at by adding a risk premium to the appropriate time preference rate. The size of the risk premium is chosen by the decision-maker in a more or less rule-of-thumb way. Projects are undertaken if and only if they have positive present values calculated in this way.

To see what this rule implies, consider a risky project whose net returns in periods $0, 1, \ldots, n$ have expected values of $E_0, E_1, \ldots, E_n$. If the MTPR of all shareholders is r, and if the risk premium is p, the project should be undertaken—according to the rule—if

$$E_0 + \frac{E_1}{1 + r + p} + \frac{E_2}{(1 + r + p)^2} + \ldots + \frac{E_n}{(1 + r + p)^n} > 0. \qquad 5.3$$

Reversing the argument of page 61 above, this inequality can be rewritten as

$$E_0 + \frac{(1 - p)E_1}{1 + r} + \frac{(1 - p)^2 E_2}{(1 + r)^2} + \ldots + \frac{(1 - p)^n E_n}{(1 + r)^n} > 0. \qquad 5.4$$

So this version of the risk premium approach implies that if an uncertain cost or return, occurring in some period t, has an expected value E_t, it should be treated as if it were a certain cost or return with the value $(1 - p)^t E_t$.

As far as returns are concerned, this amounts to assuming that there is risk aversion, and that the divergence between the expected value of a return and its certainty equivalent increases systematically the further into the future it occurs. On the face of it, this is a somewhat arbitrary procedure. For some projects, these assumptions might be reasonable as a rule of thumb; for others, they might be completely inappropriate.

But now consider the implications of the risk premium approach for the treatment of costs. An uncertain cost, if it is to be borne in the future, is valued at *less than* its expected value—that is, it is treated as less of a cost. The further into the future the cost occurs, the greater is the divergence between certainty equivalent and expected value. But this divergence is in the wrong direction. A moment's thought shows that a risk-averse individual would regard an uncertain cost as a greater burden than a certain one with the same expected value. (If this were not the case, people would not incur the certain costs of insuring against the uncertain costs of fire or theft.)

So as a means of incorporating risk aversion into project appraisal, the risk premium approach is unsatisfactory. Where there are reasons for supposing the certainty equivalents of the costs or returns of projects to be different from their expected values, it is sounder to make explicit judgements about how great the difference is than to conceal these judgements behind the smoke-screen of a risk premium.

5.5. Time horizons

When a project is expected to have a relatively long life, it is rare for an analyst to be able to predict with any degree of certainty exactly how long its life will be. We have already considered one way of handling uncertainty of this kind, this method being to assume a constant 'probability of failure' for the project (see Section 5.4). Often, however, such an assumption would be implausible. One might expect a project to become increasingly likely to fail, the older it became. Take, for example, the project of building a house. One might feel virtually certain that this project would have a useful life of at least 20 years—that is, that for the first 20 years the probability of failure would be close to zero. Yet, at the same time, one might be very doubtful that the project's useful life would be greater than, say 80 years.

In principle there is no reason for not treating this form of uncertainty in the same way as any other form. One could use sensitivity analysis and work out the present value of the project for each conceivable length of life. Or one could go further and attach probabilities to different project lives and then work out the expected present value of the project.

There is, however, a very good practical reason for seeking a simpler, more rule-of-thumb approach. The process of discounting typically make costs or benefits that occur in the distant future very insignificant relative to costs or benefits in the present. With a 10 per cent discount rate, for example, a claim on £1 in 50 years time has a present value of only £0·0085. So, provided that a project is expected to have a relatively long life, the decision between accepting it or rejecting it is unlikely to be sensitive to changes in the assumptions made about the precise length of its life.

For the sake of convenience, analysts often use *time horizons*. A time horizon is a date in the future beyond which all costs and benefits are ignored. It is conventional to assume that, up to the horizon, a project's costs and benefits are steady and predictable. In effect, therefore, the time horizon is an assumed date of failure for the project, 'failure' being a state in which the project produces neither benefits nor costs.

The use of time horizons must not be confused with the use of a very simple criterion for deciding whether or not to undertake projects—the *payback period* criterion. The payback period for an investment project is the period of time, from the beginning of the project, before the sum of the *undiscounted* returns, less the *undiscounted* costs, becomes zero. If, for example, project A has net returns in years 0, 1, . . ., 5 of −100, 20, 40, 40, 40, 40, its payback period is exactly 3 years. Similarly if project B has net returns in these years of −100, 50, 50, 5, 5, 5, its payback period is exactly 2 years. The payback period criterion is to rank projects by their payback periods; the shorter the period, the more acceptable the project. Thus if projects A and B were mutually exclusive, B would be preferred to A. To decide whether or not to undertake particular projects, one would compare projects' payback periods with some common standard; the rule might be that projects should be undertaken if their payback periods are less than say, 5 years.

The payback period criterion is an extremely crude rule of thumb, which simultaneously attempts to take account of the significances of time preference, of uncertainty about the life of a project, and of risk aversion. Since no explicit account is taken of time preference, the idea that earlier returns are preferable to later ones appears only in the notion that shorter payback periods are preferable to longer ones. But this notion can also be regarded as a means of taking account of uncertainty about projects' lives; because there is believed to be a high probability that projects will fail after short periods, projects with quick returns should be preferred. As with the risk premium approach, the attempt to mix within one decision rule, concepts which are quite distinct, is a recipe for muddled thinking.

A time horizon is a simplifying assumption whose meaning can be grasped quite easily. To use say, a time horizon of 30 years is to say, 'let us assume that after 30 years this project will cease to earn returns (or to incur costs); and let us investigate whether, given this assumption, the project is worth undertaking'. To consider whether this assumption might lead to grossly wrong results, one simply has to consider what returns the project might conceivably have in the years beyond the time horizon and what their present value would be when discounted at a plausible discount rate.

In contrast, the statement 'projects are acceptable if their payback periods are less than 8 years' has no obvious interpretation as a set of assumptions. Or, if it has, it is in terms of assumptions that are completely at variance with reality. The only justification for the payback period criterion is a combination of the assumption that projects cease to earn returns (or to incur costs) after the maximum acceptable payback period and the assumption that shareholders (or taxpayers) have marginal time preference rates of zero. No other assumption could justify the use of undiscounted costs and returns in calculating the payback periods of projects.

5.6. An example: Investment in oneself—labour-training programmes

Governments often take the view that it would be in the public interest to increase, or to change, the skills of the nation's workforce. In particular it is thought desirable to retrain workers whose existing skills fit them for work in industries which are in decline. Governments may run programmes under which workers are retrained at the expense—partly or wholly—of taxpayers. In the U.K., for example, 'suitable' workers can take courses at Government Training Centres, receiving money allowances during their periods of training. The financial costs of running these centres are met entirely by the government.

Setting up and running such a training programme is an investment by society —costs are incurred by taxpayers in the belief that, in the future, society will benefit from a change in the skills of the labour force. This is not, however, an investment that can usefully be considered in the light of financial appraisal, for a training programme involves financial outlays but no direct financial returns. In Part III we shall consider how such an investment might be appraised by cost-benefit analysis. (See Section 9.4.)

Training can, however, be looked at, not only as an investment by society as a whole, but also as an investment by the individual trainee. The process of training may not be costless for the trainee, for the time spent being trained could be spent in other useful ways—in particular, in working for a wage higher than the allowances paid to trainees. The trainee, then, may incur initial costs in the expectation of future benefits in the form of higher wages than he would have been able to earn had he not trained. To the extent that a worker is concerned with maximizing his money income, his choice between training and not training is one that can appropriately be subjected to financial appraisal.

A number of economists have been interested in making financial appraisals of this kind. In this book we have, for the most part, taken the purpose of project appraisal to be that of assisting a decision-making process. There are, however, other reasons for using the techniques of project appraisal and the present case provides a good example. Economists, when analysing the choice between training and not training that is faced by a worker, have tended not to see their role as being to advise the worker (who is the decision-maker in this context) how to make a rational choice. Instead, they have been interested in discovering whether or not workers, in fact, act *as if* seeking to maximize the present values of their money incomes. Knowledge of what determines the demand for training would, of course, be of great value to a government planning a training programme.

A financial appraisal of the costs and benefits to trainees of taking a training course requires information about the money incomes that potential trainees could expect, on the one hand if they took the course, and on the other hand if they did not. It is not easy to construct this information from a knowledge of wage rates, unemployment benefits and training allowances, for the experiences of different workers can differ very greatly. Some of these who enrol on training courses, for example, fail to complete their courses and thus incur some of the costs of training without receiving the benefit of a new skill. Some trainees find well-paid jobs using their new skill very quickly after the end of their course; others may be unemployed for a considerable time and may eventually take relatively poorly-paid jobs which do not use their new skill at all. The income that a worker earns following training must be compared with the income that he would have earned had he not trained, and the latter can be as difficult to predict as the former.

One common method of approach is to study the experience of trainees who took part in government programmes in the recent past. This experience is then compared with that of a control group of workers who did not receive training but who, in all important respects (such as age, previous employment and previous education) are as similar to the trainees as is possible.

Suppose, for example, that a survey is made of a sample of 100 former enrolees for a training course, which discovers the money income of each worker over a period of 2 years from the start of the course. The same information is collected from the members of two control groups, each of 100 workers. Two control groups are used because some trainees were employed immediately before enrolling and gave up their jobs to train; other trainees were unemployed before enrolling. Clearly the opportunity costs of training would be much greater for those who gave up jobs. To allow separate calculations to be made of the 'profitability' of training for previously-employed and for previously-unemployed workers, one control group is made up of workers who were employed at the time the trainees enrolled while the other is made up of workers who were unemployed at the time.

One way of presenting the information collected from these three groups of workers is shown in Table 5.3, which gives the average money income of the workers in each group in each of the 2 years. The average income of trainees is relatively low in year 0 because a large part of the year was spent training (a typical training course takes about 6 months) and because some trainees spend a significant period at the end of the course looking for suitable jobs. The average income of the unemployed control group is greater in year 1 than in year 0 since a large proportion of those unemployed at the beginning of year 0 find jobs within the year.

Table 5.3
Expected present values of incomes of trainees and of control groups

	Average income (£ per man year)		Expected present value in year 0 of income in years 0—9 (£ per man) MTPR (per cent)			
	year 0	year 1	4	6	8	10
Trainees	1910	2389	19 673	18 159	16 834	15 668
'Unemployed' control group	1760	2018	16 764	15 486	14 366	13 382
'Employed' control group	2230	2232	18 826	17 411	16 173	15 084

All values expressed in year 0 prices.
Expected present values calculated by assuming that rates of income earned in year 1 will be maintained to year 9.

If this is the only information available, the best estimate that we can make of the average income that will be earned by each group in subsequent years is probably that in each year after year 1 the average income of any group will be equal to the average income in year 1. It would, however, be unrealistic to expect that trainees will be able to maintain their income differential above the others indefinitely, or until they retire. The demands for different types of labour are constantly changing, and the 'life' of the project of acquiring a new skill may be fairly short. We shall, therefore, use a time horizon of 10 years. That is, we shall take the income of each group to be constant in years 1 to 9 and take no account of incomes earned beyond year 9.

To compare incomes earned in different time periods we need a discount rate. Selecting an appropriate discount rate is not easy, for manual workers do not have easy access to capital markets. Men who are unemployed or who are likely to become unemployed will find it difficult to borrow money and may face very high interest rates at the margin (for example, on hire-purchase borrowing), while workers who choose to be lenders will face much lower interest rates (for example, on accounts with building societies or with banks). We cannot simply observe the market rate of interest and use this as the MTPR of every worker. Table 5.3 shows the present value of the stream of average incomes for each group, calculated for each of four discount rates. For every discount rate the present value of the income of the trainees is significantly higher than that of either of the control groups.

This finding is not, however, sufficient to show that training is a good investment for an individual worker. For the individual worker, the income that he will receive if he trains, and the income that he will receive if he does not, are both *uncertain* quantities. Our calculations have used *averages* of the incomes of large numbers of workers, balancing, for example, one trainee's luck in finding an extremely well-paid job with another's misfortune in failing to find a job at all. This approach can be regarded as an application of the expected value criterion. In year 0, for example, the average income of the 100 trainees surveyed was £1910. The most successful of the 100 trainees may have earned, let us say, £2750. Given this information, a potential trainee might well judge that there was a probability of 0·01 that he would earn £2750 in the 12 months following enrolment. Similarly, if the second most successful trainee earned £2700, our potential trainee might judge that there was a probability of 0·01 that he would earn £2700, and so on. Given this kind of relationship between the distribution of incomes in our samples and the expectations of potential trainees, it is easy to show that the average (arithmetic mean) income of a sample of workers from a particular group is equal to the expected value of income for any individual, were he to join that group. So far, then, we have shown that by choosing to train, a worker increases the expected present value of his income.

But there can be little doubt that we are considering possible changes in wealth that, relative to the total wealth of individual workers, are far from small. The expected value criterion may be inappropriate; workers' choices may be influenced by risk aversion. One way of finding out whether some workers might be so risk-averse as to prefer not to train is to use the 'cumulative probability' approach (introduced in Section 5.2).

For each of 100 workers in each of three groups we know his income in year 0 and his income in year 1. Assume that in years 2 to 9 each worker will earn the same income as he earned in year 1. The present value of this income stream can be calculated, given a discount rate (let us say, of 8 per cent). Then for each of our three groups we would have 100 separate 'present values of income'. Suppose that the results are those shown in the first three columns of Table 5.4. From this information can be deduced the cumulative probability distributions of present value of income for all individual workers who are, respectively, beginning training, unemployed, and employed at the beginning of year 0. These are shown in the last three columns of Table 5.4.

Table 5.4

**Present values of incomes of trainees and of control groups:
cumulative probabilities**

PV of income earned in years 0—9 (£ per man) (MTPR = 8 per cent)	Number of men with PV of income within range			Probability that PV of income greater than or equal to lowest value in range		
	T	U	E	T	U	E
greater than 26 000	0	0	0	0·00	0·00	0·00
24 000—25 999	2	0	0	0·02	0·00	0·00
22 000—23 999	6	0	2	0·08	0·00	0·02
20 000—21 999	10	2	3	0·18	0·02	0·05
18 000—19 999	16	7	11	0·34	0·09	0·16
16 000—17 999	24	14	32	0·58	0·23	0·48
14 000—15 999	23	34	41	0·81	0·57	0·89
12 000—13 999	12	25	9	0·93	0·82	0·98
10 000—11 999	5	12	2	0·98	0·94	1·00
8000—9999	2	6	0	1·00	1·00	1·00
less than 8000	0	0	0	1·00	1·00	1·00
Total	100	100	100	—	—	—

PV: present value   T: trainees
U: 'unemployed' control group   E: 'employed' control group

Consider a worker who is unemployed and who must choose whether or not to enrol for a training course. His problem is to choose between two cumulative probability distributions of outcomes—that faced by 'trainees' and that faced by the 'unemployed'. A study of Table 5.4 shows that the former dominates the latter. (For an explanation of this concept, see Section 5.2.) No matter how risk-averse the worker, his best course of action is to enrol for training.

Now consider a worker who has a job and who must choose whether or not to train. The cumulative probability distribution of outcomes for 'trainees' does not dominate that for 'employed workers'. Trainees are more likely to earn high incomes. (They are, for example, over twice as likely to earn incomes with present values of £18 000 or greater.) But 'employed workers' are less likely to earn very low incomes. (The probability of earning more than £14 000 in present value terms is 0·89 for 'employed workers' and 0·81 for 'trainees'.) It is, then, conceivable that a worker with a job might be sufficiently risk-averse as to prefer to keep his current job rather than enrol on a training programme.

Appendix: Utility and choice under uncertainty

This appendix sets out one approach used by economists to discuss choice under uncertainty. In Section 5.3 it was asserted that the expected value criterion was appropriate for project appraisal provided that two conditions were met: only small changes of wealth should be at risk for any individual, and risks should be independent. In this appendix it is shown that this conclusion is consistent with a particular set of assumptions about individuals' preferences between uncertain prospects.

The starting-point for this approach is the proposition that consumption confers 'utility' on the consumer. Money, since it represents claims on consumption, itself confers utility. It is assumed that, for any individual, the marginal utility of money wealth is always positive but declines as wealth increases. Individuals seek to maximize their utilities. Under uncertainty, it is further assumed, they seek to maximize 'expected utitlity'—the mathematical expectation of utility. It follows from this that, if firms and public agencies are to pursue the interests of shareholders and taxpayers, the correct criterion to use in project appraisal is that of undertaking those projects that increase the expected utilities of shareholders or taxpayers.

Suppose that there are two mutually exclusive states of the world, A and B. In the judgement of some individual, the probability that state A will occur is p; the probability that state B will occur is $1 - p$. A project provides, for this individual, the prospect of a net monetary gain of g_A if A occurs and a net monetary gain of g_B if B occurs. (Either or both of g_A and g_B may, of course, be negative.) The expected net monetary gain is positive if and only if

$$pg_A + (1-p)g_B > 0. \qquad\qquad 5.5$$

That this inequality should be satisfied for the project to be undertaken is the expected value criterion.

Suppose that g_A and g_B are both small relative to the individual's wealth, so that the marginal utility of his wealth can be taken to be unaffected by changes of these magnitudes.

Suppose, first, that the risk involved in the project is 'independent'. If the project were not undertaken, our individual's wealth would be $\overline{W}$ irrespective of whether A or B occurred. Let us write the marginal utility of wealth as $MU(W)$ where W is wealth. Thus, in the present case, the marginal utility of wealth would be $MU(\overline{W})$ whichever state occurred. Undertaking the project would lead to an increase in expected utility if and only if

$$pg_A MU(\overline{W}) + (1-p)g_B MU(\overline{W}) > 0. \qquad\qquad 5.6$$

The term $MU(\overline{W})$ cancels out, leaving a restatement of the previous Expression 5.5. In words, the condition that the project should be undertaken if and only if it leads to an increase in expected utility is identical with the expected value criterion.

This result would not hold, however, if g_A or g_B were sufficiently large as to affect the marginal utility of wealth—that is, if $MU(\overline{W} + g_A)$ or $MU(\overline{W} + g_B)$ were significantly different from $MU(\overline{W})$. Suppose, for example, that g_A is large and positive and that g_B is large and negative. Then, if the project were undertaken, the marginal utility of wealth would be greater if B occurred than if A occurred. The expected value criterion would be insufficiently stringent a criterion for appraising the project (given that the individual's object is to maximize expected utility).

Now suppose instead that the risks involved in the project are small but not 'independent'. In the absence of the project, our individual's wealth would be W_A if state A occurred and W_B if state B occurred. The marginal utility of his wealth in each case would thus be $MU(W_A)$ and $MU(W_B)$. Undertaking the project will lead to an increase in expected utility if and only if

$$pg_A MU(W_A) + (1-p)g_B MU(W_B) > 0. \qquad\qquad 5.7$$

This condition is no longer identical with the expected value criterion (Expression 5.5). If, for example, $W_A > W_B$, and thus $MU(W_A) < MU(W_B)$, the expected value criterion is giving too great a relative weight to changes in wealth in state A and too small a weight to changes in state B. Thus if the project would lead to an increase in wealth if state A occurred and a decrease if state B occurred, the expected value criterion is insufficiently stringent. Conversely, if the project would produce an increase of wealth in state *B* and a decrease in state *A*, the expected value criterion is too stringent.

In general, the expected value criterion is insufficiently stringent for appraising projects whose gains accrue in states of the world in which the recipients are relatively wealthy and whose losses are borne in states in which the bearers are relatively poor. Conversely, if gains accrue when recipients are relatively poor, and losses when bearers are relatively wealthy, the expected value criterion is too stringent.

Problems

1. Reconsider Problem 3 of Chapter 3 (concerning a choice between two locations for a hospital). (See p. 40).

Suppose that the health authority has decided to build at site B, on the grounds that the financial costs of building at B are less than those of building at A. In the original presentation of the problem it was stated that the authority considered it 'preferable' to buy a site of 18 hectares rather than one of 12 hectares, on the grounds that this would make it less costly to build extensions to the hospital in the future. No supporting evidence was given.

Suppose that enquiry suggests that an extension, if built at all, would be begun in year 6. The cost of building an extension would be £1·2 m greater if only the 12-hectare site could be used than if the 18-hectare site could be used. These additional costs would be spread evenly over the three years 6—8. There is no possibility that additional land could be bought after year 0; the site must be bought now or never. If, however, the health authority decided in year 6 not to build an extension to the hospital it would be able to sell its surplus 6 hectares of land at the current market value of £70 000 per hectare. (All values are expressed in terms of the price level in year 0.) What judgement(s) about the probability of the extension being built would justify the decision to buy the larger site in year 0? (It may be assumed that the probability of the extension being built is not affected by whether or not the larger site is bought.) The market rate of interest, which the health authority uses as its discount rate, is 10 per cent.

2. A state-owned railway undertaking has received the approval of the government to resignal a length of railway line. The estimated cost is £1·2 m, divided equally between years 0 and 1. Since this approval was given, but before re-signalling work has begun, it has been agreed that this railway line will be given a high priority in a programme of railway electrification. On an electrified railway it is essential to provide special cables and equipment for the signalling system in order to immunize it against induction effects. The railway undertaking consequently asks the government to approve additional spending on the resignalling work so that an immunized system can be installed. The additional cost of installing an immunized system rather than a non-immunized one would be £0·3 m; the total cost of resignalling would thus be £1·5 m (again, divided equally between years 0 and 1). In addition, once installed, the immunized system would cost £3000 per year more to maintain than the non-immunized system. If an immunized system is not installed at the outset, it will cost £0·6 m subsequently to convert the signalling system, this cost being divided equally between the two years in which electrification work takes place.

Suppose that you are asked to give advice to the decision-maker whose responsibility it is to approve or turn down the railway undertaking's request. You consult the government officials who are most closely concerned with the electrification programme and are convinced that it is virtually certain that the railway will ultimately be electrified, and that the most likely date for the electrification work is years 7 and 8. Having consulted these officials, it is your judgement that the probability distribution of possible dates of electrification is that given in Table (i). The government has stated that it expects public agencies to appraise projects by using a discount rate of 8 per cent.

Table (i)

Electrification takes place in years:	Probability
before 5 and 6	0·00
5 and 6	0·05
6 and 7	0·10
7 and 8	0·20
8 and 9	0·15
9 and 10	0·12
10 and 11	0·10
11 and 12	0·08
12 and 13	0·06
13 and 14	0·05
14 and 15	0·04
after 14 and 15, or never	0·05

Carry out whatever calculations you think appropriate and present your findings in a way that would allow the decision-maker easily to make a rational and informed decision about whether to approve the railway undertaking's request. If possible, give a recommendation as to what this decision should be.

3. A local authority is currently carrying out a programme of slum clearance. As a result of this programme it finds itself the owner of a plot of land which will become vacant in the near future (when demolition work is finished). It is considering how best to use this land and instructs its chief financial officer to investigate the alternatives open to the authority. He reports:

The simplest course of action (course A) would be to sell the land to a private developer. As soon as slum clearance work finishes (year 0) we could sell the land for £600 000.

I have investigated the possibilities of our authority retaining ownership of the land and developing it in partnership with a property development company. A certain company is interested in this possibility and has stated the terms on which it would be prepared to work with us. It is willing to enter either of two schemes of partnership (B and C). Both schemes involve the same building work being carried out, but they involve different financial arrangements. Under either scheme, our authority would use its statutory powers to acquire additional land adjoining the site already owned. This would imply an outlay of £400 000 in year 0. The development company would then build shops and offices on the enlarged plot of land.

Under scheme B, our authority not only would contribute the land required for the development but also would pay some of the development costs—a total of £1 000 000, of which 50 per cent would be paid in year 0 and 50 per cent on the completion of building by the company. As a return on our investment we should be given the ownership of a proportion of the shops and offices. If we were to adopt this scheme we could reduce the risks involved in the venture by making contracts in year 0 to sell the property we should own. In my judgement we should be able to contract to sell this property for £2 450 000, to be paid to us by the prospective occupiers in the year in which building work is completed.

Under scheme C, we should not be required to pay any of the costs of development; we should merely make the land available. The property company would bear all development costs and receive all revenue from the letting of the shops and offices. It would buy the land from the authority by making payments of £88 500 per year for 50 years, the first instalment of which would be paid in the year following the completion of building work.

I have carried out a detailed financial appraisal of the three alternative courses of action. This shows that our best policy is to adopt scheme B.

The net financial returns of the various alternatives are summarized in Table (ii).

Table (ii)

	Net financial return in year(s) (£'000)		
	0	n^1	$n+1$ to $n+50$
Course of action			
A	+ 600	—	—
B	− 900[2]	+1950[3]	—
C	− 400	—	+88·5 *per year*
Investment in adopting			
B rather than A	−1500	+1950	—
C rather than A	−1000	—	+88·5 *per year*

Notes
1. n is the year in which building work is completed.
2. 400 on buying land *plus* 500 as share of development costs.
3. 2450 from sale of property *minus* 500 as share of development costs.

There is considerable uncertainty as to when building work would be completed. The later the date of completion, the less favourable would be either of courses B and C, relative to the certain and immediate returns of course A. There is no possibility of the year of completion being earlier than year 2. Any later year is possible but it is most likely that work will be completed in year 3. Accordingly I have assumed that this will be the case.

It would be possible for our authority to finance its investment in schemes B or C by borrowing at the market rate of interest of 6 per cent. To adopt either of these schemes would, however, be to undertake a risky investment. It is the policy of our authority to avoid taking risks with the electors' money. I think it prudent, therefore, to appraise the two projects of investing in scheme B (rather than A) and of investing in C (rather than A) by using a discount rate of 8 per cent. That is, a risk premium of 2 percentage points is used.

Discounted to year 0 at a discount rate of 8 per cent, the present value of the investment of adopting scheme B rather than scheme A is £47 900. The present value of the investment of adopting scheme C rather than scheme A is *minus* £140 600. I therefore recommend that we adopt scheme B.

Do you agree with the conclusions that have been drawn from the facts available?

Notes

[1] The 'subjective' interpretation of probability can be traced back to Thomas Bayes. See Bayes (1763).

Further reading

The foundations of the subjective probability approach are set out in an essay by Ramsey (1931). The expected utility approach (introduced in the appendix) derives from von Neumann and Morgenstern (1947). Expositions of this approach can be found in Alchian (1953), Green (1971), Chapters 13 and 14, and Laidler (1974), Chapter 9.

A general introduction to what is involved in structuring decisions in the face of uncertainty is produced by Raiffa (1968). A clear summary of the main ways in which uncertainty can be taken account of in project appraisal is given in Dorfman (1962). For a discussion of uncertainty in relation to the appraisal of projects by private firms, see Merrett and Sykes (1973), Chapters 6 and 7.

There is a large literature on the appraisal of labour-training programmes, both from the viewpoint of the trainee and from the viewpoint of 'society'. Selected references are given as 'Further Reading' for Chapter 9, which considers some of the problems involved in making a cost-benefit analysis of a labour-training programme. A closely related problem, the appraisal of higher education courses from the viewpoint of the students who take them, is analysed in Ziderman (1973).

6. Input Constraints

6.1. The nature of input constraints

It has been argued already that the true, or opportunity, cost to a firm or agency of using an input may not be measured by any market price. (See Chapter 3.) Market prices necessarily correspond to opportunity costs only where the firm or agency is able to buy and sell freely at these prices.

This statement requires some further explanation. Consider a project that uses a certain quantity of some input—say, the use of one truck for one year. The agency undertaking the project may face two kinds of price for 'truck years'. First, there is the price at which truck years can be bought (that is, the price at which trucks can be hired). If the agency is free to buy as many truck years as it chooses at this price, it is clear that the opportunity cost of using one truck year in the project can be no greater than this price (provided, at least, that the agency acts rationally). Second, there is the price at which truck years can be sold by the agency. If the agency owns a number of trucks, it can act as a seller as well as a buyer. If the agency is capable of selling truck years at a certain price, the opportunity cost of using one truck year in a project must be at least as great as this price (since once alternative to using the truck in the project is that of hiring it to someone else). Putting these two results together, if there is a single market price at which the agency can freely buy *and* sell truck years, the opportunity cost of using one truck year in a project must be equal to the market price.

Problems start to arise whenever the price at which additional units of an input can be bought is greater than the price at which additional units can be sold. It then ceases to be obvious immediately what the opportunity cost of using the input is; it could be anything in the range between the two prices. Obviously, this problem is the more acute the greater the difference between the two prices.

An extreme case of this problem occurs when an agency cannot buy, or cannot sell, freely at *any* price. If an agency is unable to buy additional units of an input, this is equivalent to its facing a buying price of infinity. It is is unable to sell units of an input it owns, this is equivalent to its facing a selling price of zero.

This family of problems may be called problems involving *input constraints.*

We have already considered problems of this kind. In Section 3.2 we discussed the case of a railway undertaking and the input 'trains'.

Here the constraint was that the price at which additional trains could be bought (or the cost at which they could be constructed) was much greater than the price at which they could be sold—their scrap value. Without examining the uses to which trains could be put within the undertaking it was not possible to say whether the opportunity cost of using a train in a particular project was the high buying price, the low selling price, or some figure in between. This kind of constraint is common wherever a firm uses inputs of a specialized kind, since this specialization limits the role of markets and prices. (Compare the position of a monopoly railway undertaking with that of a private-hire coach operator, who may buy vehicles from, or sell them to, a large number of other operators.)

Related problems arise where buying or selling takes a long period of time. Suppose, for example, that it takes two years from ordering a certain type of machine to being able to use it. Then, whatever the number of machines a firm has at the moment, it must use this number or less for the next two years.

Input constraints may arise out of regulation of market prices. For example, the wage that a local authority can pay for particular kinds of labour may be regulated by central government, or by a central agreement between all local authorities and a trade union. If the regulated wage is sufficiently low, a local authority will find that it cannot hire as much labour as it wishes to hire at that wage. There is a limit on the maximum amount of labour that can be used, which is set by the level of the wage and by the willingness of workers to offer their labour.

Or again, constraints may simply be imposed on a public agency by a higher authority. As was mentioned in Chapter 4, central governments often insist on controlling the amount of investment made by public agencies, and maintain this control by rationing the amount of money that may be spent on investment in a particular period.

In our earlier discussion of opportunity cost, in Chapter 3, we focused on individual projects. At this level it is difficult to say much more than that the opportunity cost of using units of an input in one project is the sacrifice of the benefits of whatever use to which they would otherwise have been put. Beyond this statement of principle the problem becomes a practical one, specific to the individual project, of discovering what these benefits are worth. In this chapter we shall look at the problem of input constraints in a wider framework. We shall discuss how a firm or agency facing a constraint on the use of an input should allocate that input between competing uses. The problem to be solved is not whether or not to undertake an individual project, given the uses to which the input is put elsewhere in the firm or agency. Instead it is to determine the best use of the input in the firm or agency as a whole.

Input rationing problems can be very complex. Many of them can most conveniently be solved by using the techniques of mathematical programming, which tend to be associated with the discipline of operations research. Such an approach would involve mathematics beyond the scope of this book. If however a rationing problem takes certain forms, it can be tackled with a simpler set of analytical tools. Three such cases will be considered in this chapter. These cases are useful because practical project appraisal problems often approximate to them. They are useful also because they illustrate the rationale of 'shadow pricing'.

6.2.   The simplest form of input constraint: one input rationed in one period

Suppose that our agency, in a particular time period, has the opportunity to undertake each of a number of independent projects. Each project uses some quantity of an input of which the agency may use no more than some given total quantity during the period. Projects cannot be deferred; they must be begun within this time period or not at all.

The agency's objective is to maximize its financial surplus, subject to the constraint imposed by the input limitation. Clearly it should undertake the set of projects whose total present value is greatest. This implies that it should undertake those projects with the highest present value *per unit of the constrained input* that they use.

Consider a public agency which is allowed by central government to spend up to £1·8 m on capital investment in year 0. (To avoid confusion later, we shall call £1 m spending on investment '1m units of capital'.) How this capital ration is used will have no effect on the amount that the agency is able to spend in future years.

Table 6.1

Project	Cost in year 0 (to be paid from capital ration) £m	Net returns per year: year 1 onwards £m	Life of project (number of years in which net returns occur)
A	1·0	0·14	20
B	1·0	0·13	50
C	2·0	1·00	3
D	1·0	0·25	8

Four independent projects are under consideration. Details are given in Table 6.1. Each project is of a kind such that any proportion of it may be undertaken. (For example, spending £0·5 m on project A in year 0 would bring net returns of £0·07 m per year for 20 years.)

This is a case of input rationing, the rationed input being capital. The projects that should be undertaken are those that have the highest present value per unit of capital used. Using a time preference rate of 10 per cent, the results shown in Table 6.2 can be calculated. The most efficient way to allocate the capital ration is to invest £1·0 m in project D (the project with the highest present value per unit of capital) and to invest the remaining £0·8 m of the ration in project B. This produces a total present value of £0·56 m, the highest attainable.

Table 6.2

Project	Present value of project in year 0 £m	Present value per unit of capital £	Internal rate of return (%)
A	0·19	0·19	13
B	0·29	0·29	13
C	0·49	0·24	23
D	0·33	0·33	19

If an additional unit of capital were made available, this could most efficiently be used to increase investment in project B, increasing the present value of the agency's financial surplus by £0·29. Thus one unit of capital, whose nominal value is £1, has at the margin a value of £1·29 to this public agency. This implies that the marginal opportunity cost of using a unit of capital is also £1·29. We could take explicit account of this opportunity cost by 'charging' this higher value as a notional charge, or *shadow price*, for the use of capital in projects. This would give the results shown in Table 6.3, which shows that, after taking account of opportunity costs, project D still has a positive present value, project B has a present value of zero, and the other two projects have negative present values. This indicates that D should be undertaken, that A and C should not be undertaken, and that B is on the margin between acceptance and rejection. It has been

Table 6.3

Project	Notional cost in year 0 (£m)	Net returns per year (£m)	Life of project (years)	Notional present value in year 0 (£m)
A	1·29	0·14	20	−0·10
B	1·29	0·13	50	0·00
C	2·58	1·00	3	−0·09
D	1·29	0·25	8	0·04

shown already that the best strategy for the agency to pursue is to undertake project D and then to invest the remainder of its capital ration in project B; the shadow-pricing approach is simply another route to the same result.

Shadow prices are a convenient device for allowing decentralized decision-making in a large organization, or hierarchy of organizations, which faces input constraints. The central, or highest level, decision-makers of the organization can ensure that a rationed input is used efficiently in the organization as a whole by determining a shadow price and then instructing all other decision-makers to behave as if the shadow price were the 'real' price.

The rationale of shadow pricing may be illustrated by using Figure 6.1. This presents in diagram form the rationing problem that we have been considering.

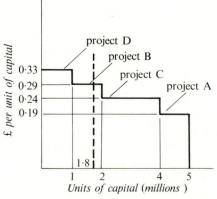

Fig. 6.1

On the vertical axis is measured the present value of projects per unit of capital used; the horizontal axis measures units of capital. The downward-stepped schedule shows the available uses for capital in descending order of value (measured by present value per unit of capital). In this sense the schedule shows the *marginal value* of capital. Given that capital is always used in the way that maximizes the present value of projects undertaken, this schedule shows the additional present value that could be achieved by using one more unit of capital, as a function of the amount of capital already in use. Using the ration of 1·8m units of capital, the marginal value of capital is £0·29 per unit. (This, of course, is in addition to the nominal value of £1 per unit which has been used in calculating the present values of projects.)

The schedule may, however, be interpreted in another way—as a *demand schedule* or *demand curve*. Reading from the vertical axis to the horizontal axis, it shows how much capital would be demanded at any given price per unit. If a surcharge of, say £0·40 over the nominal price of £1 per unit were charged for capital, none would be demanded, since this surcharge is greater than the marginal value of capital in its best use (project D). If the surcharge were in the range between £0·33 and £0·29, 1m units would be demanded (to invest in project D, the only project to produce returns in excess of this price), and so on.

Thus the value £0·29, determined by the intersection of the demand schedule and the line representing the input constraint, has a double meaning. On the one hand, it is the marginal value of capital when the supply available (1·8m units) is allocated between projects as efficiently as is possible. On the other, it is the only surcharge for the use of capital at which the agency would choose to buy the quantity that in fact is available to it. So the problem of selecting, subject to the input constraint, those projects with the highest total present value is equivalent to that of selecting a shadow price for the input such that the quantity demanded at that price is just equal to the quantity available.

It may seem strange that the shadow price (or opportunity cost) of capital is being measured in units of money rather than in percentage points. The 'cost of capital' is, after all, normally measured as so many per cent per year.

It would be possible to ration capital by using a shadow 'cost' measured in per cent per year; this would amount to using a shadow discount rate or to ranking projects by their internal rates of return. In the rationing problem we are considering this procedure would not be consistent with the agency's objectives.

Table 6.2 (p. 77) shows that a shadow discount rate of 23 per cent would be required to ensure that the capital requirements of 'acceptable' projects were in balance with the capital available. At this discount rate, all projects except C would be 'unprofitable'. This *seems* to imply that the 1·8m units of capital should be invested in project C. This implication is different from that of our original approach of shadow pricing capital in money units—for the original approach led to the conclusion that the capital ration should be invested in projects B and D.

The MTPR, it will be remembered, was taken to be 10 per cent. It is by the use of this rate that the value of projects must ultimately be judged. It is easy to calculate that a decision to invest the capital ration in project C would give a total present value of £0·44 m, which is considerably less than the present value that could be achieved by investing in B and D (£0·56 m).

The underlying error of the 'shadow discount rate' approach is that it confuses the two distinct concepts of time preference and opportunity cost. In our example, a high time preference rate favours project C relative to project B, because the former produces large returns for a short period while the latter produces small returns for a long period. A shadow discount rate of 23 per cent is high enough to make C preferable to B. But to say that capital is rationed in year 0 does not imply anything about time preference; it provides no justification for weighting earlier returns more heavily in relation to later ones.

6.3. Postponement of projects

The input rationing problem to be considered now retains all the features of the first problem (discussed in Section 6.2) with one exception. This is that projects that are not undertaken in year 0, when the input constraint is effective, may be postponed to the next year. In this second year there is no constraint on the use of the input.

To illustrate this case, consider again the example analysed in Section 6.2, of a public agency facing capital rationing. In the original analysis it was assumed that projects could not be postponed. Now suppose instead that each of the four projects may, if desired, be begun in year 1 instead of in year 0. For the purposes of the present discussion, let us assume that the effect of postponing a project is to defer the capital cost from year 0 to year 1 and to lose the returns that could have been earned in year 1 had the project been begun in year 0. There is no compensating lengthening of the project's life. (Thus, for example, if undertaken in year 1, project A will earn net returns of £0·14 m per year for 19 years, beginning in year 2.)

The problem is to select a set of projects to begin in year 0, subject to the constraint that no more than 1·8 m units of capital may be used. Those projects not begun in year 0 will be begun in year 1— provided, of course, that they are still worth undertaking. The objective is to maximize the total present value of the projects begun in both years.

It is convenient to look at this another way. Each project has two present values: the present value of undertaking it in year 0 (the non-postponed present value), and the present value, discounted to year 0, of the opportunity to undertake it in year 1 (the postponed present value). The excess of the first over the second is the net gain from undertaking the project in year 0, relative to the effective alternative of postponing to year 1 a decision about whether or not to undertake it. The criterion for selecting which projects to undertake in period 0 is to select those projects with the highest 'net gains *from not postponing*' per unit of capital used. This rationing problem is now in a form which makes it simply another example of the general class of problems discussed in Section 6.2.

The calculations necessary to identify which of the four projects should be undertaken in year 0 are summarized in Table 6.4. The project with the highest 'net gain from not postponing' per unit of capital is C. Thus the whole of the 1·8m units of capital should be allocated to this project. Projects A, B and D all have positive 'postponed present values' and so should be undertaken in year 1 when the capital rationing constraint no longer exists. Project C has a negative 'postponed present value' and so the outstanding 0·2m units of investment in this project should never be made.

Table 6.4

Project	Non-postponed present value	Postponed present value	Present value of net gain from not postponing	Capital requirement	Net gain per £ of capital
	(£m)	(£m)	(£m)	(£m)	(£m)
A	0·192	0·156	0·036	1·0	0·036
B	0·289	0·262	0·027	1·0	0·027
C	0·487	−0·241	0·487	2·0	0·243
D	0·334	0·197	0·137	1·0	0·137

If an additional unit of capital were available in year 0, it could best be used to increase the level of investment in project C. Since the net gain per unit of capital invested in this project is £0·243, the correct shadow price for capital in year 0 is £1·243 per unit.

6.4. Multi-period rationing

If an input is rationed in more than one time period, this is equivalent to there being more than one rationed input. Units of a commodity in one period, it will be remembered, can be regarded as a different good from units of the same commodity in another period. Input rationing problems become complex whenever decisions taken about projects in one period affect the availability of, or the uses for, rationed inputs in other periods. Such problems require a number of shadow prices to be determined simultaneously.

One common example of this kind of problem stems from certain kinds of capital rationing. In the examples of capital rationing used so far in this chapter, capital used by projects was shown to have an opportunity cost higher than its nominal value. The returns of projects, however, did not have similarly high shadow values. This was because it was assumed that capital would not be rationed in the periods in which the returns occurred. Not shadow pricing returns may also be correct, even if capital *is* rationed in the periods in which they occur, if for some reason these returns cannot be used to supplement capital rations. Restrictions of this kind may be imposed on agencies by higher authorities.

If, however, a project earns returns that are available for reinvestment in periods when investment funds from other sources are rationed, then these returns must be shadow priced at whatever the marginal value of capital will be in these periods. It is often argued that this situation of permanent capital rationing is normal in the public sector. Because of the unwillingness of governments to increase taxes, the funds available for the investment projects of public agencies are permanently subject to rationing. (The implications of this argument will be explored further in Chapter 15 below.) The financial returns of public projects are thus particularly valuable since they provide funds for further investment projects without requiring additional taxation.

Working out the correct shadow prices of capital for different future periods could be an extremely complex task. In principle, what is required includes knowledge of the sizes of future capital rations and knowledge of the characteristics of all the investment projects that will be considered in future periods.

There are many different ways of making the problem tractable by introducing special simplifying assumptions. One such set of assumptions is worth considering because of its plausibility and because of the simplicity of the implications that follow from it.

Suppose that capital is rationed in the present year and will be rationed in all subsequent years. Assume that in each subsequent year, rationing will be of exactly the same degree of stringency as it is in the present year. That is, if some project (a marginal project) is exactly on the margin between acceptance and rejection in one year, an identical project, if considered in any other year, would also be exactly on the margin between acceptance and rejection. Now consider a particular project which has net returns of $X_0, X_1, X_2, \ldots$ in years $0, 1, 2, \ldots$. (For the purposes of exposition, suppose that there is a capital cost in year 0 followed by returns in the following years; that is, X_0 is negative, while $X_1, X_2, \ldots$ are positive.)

The opportunity cost of undertaking this project in year 0 is that the sum of X_0 cannot be invested in other projects. If capital were allocated efficiently between projects, a decision to undertake this particular project would imply a diversion of X_0 away from a *marginal* project. Let us denote by S_0 the marginal value (or shadow price) of capital in year 0. Thus the opportunity cost of our project is $S_0 X_0$ in year 0.

Now suppose that the return of X_1 in year 1 can immediately be reinvested. The best available use for these funds will be to invest them in a marginal project. If the marginal value of capital in year 1 is S_1, then the real value of this return is $S_1 X_1$ in year 1. Similarly, if the marginal value of capital in year 2 is S_2, the real value of the return of X_2 in year 2 is S_2X_2; and so on. Thus, valuing both the outlays and the returns of our project at shadow prices, the project is equivalent to a stream of net changes in consumption of S_0X_0, S_1X_1, S_2X_2, . . . in years 0, 1, 2, ... If the common MTPR of all taxpayers (or shareholders) is r, the present value of this steam is

$$S_0X_0 + \frac{S_1X_1}{1+r} + \frac{S_2X_2}{(1+r)^2} + \ldots$$

in period 0. The project should be undertaken if, and only if, this sum is positive.

But we have assumed already that capital rationing is of exactly the same degree of stringency in all years. Thus S_0, the present value in year 0 of the returns to be expected from investing one unit of capital in a marginal project in that year, must equal S_1, the marginal value of capital in year 1; and S_1 must equal S_2, and so on. Writing

$$S = S_0 = S_1 = S_2 = \ldots,$$

the condition for accepting our project is that

$$S \left[X_0 + \frac{X_1}{1+r} + \frac{X_2}{(1+r)^2} + \ldots \right] > 0. \qquad 6.1$$

S cancels out of the inequality, leaving the result that the project should be undertaken if and only if its net returns, when discounted at the taxpayers' (common) MTPR, have a positive present value. There is no need to know anything at all about the magnitude of the marginal value of capital to decide whether or not to undertake an individual project; it is sufficient to be willing to assume that this value will remain constant over time.

Problems

1. A local authority employs a labour force for use on small-scale construction projects. The wage rate that it can offer to its workers is controlled by a national agreement between all local authorities; consequently the authority is able to hire no more workers than the number that are willing to work at the current wage. During the coming year it will be able to hire no more than 30 man years of labour.

During the year, 6 projects must be carried out. If the authority's own labour force is not used to undertake a project, the project must be undertaken by private contractors. Details of the costs of these projects are given in Table (i).

Which projects should the authority undertake with its own labour force and which should it hire contractors for? (Projects may be undertaken partly by the authority's labour force and partly by contractors. For example, the authority could undertake one-half of project A, using 10 man years of labour and at a cost of £30 000; the remainder of the project could be undertaken by contractors at a cost of £30 650.)

Suppose that the authority considers ways of attracting more workers to join its labour force, other than increasing wages. What is the maximum sum that it would be worthwhile for the authority to pay, over and above the current wage, to induce one additional man year of labour to be supplied?

Table (i)

Project	If undertaken by authority's labour force		If undertaken by contractors
	Labour required (man years)	*Cost (including cost of labour) (£'000)*	*Cost (£'000)*
A	20	60·0	61·3
B	15	51·1	54·8
C	12	40·6	41·9
D	10	58·0	59·8
E	5	18·3	18·6
F	2	7·0	7·3

2. A public agency has planned to spend £180 000 in year 0 on minor investments. The planned investments are of two kinds. The first (project A) is a programme of making minor modifications to existing, aging equipment. It was planned to spend £2500 on each of 32 pieces of equipment. This, it was expected, would produce cost savings of £800 per year for each piece of equipment from year 1 to year 5 inclusive. (The equipment, whether modified or not, will be scrapped after year 5.) The second type of investment (project B) involves buying labour-saving equipment. Each of these pieces of equipment costs £10 000 and produces cost savings of £6000 for 3 years, after which it must be replaced. The agency planned to buy 10 such pieces of equipment. The net financial returns of these projects are summarized in Table (ii).

Table (ii)

	Net financial return to agency (£'000 per piece of equipment) in year:								
	0	1	2	3	4	5	6	7	...
Project A	− 2·5	+0·8	+0·8	+ 0·8	+0·8	+0·8			
Project B									
Initial equipment	−10·0	+6·0	+6·0	+ 6·0					
1st replacement				−10·0	+6·0	+6·0	+ 6·0		
2nd replacement							−10·0	+6·0	...
Total	−10·0	+6·0	+6·0	− 4·0	+6·0	+6·0	− 4·0	+6·0	...

The agency is then told by the central government that its capital spending in year 0 must not exceed £120 000. It is assured that capital will be available in year 1 to undertake any planned investment that has to be postponed from year 0.

If spending on project A were postponed, in year 1 the agency would still be able to make its planned modifications at a cost of £2500 per piece of equipment, but the cost savings of £800 per year per piece of equipment would be enjoyed only in years 2 to 5 inclusive. If spending on project B were postponed the whole expected stream of net returns (shown in Table (ii)) would be shifted forward by one year.

The agency is instructed by the government to use a discount rate of 10 per cent.

How should the agency cut its planned investment spending from £180 000 to £120 000? What is the marginal value (or shadow price) to the agency of capital in year 0?

(*Note*: Calculating the present value of the stream of net financial returns from project B may appear a tedious task. There is, however, a very convenient short cut to be used in cases like this. Take, for example, the problem of calculating the present value of a stream of income of 3, 2, 1, 3, 2, 1, 3, 2, 1, . . . in years 0, 1, 2, 3, ... If the discount rate is 10 per cent, the present value in year 0 of a stream of income 3, 2, 1 in years 0, 1, 2 is 5·6446. Consider the stream of income x, x, x in years 0, 1, 2, such that this too has a present value in year 0 of 5·6446. It is easy to show that

$$x = \frac{5 \cdot 6446}{1 + a_{2, \, 0 \cdot 10}} = 2 \cdot 0635.$$

Thus a stream of income of 3, 2, 1, 3, 2, 1, 3 . . . has the same present value as one of 2·0635, 2·0635, 2·0635, 2·0635, ... Taking year 50 to be our time horizon, the present value of this stream of income is $2 \cdot 0635(1 + a_{50, \, 0 \cdot 10})$ or 22·5227.)

3. An agency uses a large number of items of a certain type of equipment. This equipment costs £10 000 per item, which is paid during the first year in which the equipment is in use. In addition the equipment is costly to maintain. Maintenance costs increase steeply with the age of the equipment, being £1000 in the first year of its life, £2000 in the second, £5000 in the third and £8000 in the fourth. It is the agency's policy to scrap and replace equipment after 3 years of use. (It can be shown that, given the discount rate of 10 per cent that the agency uses, the policy of replacing equipment every 3 years is less costly than using any other interval between replacements.)

At the beginning of year 0, 50 such items of equipment are due for replacement. The agency thus expects to spend in year 0, £500 000 on buying new equipment and a further £50 000 on maintaining this. The agency then is told that it is the government's policy that public spending in year 0 should be reduced significantly below the level previously planned. As part of a programme of cuts in public expenditure, the agency is instructed to postpone by one year its replacement of the 50 items of equipment. From year 1 onwards, the agency will (it is assured) be able to continue with its normal policy of replacing equipment every 3 years.

The managers of the agency wish to resist the government's proposal. They know that another agency very recently received the government's approval for an investment project which involved a cost of £400 000 in year 0 followed by returns of £100 000 per year in each of years 1 to 10. The managers would like to be able to argue that the government's decision in favour of the investment project just mentioned is inconsistent with its decision that the replacement of our agency's equipment should be postponed.

Suppose that you are asked to investigate this matter to find out whether there is any inconsistency. What would your conclusion be?

(You may assume that the government expects both the agencies involved to take decisions on the criteria of financial appraisal and to use a discount rate of 10 per cent. The only relevant constraint is that the total amount of public spending in year 0 should not exceed some given quantity. The 'Note' to Problem 2 should be consulted.)

Further reading

For discussions of the implications of capital rationing for project appraisal by private firms, see Bierman and Smidt (1975), Chapter 8, and Merrett and Sykes (1973), Chapter 4.

Introductions to mathematical programming and its economic applications can be found in Dorfman, Samuelson and Solow (1958) and in Dorfman (1953). For applications of mathematical programming to capital rationing problems, see Baumol and Quandt (1965) and Charnes, Cooper and Miller (1959).

Part III: Cost-benefit Analysis

7. The Objective in Cost-benefit Analysis

7.1. Introduction

So far, the objectives that we have attributed to decision-makers have been financial ones. That is, project appraisal has been concerned only with entities which are registered in financial accounts. The projects of public agencies have been appraised on the criterion of maximizing an agency's financial surplus or, equivalently, of minimizing its net subsidy requirement.

It was admitted at the outset that a financial objective was a narrow one for a public agency to pursue and that, for most public decisions, a broader, 'social' objective would be more appropriate. It is now time to discuss such objectives—that is, to discuss cost-benefit analysis.

Immediately we encounter difficult terrain. The very idea of a social objective is problematical. There are many shades of meaning to the words 'social objective' and hence many different interpretations of cost-benefit analysis. Fortunately, however, most practitioners of cost-benefit analysis, despite their often varied interpretations of what their work 'means', use at least a core of common principles and analytical techniques. They produce analyses that are recognizably akin.

7.2. The potential Pareto improvement criterion

At the most basic level, a cost-benefit analysis of a project requires the identification of all the effects of the project on the individual welfare of all members of the community. It then requires these effects to be measured in some common unit so that aggregate benefits can be compared with aggregate costs. This much, at least, is fairly uncontroversial.

There are various ways in which one might set about identifying, measuring and comparing changes in people's welfare. One particular system of dealing with welfare changes lies at the heart of cost-benefit analysis. This is the *potential Pareto improvement criterion.*

In the language of welfare economics, a change that makes at least one member of a community better off and makes none worse off is a Pareto improvement.[1] Undertaking a project provides a *potential Pareto improvement* if it is *in principle possible* to secure an actual

Pareto improvement by linking the project with an appropriate set of transfers of money between gainers and losers—even if *in fact* these transfers will not take place. In other words, a project provides a potential Pareto improvement if the total sum of money that the gainers from the project would be prepared to pay to ensure that the project were undertaken exceeds the total sum of money that the losers from it would accept as compensation for putting up with it. (For the purposes of discussing potential Pareto improvements it is conventional to assume that making transfers of money between individuals is not costly in itself; for example, there are assumed to be no administrative costs in organizing transfers.)

The rule that projects should be undertaken if, and only if, they produce potential Pareto improvements is, unsurprisingly, known as the potential Pareto improvement criterion.

To fix ideas, consider the example, introduced in Section 2.6, of a river development authority considering whether to build hydro-electric power dams in a river valley. There are two available sites, A and C. A is upstream of a dam owned by a private company; C is downstream of it. A decision to build a dam at A would provide a benefit to the owners of the private company. If the river authority uses financial appraisal it is taking the position that any benefits of its actions which accrue directly to private firms are none of its concern. Financial appraisal would imply the decision to build only the dam at C. To build A in addition to C would involve net financial costs with a present value of $0·874 m, which, if the river authority is publicly owned, will ultimately be borne by taxpayers.

But the building of a dam at A would increase the profits of the private firm, providing benefits to the firm's shareholders which have a present value of $6·305 m. These shareholders, who would be the gainers from a decision to build at A, would presumably be willing to pay any sum up to $6·305 m to ensure that the dam was built. The losers—the taxpayers—would agree to the dam being built if a sum at least as great as $0·874 m were appropriately shared out amongst them. In principle, then, there is scope for a package deal, combining the building of the dam with the transfer of sums of money between individuals, to which all members of the community would assent. That is, to build at A as well as at C, rather than only at C, is to produce a potential Pareto improvement.

In essence, the potential Pareto improvement criterion requires that changes in people's welfare should be measured by their 'willingness to pay'—that is, by the amount that they are willing to pay for the benefits of a project and by the amounts they are willing to accept as compensation for harm inflicted on them. These benefits and costs borne by individuals are aggregated into 'social benefits' and 'social costs' by simple addition; a project is to be undertaken if its social benefits exceed its social costs—that is, if its 'net social benefit' is positive.

Almost every cost-benefit analysis makes some use of the potential Pareto improvement criterion, even if only implicitly. The relative simplicity of the criterion is a further reason for making it the starting point of a discussion of cost-benefit analysis. For the present we shall take the securing of potential Pareto improvements to be *the* social objective. The possibility of using other social objectives will be considered from Chapter 13 onwards.

So far we have said nothing to justify, at the level of principle, the use of the potential Pareto improvement criterion as a statement of the social objective. We cannot do this without first interpreting the concept of a 'social objective' and, as noted above, many different interpretations are possible. Very broadly, however, two schools of thought can be distinguished.

To one school,[2] a social objective is an objective pursued by a social decision-maker—that is, by someone responsible for making decisions in the public interest. The objective is 'social' in the sense that it is used to determine decisions which affect society as a whole. Some would go further and argue that such an objective can properly be thought of as society's objective. The decision-maker, it is argued, occupies his position by virtue of a socially approved political process. He has been entrusted with the task of making choices on behalf of the general public, and this trust implies that he will formulate objectives for society. He is accountable to the public for carrying out this task to their satisfaction. With this approach, then, cost-benefit analysis is seen as a process of appraising decision problems in the light of objectives chosen by the decision-maker. We shall call this approach the *decision-making approach* to—or decision-making interpretation of—cost-benefit analysis. It has much in common with the approach that we used in our discussions of financial appraisal in Part II of this book.

The other main school of thought[3] about the proper function and nature of cost-benefit analysis looks at appraisal from a rather different viewpoint. It starts from a distinct position about what the objectives of social decision-makers ought to be. These objectives should be distilled from a consensus of the value judgements of the individuals who make up society, and they should be propositions which would command universal, or at least very wide, assent. This interpretation of cost-benefit analysis sets it apart from the process by which actual decisions are taken in practice at any point in space or time. The analyst works independently of the political decision-making process and brings to his work his own independent norms.

The strongest advocates of this approach have argued that 'consensus value judgements' can be identified with a particular body of doctrine in welfare economics (that branch of economics that deals with ethical propositions). These doctrines may, for want of a better word, be called Paretian; for this reason we shall call this approach the *Paretian approach.*

Let us now consider how the use of the potential Pareto improvement criterion can be justified according to the principles of each of these two approaches to cost-benefit analysis.

7.3.   The decision-making approach

Given this approach, the relevant question to ask is 'what objective would a social decision-maker choose to pursue?' There is a strong argument that, at least in a fairly centralized public decision-making system, the objective chosen normally will correspond to that implied by the potential Pareto improvement criterion. The key to this argument is the proposition that a national government, because of its control of the tax system, has control of the distribution between individuals of the community's income. Given this proposition, it follows that the government has the power to convert potential Pareto improvements into actual Pareto improvements. For the government, then, the word 'potential' refers not simply to a theoretical possibility but to a practical policy option. A project that satisfies the potential Pareto improvement criterion is one that the government can use, in conjunction with tax changes, to make everyone better off. And it is very plausible to suppose that this is something that most governments, in most circumstances, would want to do.

The idea of governments having complete control over the distribution of income may seem far-fetched. It is obvious that governments do not think it practical to change taxes every time a project is undertaken. A decision to build an urban motorway in Leeds, for example, would not be followed by the introduction of a special tax to be paid by Leeds motorists. But it may be that at a broad strategic level, something of this kind takes place. If, over a period of time, there was a systematic tendency for public projects to favour the members of some identifiable group, such as motorists or city dwellers, the government might restore the balance by appropriate changes in taxes and subsidies. (This issue will be returned to in Chapter 14.)

Undoubtedly there are circumstances where governments, for one reason or another, wish to pursue objectives other than that of securing potential Pareto improvements. In later chapters we shall explore why this is so and how cost-benefit analysis can take account of such additional objectives. But for the present we shall take the potential Pareto improvement criterion to be the sole definition of government or social objectives. As a first approximation to a full statement of government objectives, the criterion has much to recommend it. Not least amongst its merits is that it is relatively simple to understand and to use.

7.4. The Paretian approach

The advocates of this approach maintain that social objectives should be statements of consensus ethical judgements, and that a body of such judgements are to be found in one of the dominant streams of welfare economics—the Paretian stream.

In welfare economics there is a long tradition of considering social welfare as having (at least) two dimensions—those of *economic efficiency* and *distributional justice.*

In essence, economic efficiency concerns the size of the total of the wealth of all members of the community, while distributional justice concerns the way that this total is shared amongst individuals. 'Wealth' here is to be interpreted in its broadest sense; if someone would prefer A to B he is 'wealthier' if he has A than if he has B. (Thus, for example, a man might choose to work 40 hours per week for a wage of £50 rather than to work 50 hours for £65. In our present sense he is at least as 'wealthy' in the first situation as in the second, for he has revealed in his choice that the extra 10 hours of leisure are worth at least £15 to him.) The potential Pareto improvement criterion is a criterion for identifying changes in economic efficiency; a change that produces a potential Pareto improvement is one that increases economic efficiency. Formally, this is simply a matter of definition; the two expressions 'potential Pareto improvement' and 'increase in economic efficiency' mean precisely the same. Alternative distributions of a given total of wealth may, in principle, be ranked as 'better' and 'worse' or 'more just' and 'less just'. How such a ranking should be made is a controversial question, but for our present purposes that is not important.

The fundamental value judgement on which the Paretian approach to cost-benefit analysis rests is that, *other things being equal,* an increase in economic efficiency is a good thing. That is, if social welfare has just the two dimensions of economic efficiency and distributional justice, an increase in economic efficiency is a good thing provided that it is not associated with a decrease in distributional justice. (Some writers also admit the possibility of further dimensions of social welfare. For example 'national greatness'—perhaps the quality of a nation's cultural heritage or its degree of influence in world affairs—may be asserted to have an ethical significance in its own right, entirely independent of its significance for efficiency and justice.)

Thus, if cost-benefit analysis is purely and simply the appraisal of projects by reference to the potential Pareto improvement criterion, it goes part of the way to identifying increases in social welfare.

The exponents of the Paretian approach argue that cost-benefit analysts should, as a matter of principle, confine themselves to using the potential Pareto improvement criterion and hence to measuring changes in economic efficiency. They argue that a cost-benefit analysis should aim to answer one question only: 'by how much does the total sum of money that the gainers from a project would be prepared to pay to ensure that the project is undertaken exceed the total sum of money that the losers from the project would accept as compensation for putting up with it?' The answer to this question does not amount to a statement about whether the project will increase or decrease social welfare; but it is a significant piece of information. It narrows the area of debate about the merits and demerits of the project. If, for example, a project is shown to cause a decrease in economic efficiency, then someone who argues that the project ought to be undertaken must argue that the decrease in efficiency is outweighed by an improvement along some other dimension of social welfare—perhaps that of distributional justice.

In support of this approach, with its implication that cost-benefit analysis should not concern itself with any dimensions of social welfare other than that of economic efficiency, it may be argued that to attempt to go further is to attempt the impossible. It may not always be possible, even in principle, to identify increases and decreases in social welfare by using 'consensus' ethical judgements. Some writers, for example, argue that the different dimensions of social welfare are inherently incommensurable.[4]

This sets the Paretian approach apart from the decision-making approach. The welfare economist may legitimately declare that it is not possible to know which of two social states would produce more social welfare. The decision-maker, however, is not free to declare that it is impossible to choose between two alternative courses of action. It is his job to choose. According to the decision-making approach, cost-benefit analysis exists to assist him in choosing; it may, therefore, have to explore social objectives other than that of increasing economic efficiency. In this sense the decision-making approach is the more ambitious of the two approaches, since it permits a wider range of the effects of a project to be taken account of in cost-benefit analysis.

The main thrust of this book is to pursue the decision-making approach to cost-benefit analysis. Consequently a good deal of space will be devoted to exploring the implications of social objectives other than, or in addition to, that of increasing economic efficiency.

However, the whole of Chapters 8—12 and much of the remainder of this book are concerned with the implications of using the potential Pareto improvement criterion in cost-benefit analysis. The discussion in these parts of the book is equally relevant to either approach to cost-benefit analysis.

7.5.   The scope of analysis

If the cost-benefit analyst adopts the potential Pareto improvement criterion he is committed to taking account of the effects on the welfare of all members of the community of every transaction that enters into his analysis. Stated like this, the task seems extremely difficult; and indeed in many circumstances it is. However there also are many circumstances in which cost-benefit analysis differs very little from financial appraisal.

Consider for example a public project which requires the government to buy and to use 1000 tons of bricks. For a financial appraisal we need know only the market price of this quantity of bricks. But for a cost-benefit analysis we must take account also of the effects of the government's purchase on the welfare of owners of brickworks, of other users of bricks, of employees in the brick industry, and so on. Fortunately, however, it can be deduced from economic theory that in a competitive economy the welfare of none of these people will be affected, provided that the purchase is not so large as to cause changes in any prices or wages.

Using the economic model of 'perfect' or 'atomistic' competition, the price of a good equals the marginal cost of producing it. (Otherwise firms would want to produce more or less of it.) So the price of 1000 tons of bricks measures the extra costs borne by firms in producing them; the net gain to brickwork owners is zero. The price of bricks also measures their 'marginal value' to their users—that is, how much brick users would be willing to pay 'at the margin' for extra bricks. (If price did not equal marginal value, brick users would want to buy more or less bricks.) So if, as a result of the government's purchase, other brick users use slightly fewer bricks, their net loss is also zero.

Similarly, the price of labour measures the amount that it is necessary to pay to compensate additional or marginal workers for giving up their leisure to work. (Otherwise, more or less workers would want to work.) So if additional workers are employed, the net effect on their welfare is zero. And the price of labour also measures the value of the 'marginal product' of labour—that is, the value of the extra output that would result from hiring the labour. (Otherwise, more or less labour would be demanded.) So if labour moves to the brick industry from other industries, the net loss to its former employers is again zero.

In a 'perfectly competitive economy', then, the price paid for a good measures the marginal social cost of using an additional unit of the good; and the price at which a good can be sold measures the marginal social value of producing an additional unit. ('Social cost' and 'social value' are to be interpreted relative to the potential Pareto improvement criterion.) Thus a financial appraisal of a project and a cost-benefit analysis of it would be identical (provided that undertaking the project did not lead to a significant change in the market price of any good).

It is because perfect competition cannot always be assumed to exist, and because prices cannot always be assumed to be independent of whether or not a project is undertaken, that cost-benefit analysis is something different from financial appraisal. In the following chapters we shall consider the implications of relaxing the assumptions that make cost-benefit analysis and financial appraisal identical.

An important problem has to be faced here. Many of the ways in which economies diverge in reality from the idealized model of perfect competition reflect man-made arrangements which in principle could be altered by appropriate public policies. In the next chapter, for example, we shall consider the implications of 'managed' foreign exchange rates, of trades union determined wage rates, and of taxes imposed on the consumption of specific goods. All these can be regarded as divergences from perfect competition; all are the products of, or are subject to influence by, public policy.

An analyst might respond to this problem in one of at least two ways.

One approach would be for him to address himself to 'the government' and take virtually everything that could conceivably be influenced by public policy as being within the government's discretion. Then only the most fundamental and unchangeable facts of economic life would be accepted as constraints on his analysis. He would seek to make very general prescriptions as to how the government should act to maximize social welfare. A good example of this kind of approach is the analysis that has been made of the problem of 'optimal taxation'.[5] In one version of this problem the fundamental constraint is that the government must raise revenue and the only means available are taxes on goods and services (including labour). The result of the analysis is a set of recommendations about the structure of the tax system, which maximizes social welfare subject to the given constraint. Since any system of taxes on goods and services will imply the acceptance of some divergence from the perfectly competitive ideal, such a solution is known to economists as a 'second best' solution.[6] This kind of approach can be very enlightening, but it is not what we understand to be the role of cost-benefit analysis.

We shall adopt a different approach. We shall accept divergences from the perfectly competitive ideal simply as facts. We shall not attempt to decide in a generalized framework whether social welfare would be increased or reduced by the removal of these divergences, nor whether or not it would be possible for a government to remove them, although *one or other* of these divergences might happen to be the subject of a particular cost-benefit analysis. For us, cost-benefit analysis is a technique to be applied to limited and tightly defined problems. In making any specific and small-scale decision—let us say, whether to build a new hospital at one site or another—it is inevitable that very many features of economic life are treated as constants. This is not to say that these features of the world should *never* be treated as variables in cost-benefit analysis. Our point is simply that cost-benefit analysis is best understood as part of a piecemeal approach to decision-making.

Although it is possible to limit the scope of a problem by limiting the number of alternative courses of action to be considered it is never possible to contain the relevant *effects* of these actions within neat boundaries. Any decision sets in motion a ripple of effects which spreads outwards to affect the whole economy. The location of a hospital, for example, affects the travelling patterns of people, which affect the demand for cars, which affects the demand for steel, and so on. The analyst clearly cannot take explicit and detailed account of all of such a chain of effects. The only practical way to proceed is to adopt some simple theory of the workings of the economy in general and then to use this whenever it is not possible, or too costly, to work out more exactly the precise repercussive effect of a decision. We shall use the theory of perfect competition in this way.

There are many reasons for selecting this particular theory. It is—at least in comparison with most of its rivals—very simple. It has been studied in great detail and thus its main properties are not controversial and are part of the body of received economic doctrine. Perhaps most important in the context of this book is the relationship between perfect competition and financial appraisal—that in a world of perfect competition, cost-benefit analysis and financial appraisal would be identical. Thus to adopt the working rule that the economy should be regarded as, on the whole, competitive is to accept that a financial appraisal is a first approximation to a cost-benefit analysis. This is very valuable for the purposes of exposition. While we shall, in the course of this book, progressively introduce more and more reasons for the divergence of cost-benefit analysis from financial appraisal, we shall maintain the working assumption that prices measure marginal social costs and marginal social values whenever there is no specific reason to suspect that this assumption is significantly wrong.

It must be admitted that, although our approach is fairly conventional, some writers have proposed working rules of rather different kinds. Little and Mirrlees, for example, seem to advocate using the general assumption that the economy is in an 'optimal' state in the second-best sense. That is, it should be assumed that certain fundamental constraints prevent the existence of perfect competition but that the government has ensured that, subject to these constraints, the economy is arranged in a socially optimal way. It is a bold step to attribute to the government such skill in economic management. On balance we do not think that the argument in favour of this approach is sufficiently compelling to justify the added complexity that it would introduce. However, it does represent an alternative working rule which some analysts may adopt and which the interested reader may therefore wish to pursue elsewhere.[7]

Notes

[1] Named after the Italian economist and sociologist, Vilfredo Pareto (1848–1923).

[2] This approach underlies two recent works on project appraisal in developing countries—by Dasgupta, Marglin and Sen (1972) and by Little and Mirrlees (1974). A case for this approach has been made by one of the present authors (Williams, 1972).

[3] This approach is adovocated very strongly by Mishan. See Mishan (1971a), especially Chapters 45–47, and Mishan (1974).

[4] Mishan (1971a), p. 314.

[5] See, for example, Diamond and Mirrlees (1971).

[6] Modern discussion of the problems of the second-best derives from Lipsey and Lancaster (1956).

[7] This approach underlies Little and Mirrlees (1974). See especially their discussions of indirect taxes (pp. 223–5) and of the economics of the second-best (pp. 367–73).

Further reading

Surveys of the theoretical framework of received welfare economics can be found in Mishan (1960), Nath (1969) and Winch (1971). All three discuss the potential Pareto improvement criterion (which sometimes is known as the Kaldor-Hicks compensation test).

The arguments of Section 7.5 were based on a use of the model of 'perfect competition'. The properties of this model are explained in almost every textbook of microeconomics. The argument that, in a perfectly competitive economy, cost-benefit analysis and financial appraisal would be identical is very closely related to the theorem of economics that the outcome of a perfectly competitive economy would be Pareto-optimal (that is, would be a state from which no further Pareto improvements could be made). For a formal exposition of this theorem see, for example, Winch (1971).

8. Shadow Pricing in Cost-benefit Analysis

8.1. Introduction

In this chapter we shall consider various factors which can make market prices inappropriate as measures of the marginal social costs, or marginal social values, of goods and services. When such factors are important, the cost-benefit analyst may have to use in his accounts some valuations that are not taken directly from market prices. Such valuations we shall call by the general name of *shadow* or *accounting prices*. They are valuations that replace market prices in a cost-benefit analysis.

The examples which follow are intended to illustrate the general principles involved in working out shadow prices. In each example we inevitably use a number of simplifying assumptions. Since different authors make different simplifying assumptions, the formulae that result from our analysis may not always be the same as those that result from the analyses of other writers. Such differences do not necessarily reflect any important differences in method, and it is the method and not the detailed form of the results that is important.

8.2. Price and quantity constraints

The significance of market prices as measures of social costs and social values depends on the ability of individuals to buy and sell goods freely at their market prices. Thus, for example, it was argued in Section 7.5 that the price of bricks measured the marginal cost of producing them. This was inferred from the (assumed) fact that each brick producer was free to sell as many bricks as he chose at the market price; a producer would be irrational not to produce and sell that quantity of bricks whose marginal cost was equal to the price. Similarly, each brick user was assumed to be free to buy as many bricks as he chose at the market price; he would be irrational not to buy that quantity at which the marginal value of bricks equalled the price.

In a competitive market, the price of a good tends to that level at which supply equals demand—that is, to the level at which everyone is able to buy and sell the quantities he wishes to buy or sell. For the cost-benefit analyst, problems begin to arise when the workings of a market are constrained in ways that prevent it from reaching such an equilibrium, and thus everyone is *not* able to buy or sell the quantities he would choose.

We have already considered very similar problems in our discussion of financial appraisal. In Chapter 6 we considered situations in which a firm or public agency was unable to buy as much as it wished of some input, given its nominal price. We looked at constraints both on the availability of capital and on the availability of labour. A number of problems in cost-benefit analysis can be tackled by extensions of this analysis.

Foreign currency rationing

Projects often require the buying of inputs from abroad. Since foreign goods must be bought by spending foreign currency, it is often convenient to regard foreign currency, rather than the goods bought with this currency, as the input to a project. Conversely, projects may produce outputs which are sold abroad, or which in-directly lead to a reduction in imports from abroad. In either of these cases, foreign currency can be regarded as an output of the project.

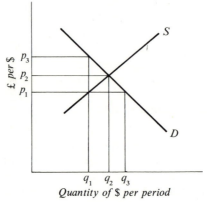

Quantity of $ per period

Fig. 8.1

Foreign currency, like other goods, has a price. The price of foreign currency—say, dollars—in terms of domestic currency—say, pounds—is the *exchange rate*. The lower the price of foreign currency, the greater will be quantity of it that is demanded. This relationship is represented by the demand curve, D, in Figure 8.1. This curve may also be interpreted as showing the marginal value (measured on the vertical axis) of any given quantity of foreign currency. If, for example, the quantity q_1 is available and is allocated to those uses in which it is most highly valued, an additional unit of foreign currency would be worth p_3 to the user who would be willing to pay most to have that unit. In other words, the marginal value of foreign currency is p_3 when the quantity is q_1. (The idea of a marginal value curve was introduced in Section 6.2.)

The greater the price of foreign currency, the greater is the quantity that people wish to offer for exchange into domestic currency. This relationship is represented by the supply curve of foreign currency, S in Figure 8.1. If there were a competitive market for foreign currency (the institution of 'floating' exchange rates), the price of dollars would tend to the level p_2, which equates the quantity of dollars demanded with the quantity supplied. At this price all buyers of dollars would be able to have the quantities they wished to buy, and the price of dollars would equal their marginal value.

However, national governments are sometimes reluctant to allow the price of foreign currency to be determined by the forces of a competitive market. An increase in the price of foreign currency corresponds to a devaluation of domestic currency and, rather than allow such a devaluation to happen, governments sometimes fix the price of foreign currency below the level it would reach in a competitive market. For example, the price might be fixed at the level p_1, at which the quantity of foreign currency demanded, q_3, exceeds the quantity supplied, q_1. For a limited time it would be possible for all of this demand to be met by running down stocks of foreign currency. But in the long run, the exchange rate can be maintained at the level chosen by the government only if the available supply of foreign currency, q_1, is rationed amongst competing users.

This can be regarded as a problem of input rationing of the kind discussed in Chapter 6. Here, however, it is not a single firm or institution but a whole community that cannot buy as much of an input as it would choose to, given the price of the input. The problem for the community is to ensure that the available foreign currency is allocated to those uses where its social value is greatest.

We have argued already that, in a competitive economy, the sum that a user is willing to pay for additional units of an input is a measure of the marginal social value of that input in that use. Thus the demand curve for foreign currency, D, does not show simply the marginal value of foreign currency to its immediate users; it also shows the marginal *social* value of foreign currency.

Following the arguments introduced in Section 6.2, the available quantity of foreign currency, q_1, would be allocated to its socially most valuable uses if users of foreign currency behaved *as if* the price were p_3. In other words, a *shadow price* or *accounting price* should be used. To ensure that such a shadow price actually was used, a government might impose a tax on the use of foreign currency, such that the gross cost of foreign currency equalled the optimal shadow price. Imports are commonly subjected to tax for this purpose.

If all users of foreign currency behaved as if its price were p_3, then the social value of marginal units of foreign currency would also be p_3. Each dollar used by a project would impose a social cost of p_3, since this would be the marginal social value of foreign currency in the uses from which it would have to be diverted. Conversely, each dollar earned by a project would have a social value of p_3.

If, however, all users of foreign currency do not take decisions by using the shadow price, this simple conclusion is no longer valid. If, for example, foreign currency is rationed amongst competing users in a haphazard way, the value p_3 has no special significance for the appraisal of particular projects.

Unemployment of labour

According to the argument presented in Section 7.5 above, the social cost of using additional units of labour for a project is exactly measured by the price at which labour is bought. If this argument is correct, the fact that a particular project leads to an increase in the total number of people in the community who are employed is, in itself, neither a reason for undertaking the project nor a reason for not undertaking it. Yet in reality, particular projects are often advocated on the grounds that (amongst other advantages) they create jobs or save jobs.

The difficulty with the original argument is that it depends upon workers being able to choose whether or not to supply labour at the prevailing wage. This clearly is not the case if some workers are involuntarily unemployed—that is, would like to work at the going wage rate but cannot find jobs. Involuntary unemployment is not uncommon in particular labour markets—that is, for workers with particular skills living in particular regions. The mechanism that would eliminate unemployment in a labour market is that of unemployed workers bidding down the wage rate until it is at a level that equates the quantity of labour demanded with the quantity supplied. In practice, strong labour unions are often able to prevent individual unemployed workers from taking work at less than the union rate.

Analytically, this case is the opposite of the case of the market for foreign currency. Here a minimum rather than a maximum price has been fixed for a good (labour services) and the result is excess supply rather than excess demand. This is shown diagrammatically in Figure 8.2. For convenience, we take as our unit of quantity *numbers* of workers, assuming that a worker can, at best, choose only whether or not to work; the number of hours per week that he must work if he takes a tob is given and is the same for each job. The curve D represents the demand for labour; this curve may also be interpreted as representing the marginal social value of any given quantity of labour.

The curve S represents the supply of labour. The higher is the wage rate, the greater will be the number of people offering to work. We shall suppose that, for our workers, the alternative to working in this labour market is not working at all. Given these two alternatives, each worker will, when considering whether to offer his labour, compare the going rate with his own valuation of his leisure time, and will offer to work only if the wage rate is at least as great as his valuation of the leisure he must forgo to work. Thus the curve S can be reinterpreted as showing the marginal value of leisure. (For example, if workers are ranked in ascending order of their valuations of leisure, the n_1 th worker values his leisure at w_1.) In a competitive market, the wage rate would tend to the level w_2, at which rate n_2 workers would be employed. Both the marginal social value of labour and the marginal value of leisure would be equal to this market wage rate.

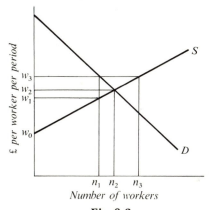

Fig. 8.2

But suppose that the wage instead is fixed at the level w_3. At this wage, only n_1 workers are demanded but n_3 offer to work; n_3-n_1 workers are involuntarily unemployed.

As in the previous example of the market for foreign currency, we could try to find an optimal shadow price of labour. For example, given that the quantity of labour demanded is n_1, the available jobs would be allocated to those workers who value leisure least if workers behaved *as if* the wage were w_1. Alternatively (and this would be more difficult, for reasons which will become clear shortly) we could take as given that n_3 workers offer to work and try to find out what shadow price it would be optimal for employers to use. Governments sometimes try to induce participants in labour markets to act in accordance with shadow wage rates. (The British Regional Employment Premium, introduced in 1967, subsidized the use of labour in regions with high unemployment rates so as to induce employers to behave as if wage rates were less than those that workers received.)

The problem most commonly faced by the cost-benefit analyst, however, is to evaluate the social cost of using labour in a particular project when in the labour market as a whole there is unemployment but no systematic use of shadow prices. (The converse of this problem, which also is very common, is that of evaluating the saving to the community that results from employing less labour.) It is tempting to deduce from Figure 8.2 that if the wage is w_3 and the number of men employed is n_1, and if a project then provides a job for an additional worker, the value of the leisure that this worker forgoes is w_1, the 'marginal value of leisure'. This deduction would be correct *if* there were some mechanism to ensure that, when the number of people wishing to work exceeded the number of jobs available, jobs were always allocated to those workers who had the lowest valuations of leisure. In reality, however, jobs may be allocated on other criteria, such as 'first come, first served' or 'knowing the right people'. All that we can deduce immediately is that the social cost of labour is *at least* w_0 (since no one values his leisure less than this) and is *no greater than* w_3 (since no one who valued his leisure more than this would offer to work at the existing wage of w_3).

For the purposes of discussion, suppose that a project requires a small number of additional workers to be employed, and that the average valuation of leisure amongst these workers is known—say, w^*, which is less than the wage, w_3. From the viewpoint of the organization that undertakes the project, the cost of labour is its financial cost, w_3 per worker. But this is partially offset by a benefit to the workers who are employed. Each worker receives w_3 in return for giving up leisure which, on average, is valued at only w^*. There is, then, a benefit of $(w_3 - w^*)$ per worker. The net *social* cost of using labour is only w^*. This is the valuation that would be used in a cost-benefit analysis.

8.3. Taxation

In a competitive economy, there are two ways in which market prices are significant as measures of social value. If buyers are free to buy as much of a good as they choose at its market price, this price measures the good's *marginal value* to consumers. If producers are free to produce as much as they choose of the good for sale at its market price, this price measures the *marginal cost* of producing the good. (In the case of labour markets, the equivalent statement is that if workers are free to choose whether or not to work at the market wage rate, this wage rate measures the marginal value of leisure to workers.)

So far we have assumed that the price paid by buyers—the *demand price*—is the same as the price received by suppliers—the *supply price.* But frequently this is not so. The reason is that governments raise revenue by taxing goods. As a result, the buyer of a good pays a price which includes a tax payment; he will buy the quantity that equates the good's marginal value with its gross-of-tax price. But the producer of the good receives only the price paid by the buyer, net of tax. He will produce the quantity that equates the marginal cost of producing the good with its net-of-tax price. There are, then, two prices for any taxed good, each of which carries some information for the cost-benefit analyst.

Suppose that some project requires one unit of a good (say, trucks) which is subject to indirect tax. The analyst's problem is to evaluate the social cost of this unit.

If the project's requirement is met entirely by an increase in the production of trucks, the net social cost is the marginal production cost, and this is measured by the net-of-tax supply price. The *financial* cost to the buyer is the gross-of-tax price, but the tax element in this price is simply a transfer to the government, and hence, we may assume, to taxpayers in general.

Alternatively, the project's requirement might be met without there being any increase in the production of trucks. Instead, potential truck users may have forgone the use of trucks to an extent equal to the project's requirement. In this case, the social cost is the marginal value of the good to its consumers—that is the gross-of-tax price. This time the government makes no net gain which can be offset against the financial cost of trucks which is paid by whoever undertakes the project. (The government makes no net gain because the total consumption of the taxed good remains unchanged.)

More generally, suppose that each extra unit of the good used by the project implies a decrease of a units in the consumption of the good outside the project and an increase of $1 - a$ units in the total production of the good. Clearly the social cost of each unit of the good used in the project is

$$a(\text{gross-of-tax price}) + (1 - a)(\text{net-of-tax price}). \qquad 8.1$$

The main remaining problem is to estimate, for any particular case, what the value of a will be. Consider Figure 8.3. In this diagram, the curve S represents the supply of a taxed good and the curve D_1 the initial demand for it. (Both curves relate to the gross-of-tax price of the good.) The market price initially is p_1. Now suppose that a project requires an additional unit of the good. This shifts the demand curve to the right by one unit, to D_2. The result is an increase in the price to p_2, a reduction of a units in the quantity demanded outside the project, and an increase of $1 - a$ units in the quantity supplied.

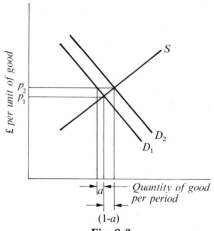

Fig. 8.3

The value of a is determined by the slopes of the supply and demand curves in the relevant ranges. It is conventional to express the responsiveness-to-price of the quantity demanded of a good, and of the quantity supplied of a good, by use of *elasticities*. If, given some initial combination of price and quantity demanded, an increase in the price by 1 per cent would induce a reduction of 2 per cent in the quantity demanded, the *(price) elasticity of demand* is -2. Similarly, if an increase in the price by 1 per cent would induce an increase of 3 per cent in the quantity supplied, the *(price) elasticity of supply* is 3. It is easy to show that

$$\frac{a}{1-a} = \frac{-e_d}{e_s} \qquad\qquad 8.2$$

where e_d is the price elasticity of demand at the initial combination of price and quantity, and e_s is the price elasticity of supply.

By slight revisions of the above argument it can be shown that, if a project produced one additional unit of the good (instead of requiring one additional unit), the resulting increase in the quantity consumed would be a units and the decrease in the quantity produced outside the project would be $1 - a$ units. (a has the same numerical value as before.) Thus the social value of the unit of the good produced by the project would again be

$$a(\text{gross-of-tax price}) + (1 - a)(\text{net-of-tax price}). \qquad 8.3$$

Since this expression represents both the social value of producing an additional unit of the good and the social cost of using an additional unit (see Expression 8.1), it may be called the *shadow price* of the good. In a cost-benefit analysis this shadow price would be used in place of financial valuations of the good.

It is worth considering briefly two extreme assumptions that could be made about the elasticity of the supply curve, each of which is in some circumstances a good approximation to reality. First, consider the case of a good whose price elasticity of supply is zero. (This implies that the quantity supplied is independent of the price and that the supply curve is a vertical line.) In this case $a = 1$ and the correct shadow price for the good is its gross-of-tax price. Second, consider a good whose price elasticity of supply is infinite. (This implies that producers would not require any increase in the price of the good to induce them to produce greater quantities; the supply curve is a horizontal line.) In this case $a = 0$ and the correct shadow price for the good is its net-of-tax price.

The arguments of this section have been made in relation to taxes on goods. But since labour is itself a good, the same arguments can be applied to income taxes. An income tax is, in effect, a tax on the good 'labour'. Our conclusions can be reinterpreted quite simply so as to relate to income taxes, provided only that we are considering a labour market in which wages are determined by the forces of competition (and thus in which there is no involuntary unemployment).

An employer will buy labour up to the point at which the value of the additional output that would be achieved by employing an additional worker (the *marginal product* of labour) is equal to the gross wage. A worker will offer his labour if the net-of-tax wage is high enough to compenstate him for forgoing his leisure. If a project requires one worker and this requirement is met by some other employer forgoing a worker, the social cost of labour is measured by the gross wage. If instead the requirement is met by an additional worker entering the labour market, the social cost of labour is measured by the net-of-tax wage.

Throughout this section it has been assumed that the good with which we were dealing at any time was the only one subject to tax. This assumption allows the analysis to be made relatively simple, but it is hardly realistic. In an appendix to this chapter we show how a shadow price can be derived for a taxed good in an economy where many other goods are also subject to tax.

8.4. Producers' market power and public control of prices

At various points in this chapter it has been argued that the supply price received by the producers of a good measures the marginal social cost of producing it. The logic of this argument, it will be remembered, is that if the marginal cost were greater than the price, producers would want to produce less, whilst if marginal cost were less than price producers would want to produce more.

This argument, however, assumes that producers take as given the price at which they can sell their output. But in many cases firms have a degree of 'market power' or 'monopoly power': the price at which they sell their output depends on how much they decide to supply. Thus if a firm decides to increase the amount of a good which it produces, this will bring about a fall in the price at which the whole of the firm's output can be sold. So in deciding whether or not to increase production, the firm will take account not only of additional production costs but also of the loss of revenue brought about by the fall in price. While additional production costs can be taken to measure corresponding social costs, the loss of sales revenue is not a social cost. It is a transfer from the firm to consumers, the loss by the one being exactly countered by the gain to the other. For such a firm we should expect the marginal social cost of its output to be less than the price at which it is sold. (This is simply a restatement of the well known theorem of economics that for a profit-maximizing monopoly firm, price will exceed marginal cost.)

If a firm has a strongly entrenched monopoly position in a market, governments often respond either by introducing some form of public regulation of the firm's behaviour, or by bringing the firm into public ownership. These forms of organization are common in such 'natural monopoly' industries as postal services, telecommunications, railways, and gas and electricity supply. When a firm's price and output decisions are being influenced by government we can no longer presume profit-maximizing behaviour. But nor can we assume, as a matter of fact, that price will equal marginal social cost. On many rural public transport services, for example, the marginal social cost of carrying passengers is virtually zero (since buses and trains run with many empty seats), but publicly owned transport undertakings rarely charge zero prices.

So in some circumstances the cost-benefit analyst cannot simply accept a supply price as a measure of the marginal social cost of a good. Instead he must try to measure marginal social cost in some other way—for example, by studying the financial accounts of firms.

Again, the social cost of units of a good required by a project depends on how far this requirement is met by increased production and how far it is met by reduced consumption outside the project. To the extent that it is met by increased production, the social cost is the marginal social cost of producing the good. To the extent that it is met by reduced consumption, the social cost is measured by the sum that those who forgo consumption would have been willing to pay for what they forgo. That is, it is measured by the price at which the good sells to consumers.

Appendix: Shadow pricing a taxed good when many goods are taxed

In Section 8.3 we derived an expression (Expression 8.3) for the shadow price of a good that was subject to a tax. This derivation was based on an implicit assumption that the good under consideration was the only one subject to tax. It is a little more difficult to derive the correct shadow price for a particular taxed good in an economy where many goods are taxed.

In our original examples, we were able to regard an increase of £1 in the government's tax revenue as being equivalent to a gain of £1 by taxpayers. But if many goods are taxed we can no longer do this; £1 in the hands of the government has a greater social value than £1 in the hands of the taxpayers.

To illustrate this argument, consider an economy in which all goods and services sold for consumption are taxed at the rate t. (That is, a net-of-tax price of £1 corresponds to a gross-of-tax price of £$(1 + t)$.) Now suppose that the government suddenly needs an additional one million pounds, let us say to pay a foreign debt, and that it chooses to raise this money by increasing direct taxation of incomes. (To simplify the argument, it is assumed that the supply of labour is completely unresponsive to the net-of-tax wage, and thus an increase in direct tax rates has no effect on the quantity of labour supplied.) The government would need to increase direct taxation by £$(1 + t)$ million to ensure a net increase of one million pounds in its tax revenues, since every extra £1 raised in direct taxation implies that £1 less is available for spending on consumption goods, and thus that the government's revenue from indirect taxes will fall by £$t/(1 + t)$. So each £1 gained by the government is equivalent to a gain of £$(1 + t)$ to taxpayers.

Now let us return to the original problem of a project which requires one unit of a taxed good to be bought. This good is taxed at the rate of t'. All other consumption goods are taxed at the rate t. (We assume that the particular good with which we are dealing accounts for only a small part of total spending in the economy.) Suppose that the net-of-tax price of our good—equal to the marginal cost of producing it—is p; its gross price is thus $p(1 + t')$. And suppose that the effect of the project's demand for one extra unit of the good is to reduce the consumption of the good outside the project by a units while increasing the quantity produced by $1 - a$ units.

The cost to whoever undertakes the project is the gross price, $p(1 + t')$. As a result of the increased consumption of the good, the government's tax revenue increases by $(1 - a)pt'$. But this increased spending will be offset by deceased spending on other goods. If each additional £1 spent on our good means that £1 less will be spent on other goods, expenditure on other goods must fall by $(1 - a)p(1 + t')$. Consequently the government's revenue from its taxation of these goods will fall by

$$(1 - a)\, p\, (1 + t')\, \frac{t}{1 + t}. \qquad\qquad 8.4$$

The net change in government revenue is

$$(1 - a)\, p\, \frac{(t' - t)}{1 + t}. \qquad\qquad 8.5$$

Since each additional £1 of government revenue has a social value of £$(1 + t)$, the social value of the government's net change in tax revenue is

$$(1 - a)\, p\, (t' - t). \qquad\qquad 8.6$$

Subtracting the social value of the net change in government revenue from the cost borne by whoever undertakes the project, the net social cost or shadow price of a unit of our good is

$$ap(1 + t') + (1 - a) p (1 + t). \qquad 8.7$$

In words, to the extent that a project's requirment of a good is met by reduced consumption outside the project, the social cost of the good is measured by its gross-of-tax price. To the extent that the requirement is met by increased production, the social cost is measured by the gross-of-tax price that the good would have had, had it been taxed at the same rate as other goods in the economy.

By rearranging Expression 8.7, the shadow price of the good may be written as

$$p(1 + t') - (1 - a)pt' (1 - \frac{t}{t'}). \qquad 8.8$$

The first term in the expression, $p(1 + t')$, is the gross-of tax price of the good. The second term can be interpreted in the following way. As a result of the project's requirement of one additional unit of the good, the government's revenue from its taxation of this good increases by $(1 - a)pt'$. The term in brackets, $1 - t/t'$, is a kind of shadow price; it is the net social benefit that results from an increase of one unit in the yield of the tax on the good.

Problems

1. In most developed countries, the consumption of oil is subjected to heavy taxation. There are a number of reasons for this. On the one hand, if a country is a net importer of oil, its government may wish to discourage the consumption of oil as a means of reducing the demand for foreign currency. (This policy is an alternative to allowing the national currency to devalue.) On the other hand, governments may see oil taxes simply as a convenient way of raising revenue, for it is usually believed that the price elasticity of the demand for oil is relatively low.

In the appraisal of projects that involve changes in the consumption of oil (transport projects, for example) or changes in the production of oil (exploitation of domestic oil reserves, for example), the result of the appraisal is likely to be very sensitive to the value attached to oil.

Should changes in the consumption of oil be shadow priced, for the purpose of cost-benefit analysis, at the gross-of-tax or the net-of-price in the following alternative circumstances?

(*i*) All oil consumed in our country is imported at a price fixed by oil-producing countries. Changes in the quantity of oil consumed in this country will have no significant effect on this price. Oil taxes are levied solely to raise revenue for the government. There is no excess demand for foreign currency at the current exchange rate and the government is content to allow the exchange rate to be determined by market forces. Most goods in the economy are not subject to indirect tax.

(*ii*) As before, all oil consumed in our country is imported at a price which would not be affected significantly by changes in the quantity of oil consumed. But oil taxes are levied primarily as a means of reducing the demand for foreign currency. The government has committed itself to maintaining the exchange rate at its current level; the rate is fixed at this level by the government. To prevent a net outflow of foreign currency, imported goods are taxed. Oil is taxed at the same rate as are other imports. Most home-produced goods are not subject to tax.

2. In a particular labour market there are neither strong unions nor strong employers' organizations; wages are determined in a competitive market. Currently

the gross-of-tax wage is £1·50 per hour and the total quantity of labour employed is 400 000 hours per week. It is estimated that, for wage rates in the region of £1·50 per hour, each additional £0·01 per hour would induce an additional 2000 hours per week of labour to be supplied and would induce employers to demand 4000 fewer hours per week. For an average worker, income is taxed at a rate of 33 per cent, but tax allowances amount to £33 per week. (Thus a worker earning £33 per week pays no tax; one earning £36 per week pays £1 per week in tax.) What is the appropriate shadow price for labour in the following alternative circumstances:

(*i*) Workers are not free to choose the number of hours they work each week; all must work 40 hours per week or none. Each worker chooses between working in the labour market and not working at all; there are no opportunities for employment outside this market.

(*ii*) Workers must work a minimum of 35 hours per week but, subject to this constraint, may work as many hours as they choose at the prevailing wage rate. Changes in the wage rate in the region of £1·50 per hour do not lead to any significant changes in the number of workers in employment but only to changes in the average number of hours of labour per week supplied by each worker.

(Assume that all workers receive the average tax allowance of £33 per week and pay tax at the rate of 33 per cent.)

3. In a certain developing country, providing services to tourists is an important source of foreign currency. In its capital city (a major tourist attraction) there are at present 8000 hotel rooms. The price at which these rooms are let is determined by the forces of a competitive market, and at this price all hotels are fully occupied throughout the year. A recent study has shown that 50 per cent of the room nights let in the city are let to foreign visitors, and that the price elasticities of demand for foreign and domestic visitors are respectively −2 and −1. (That is, an increase in the price of hotel rooms by 1 per cent would induce a 2 per cent reduction in the number demanded by foreigners and a 1 per cent reduction in the number demanded by domestic visitors.) It has also been found that, on average, foreign visitors spend $0·8 on other domestically produced goods and services for every $1 they spend on hotel accommodation.

A new hotel is planned, which will have 100 rooms—a relatively small addition to the present total number of hotel rooms in the city. It is expected that this hotel will earn a revenue of $360 000 per year. It can be expected that this hotel will have the same proportion—approximately 50 per cent—of foreign visitors amongst its guests as the other hotels will have; thus approximately $180 000 of its annual revenue will be received from foreign visitors.

In the judgement of the government, foreign currency earnings should be shadow priced at the value of 1·2. (That is, earnings from abroad that have a nominal value of $1 in local currency—converted at the official exchange rate—have a social value of $1·2.) This shadow price is used by the government in all its appraisals of its own projects and of private sector projects. (Most large private investment projects require government approval before they can go ahead.)

By how much does the social value of the additional foreign currency earnings generated each year by the new hotel exceed the nominal value?

(It may be assumed that all hotels sell an identical 'product' which is bought at a single, market-determined price. The quantity of this product that is supplied is given by the number of hotel rooms in the city and may be assumed to be independent of the price of rooms—at least within the relevant range of prices. As far as foreign visitors are concerned, the main substitutes for the services provided by hotels in this city are those provided by hotels in other countries.)

Further reading

For a lucid general discussion of shadow pricing, see the essay by McKean (1968).

The publication in 1969 of an O.E.C.D. manual of project appraisal methods for use in developing countries sparked off a debate about the use of shadow prices, particularly shadow prices of foreign currency. See Little and Mirrlees (1969 and 1972), Bacha and Taylor (1971) and Sen (1972).

A more formal treatment of the subject matter of Section 8.3 can be found in Harberger (1969). A very different way of treating indirect taxation is advocated by Little and Mirrlees (1974, pp. 223—5). These authors differ from us by assuming that the net-of-tax price of a good subject to a specific tax 'is a better measure of the social value of the good than the market price'. Their argument is that the government would not have taxed the good had there not been a good 'corrective' reason for doing so. This difference stems from the basic difference between their and our approach to cost-benefit analysis that was discussed in Section 7.5.

The issues raised in the appendix are discussed by Harrison (1974, pp. 150—56) and by Gwilliam and Mackie (1975, p. 208). The latter authors report how this problem was dealt with in cost-benefit analyses undertaken by the (then) Department of the Environment in the U.K. Both discussions differ from ours in not considering explicity the difference between £1 in the hands of the government and £1 of disposable income in the hands of taxpayers.

A practical study which attempts to calculate the correct shadow wage rate for the labour of coal-miners is reported in Appendix I of H.M.S.O. (1970), reprinted as Chapter 13 of Turvey (1971).

9. The Direct Effects of Price Changes: Consumers' Surplus and Producers' Surplus

9.1. Introduction

In the previous chapter we considered how market prices might be used to measure social costs or social values of goods used by, or produced by, a project. Throughout the discussion it was assumed that the existence of the project did not affect market prices. Prices were data from which social values were measured; they were not variables to be influenced by policy.

In this chapter we shall consider cases where the existence of a project affects market prices, either indirectly or directly. (A proposal to change a price charged by a public agency can be called a project in itself.)

9.2. Consumers' surplus

It is simplest to begin with the case of a price set by a public agency and to consider the social costs and benefits of changing this price.

Consider a plan to increase the price of gas charged to domestic consumers by a publicly owned gas undertaking. It is obvious that, to the extent that consumers continue to buy gas at the higher price, the financial gain to taxpayers (resulting from an increase in the gas authority's revenue) is exactly matched by a corresponding loss to consumers of gas. This is simply a transfer payment. But one would expect that an increase in the price of gas would lead to a reduction in the quantity demanded by consumers. Do consumers lose because they consume less gas, and if so, how much do they lose?

The analysis that follows is very important in the framework of this book as a whole. The concepts that are explained, and the general method of approach that is used, will be used repeatedly later in the book; they are at the heart of the methodology of cost-benefit analysis.

Consider any individual consumer. The amount of gas that he chooses to consume will depend on the price of gas, on the prices of various other goods (electricity, for example), and on his income. If we specify a particular set of prices for 'other goods' and a particular level of his income, we can draw a demand curve relating the amount of gas demanded by our consumer to the price of gas. This is shown in Figure 9.1 as the line D.

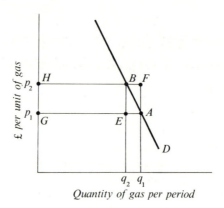

Fig. 9.1

Suppose that the initial price of gas is p_1; the initial quantity consumed is q_1. Now consider an increase in the price to p_2, which brings about a fall in the quantity consumed to q_2. (The consumer's income, and all prices, other than that of gas, meanwhile remain unchanged.) The question that concerns us is 'how much has the consumer lost?' or, more precisely, 'what increase in his money income would just compensate him for this price increase?'

To investigate this question we must take what at first sight seems a roundabout route. Consider four conceivable 'states of the world'. State A is the consumer's initial position, facing a price of p_1 and consuming the quantity q_1. State B is his final position; the price is p_2 and he consumes q_2. The other two states are hypothetical ones and represent ways in which our consumer might have behaved but chose not to. State E corresponds to the initial price, p_1, and the final quantity, q_2. Had the consumer wished to, he could have consumed q_2 rather than q_1 at the initial price, and spent more of his income on other goods. However, he chose not to do this, so we must infer that he prefers A to E. State F corresponds to the final price, p_2, and the initial quantity, q_1. Had the consumer wished to, he could have consumed q_1 at the final price, by spending less of his income on other goods. (This, of course, presupposes a certain minimum level of spending on other goods at the initial price.) Since, in fact, the consumer chooses state B rather than state F, we must infer that he prefers B to F.

Now consider the effect of moving the consumer from A to F—that is, of raising the price from p_1 to p_2 while preventing him from changing his rate of consumption from q_1. He will thereby increase his spending on gas by $(p_2 - p_1)q_1$ or by the area $GHFA$. Clearly, if he were to be paid this sum of money, he would be exactly compensated for the price increase, since he would then be able to—and would

—use his higher money income to buy the collection of 'other goods' that he bought initially. But we have deduced already that the consumer prefers his actual final position, B, to this hypothetical state F. So if the sum of money $(p_2 - p_1)q_1$ compensates him to a move from A to F it must *at least* compensate him for a move from A to B. This sum of money is, then, a *maximum estimate* of the consumer's actual loss.

Now consider starting from the initial position of state E rather than state A. That is, we begin from a position where the price of gas is p_1 but the consumer is compelled to consume the quantity q_2. If the price of gas is then raised to p_2, and the consumer continues to consume at the rate q_2 (since, at the new price, this is his preferred rate of consumption), his money loss from the price increase is his increased spending on gas—$(p_2 - p_1)q_2$ or the area $GHBE$. This sum of money would just compensate him for a move from state E to state B. But we have deduced already that the consumer prefers state A to state E; so this sum of money is a *minimum estimate* of the consumer's actual loss in moving from A to B.

(The foregoing argument requires, if it is to be strictly correct, a special assumption. We know that the consumer would choose to consume q_2 if the price were p_2, *and if his income were unchanged from its initial level*. We have assumed that, if he were to receive sufficient additional income to compensate him for the price increase, he would still consume q_2. Technically this is known as the assumption of *zero income effect*. Since in most practical applications the quantitative significance of income effects is likely to be extremely small, there is a strong case for using this assumption as a working rule in cost-benefit analysis. This is the position that will be maintained throughout this book. A more detailed treatment of this point is given in the appendix to this chapter.)

So far we have arrived at two estimates of our consumer's loss from the price increase—a maximum and a minumum estimate. It is extremely simple (in principle at least) to narrow the area of uncertainty about what the consumer's loss is. This is done by considering the price increase from p_1 to p_2 as a succession of smaller ones. Suppose that we break down the price increase into two components, an increase from p_1 to p_3 and an increase from p_3 to p_2 (see Figure 9.2). Using precisely the same arguments as before, the consumer's loss from the first price increase can be shown to be *at least* the area $GJCS$ and *no more than* the area $GJUA$. Similarly, his loss from the second price increase is *at least* the area $JHBR$ and *no more than* the area $JHTC$. The sum of the minimum estimates of the consumer's loss from the two stages of the price increase is greater than the area $GHBE$, which was our original minimum estimate of this loss.

Similarly the sum of the maximum estimates for the two stages is less than the original maximum estimate (area $GHFA$). Our maximum and minimum estimates are beginning to converge. It is easy to show that as the price increase from p_1 to p_2 is broken down into an increasingly large number of increasingly small stages, the maximum and minimum estimates will converge. Both will be measured by the area of the strip to the left of the demand curve that is shaded in Figure 9.2. This is *the* measure of the consumer's loss. Conversely, this area measures the consumer's gain from a fall in the price of gas from p_2 to p_1. Such gains and losses are known as changes in *consumers' surplus*.

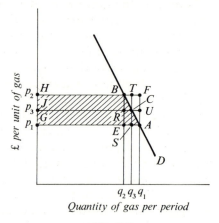

Fig. 9.2

Consumers' surplus is the value to consumers of the opportunity to buy units of a good at a particular price. Suppose, for example, that if the price of gas were 10p per unit, a particular individual would buy 100 units per month at a cost of £10. Suppose that he is then called on to pay an additional fixed charge before he is allowed to consume any gas at all. Suppose, too, that his preferences for gas are such that he would be willing to pay a fixed charge of up to £8 per month, in addition to the unit charge of 10p per unit, rather than go without gas altogether; but if the fixed charge were greater than £8 he would prefer to go without. This means that his consumer's surplus at the price of 10p per unit is £8 per month. If the price of gas were to be increased (say to 12p per unit) the maximum fixed charge he would be willing to pay would fall (say to £6·25 per month). The fall of £1·75 in the maximum fixed charge he would pay corresponds to his loss of consumer's surplus; to him, the price increase is the equivalent of a loss of £1·75 per month. That such losses can be measured by the areas of strips to the left of observable demand curves is a very important and valuable deduction.

Now consider the demand curve that relates the *total* quantity of gas demanded by a group of individuals to the price of gas. The group might, for example, consist of all those consumers served by a particular gas undertaking. Again, all other prices and the incomes of all consumers are taken to be constant. This *market demand curve* is obviously the horizontal sum of the demand curves of the individual consumers. (That is, the quantity demanded by all consumers at any price is the sum of individual demands.) Thus if we reinterpret Figure 9.2 so that the curve *D* is a market demand curve, it is easy to work out that the area of the shaded strip measures the sum of the losses borne by individual consumers as a result of the increase in the price of gas from p_1 to p_2. This is a loss of consumers' surplus.

The implication of this analysis is that a change in the price at which a good is sold affects the welfare of consumers. Thus if a public agency changes the price at which it sells its product, the *financial* effect of this change—which shows itself in the agency's financial accounts—is not the only effect that a cost-benefit analyst needs to consider.

To continue with the present example, consider a proposal to begin to supply gas to householders in a rural area that initially has no supply. Suppose that the market demand curve for gas by these householders is *D* in Figure 9.3. (It is assumed that gas is always sold at a uniform price per unit.) The average cost of supplying any quantity of gas per period of time is shown by the curve *AC*.

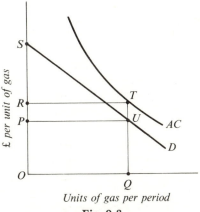

Fig. 9.3

Given the way the figure has been drawn, at all possible rates of consumption of gas, the average cost of supply is greater than the price at which that supply can be sold. Hence it is not possible to find any (single) price that would allow the gas undertaking to cover the costs of supplying gas. If financial criteria are used, this area will not be given a gas supply.

But consider the costs and benefits of supplying gas at some price, say *OP*. Not to be supplied with gas at all is, from the viewpoint of consumers, equivalent to being charged a price so high that no one would choose to buy any—that is, a price of *OS* or greater. The gain in consumers' surplus from supplying gas at the price *OP*—in effect, from lowering the price from *OS* to *OP*—is equal to the area *PSU*. This gain may be more than the financial loss borne by the gas undertaking (the area *PRTU*). In other words, consumers might be willing to pay more than enough to cover costs, if only payment could be divided amongst them appropriately.

But it is extremely difficult to convert 'willingness to pay' into actual payment, as this would mean charging different people different amounts for consuming the same quantities, and charging the same people different amounts at different times, and so on. It would require whoever administered the policy to know how much each consumer was willing to pay. There is a strong incentive for the consumer who is willing to pay a high price to conceal the fact, if there is any possibility of his being called on to pay this amount. Typically, in cases such as this, only a limited number of different pricing policies are practicable, and often a choice has to be made between supplying a good at a financial loss and not supplying it at all. In the present case, according to the criteria of cost-benefit analysis, it is better to supply gas at the price *OP* than not to supply at all if the area *PSU* is greater than the area *PRTU*.

9.3. Producers' surplus

Changes in consumers' surplus are measures of the effects on the welfare of individuals of changes in the prices of goods that they consume. Individuals may be affected in a very similar way if there are changes in the prices of 'factor services'—such as labour and the use of land and machinery—that they supply. Such changes are said to lead to changes in *producers' surplus*.

Producers' surplus to labour: variable hours of work

Consider the effects on the welfare of suppliers of labour of a change in the wage rate at which labour can be sold. We shall consider a labour market in which there is no involuntary unemployment and in which each worker is free to work as many hours per week as he chooses, earning a given hourly wage rate. With these assumptions, producers' surplus to labour is a concept which is completely symmetrical with consumers' surplus.

In Figure 9.4 the curve *S* is one worker's supply curve of labour, showing how much labour he would choose to supply at different wage rates. It is drawn on the assumption that all other prices and wages, and the worker's income from sources other than his supply of labour, are constant. An increase in the wage rate from w_1 to w_2 induces him to increase the quantity of labour he supplies from q_1 to q_2.

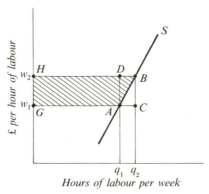

Fig. 9.4

Our problem is to deduce how much he gains from this increase in the wage rate or, to be more precise, what is the maximum sum of money that he would be willing to pay to ensure that this increase took place. As in our discussion of consumers' surplus, we shall assume that income effects are zero. (This implies that at the wage rate w_2 he would supply the quantity q_2 whether or not he was actually called on to pay to secure the wage increase.)

The argument follows extremely closely that used in the case of consumers' surplus. At the wage rate w_1 our worker chose to supply q_1; he had the option of supplying q_2 but chose not to take it. At the wage rate w_2 the reverse is true. He chooses to supply q_2 in preference to supplying q_1. His gain from the wage increase must be *at least* $(w_2 - w_1)q_1$ or the area *GHDA*, since he would have gained this if he had continued to supply q_1 after the wage increase. His gain can be *no more than* $(w_2 - w_1)q_2$ or the area *GHBC*, since this is what he would have gained if his initial position had been that of supplying q_2, and we know that in fact he chose not to be in this position. By considering the wage increase from w_1 to w_2 as a succession of small increases, it can be shown that both the maximum and minimum estimates of the worker's gain converge to equal the area of the shaded strip to the left of the supply curve in Figure 9.4. A market supply curve, showing how a group of workers respond to changes in the wage rate, is simply a horizontal sum of individuals' supply curves. Thus if the curve *S* in Figure 9.4 is reinterpreted as a market supply curve, the shaded area measures the total gain, or increase in producers' surplus, enjoyed by suppliers of labour as a whole. (In formal economic theory, the term *economic rent* is sometimes used to describe surpluses enjoyed by suppliers of factor services.)

Producers' surplus to labour: fixed hours of work

In many types of employment it is unrealistic to assume (as we did above) that each supplier of labour is free to supply as much as he wishes at any given wage rate. Instead, the number of hours per week that a worker must work is laid down by the employer. The worker is confronted with an 'all or nothing' (or 'take it or leave it') choice: *either* he supplies the predetermined amount of labour per week *or* he does not work at all. This makes the concept of an *individual's* supply curve of labour virtually irrelevant (for this curve shows how the individual would react if given the opportunity to make choices of a kind that, in fact, he is not permitted to make.) However, the *market* supply curve of labour remains as a useful and observable concept. This curve relates the *number* of people who wish to work (given the conditions laid down by employers) to the wage that is offered.

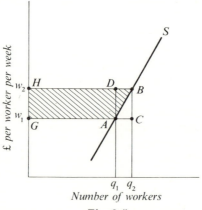

Fig. 9.5

The curve S in Figure 9.5 represents a market supply curve of labour. (Again, all other prices and wages are held constant and income effects are taken to be zero for all workers.) An increase in the wage from w_1 to w_2 induces an increase from q_1 to q_2 in the number of people offering their labour. As far as those q_1 workers who were willing to work at the lower wage are concerned, all that has happened is that they receive more money for doing the same amount of work. They receive in additional income the sum $(w_2 - w_1)q_1$, or the area $GHDA$. The remaining $(q_2 - q_1)$ workers give up leisure in return for money. Clearly they cannot be said to be worse off as a result of doing this, for they have chosen to work at the higher wage. In other words, their net gain from the wage increase is at least zero (it is not negative). But none of these workers can have gained more than $w_2 - w_1$, the increase in the wage, since we know that they chose not to work when the wage was w_1. Thus the total benefit to these $(q_2 - q_1)$ workers is *at least* zero and is *no greater than* $(w_2 - w_1)(q_2 - q_1)$ or the area $ADBC$. Adding together the benefits to the two groups of workers, the total benefit is *at least* $(w_2 - w_1)q_1$ or the area $GHDA$ and is *no greater than* $(w_2 - w_1)q_2$ or the area $GHBC$. This repeats exactly our conclusion for the case of a supply curve for labour in a market where workers were free to choose their hours of work. Again, by considering the wage increase from w_1 to w_2 as a succession of small changes it can be shown that the benefit—or increase in producers' surplus—enjoyed by workers is the area of the shaded strip to the left of the supply curve in Figure 9.5.

Producers' surplus to owners of capital

In a typical production process, labour is combined with 'capital' or 'machines' to produce output. Changes in prices and wages can affect the incomes of owners of capital.

Consider the production of a particular good, let us say, screws. This good is produced by combining labour and machines. Over some period of time we take the number of machines to be fixed (on the grounds that it takes time to build and install new ones). Firms own machines but hire labour. In other words, any revenue earned by a firm from the sale of screws which is not taken up by payments to labour is received by the firm's shareholders, who are the joint owners of the machines. This residual may be called a *producers' surplus to owners of capital*. (In economic theory it is sometimes called a *quasi-rent*.)

The size of this residual depends both on the price at which screws can be sold and on the price at which labour can be bought. An increase in the first or a decrease in the second will lead to an increase in producers' surplus to owners of capital.

Consider first an increase in the market price of screws which takes place while the price of labour is unchanged.

If the number of machines that a firm owns is fixed, increases in output can be achieved only by increasing the amount of labour used in combination with these machines. According to the well-known 'law of diminishing returns', beyond some point the more labour that is used, the less will be the additional output achieved by using additional units of labour. If the price of labour is constant, this implies that the marginal cost of output—screws—will increase as the quantity produced increases. In a competitive market, a profit-

maximizing firm will produce up to the point where the marginal
cost of producing screws equals the price at which they can be sold.
Thus the marginal cost curve relating the marginal cost of screws to
the quantity produced is the same as the supply curve relating the
quantity of screws that the firm wishes to produce to the price of
screws.

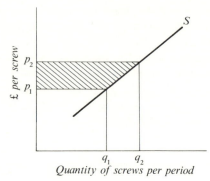

Fig. 9.6

Figure 9.6 shows a supply curve for screws, S. An increase in their
price from p_1 to p_2 will induce an increase in the quantity produced
from q_1 to q_2. The shaded area in the figure represents the increase
in the income of the firm's shareholders as a result of this increase in
price. (The proof that this is so is very similar in principle to the
proofs used in the analyses of consumers' surplus and of producers'
surplus to labour.) This is an increase in producers' surplus to owners
of capital.

Now consider the effect on owners of capital of a decrease in the
price of labour which takes place while the price of screws is unchanged.

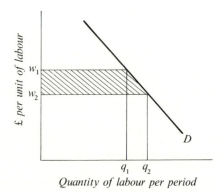

Fig. 9.7

In Figure 9.7 the line D represents the value of the marginal
product of labour—that is, the market value of the additional output

that results from employing an additional unit of labour. Since it has been assumed that the price of screws is constant, the principle of diminishing returns implies that the marginal product of labour will fall as the amount of labour used increases. A profit-maximizing firm in a competitive market will buy labour up to the point at which its marginal product is equal to the wage, and so the marginal product curve is also a demand curve for labour.

If the wage falls from w_1 to w_2, the firm will increase the amount of labour it uses from q_1 to q_2. The shaded area measures the gain to the firm's shareholders as a result of the fall in the wage. Again, this is an increase in producers' surplus to owners of capital.

9.4. An example: Evaluating a labour-training programme

In Section 5.6 it was shown how a labour-training course might be appraised from the viewpoint of a trainee. While, as we argued in that section, the results of such an appraisal would be of interest to a government that financed training courses, the government's main interest would be in the costs and benefits of courses to society as a whole. In this section we shall consider how a cost-benefit analysis might be made of a labour-training programme.

The obvious starting point is to ask in what ways a cost-benefit analysis should differ from the financial appraisal made in Section 5.6. Or, in other words, how does one man's being trained impose costs or confer benefits on other people?

To begin with, there is one straightforward difference between a financial appraisal and a cost-benefit analysis. The trainee does not pay any share of the financial costs of the training process; instead he receives a money payment from the government while he is being trained. Thus in a financial appraisal on behalf of the trainee, the costs of running training centres are ignored while the money payment counts as a benefit. In a cost-benefit analysis, this procedure is reversed. The costs of running training centres must be counted, since these are borne by taxpayers, who are part of the community. Conversely, the money payments received by trainees are transfer payments to them from taxpayers. These payments therefore count as a zero net benefit or cost to society as a whole. (To some extent these money payments are a direct compensation for costs borne by trainees as a consequence of their being trained—travelling expenses, for example. Indirectly, taxpayers bear the costs of transporting trainees to training centres just as they bear the costs of paying for instructors. In a financial appraisal, therefore, these elements of the money income of trainees would be ignored, since the benefit to the trainee of extra money is cancelled out by the costs of travelling. Conversely, these are the only elements of the money payments to trainees that would count in a cost-benefit analysis. They would count as a cost because the trainees' travel involves real costs to the community (in fuel, for example) which are borne, ultimately, by taxpayers.)

A second difference between a financial appraisal and a cost-benefit analysis is that one man's decision to supply or not to supply his labour in a particular trade may affect the welfares of others, and if it does, this must be taken account of in a cost-benefit analysis. If there is unemployment amongst the workers in a trade, one worker's leaving a job will allow another worker to become employed, while one worker's taking a job will prevent another from finding employment. (These effects are sometimes known respectively as 'replacement effects' and 'displacement effects'.) Alternatively, if wages are determined by supply and demand, a large change in the number of workers in a trade will lead to changes in the wage rate and thus to effects on the welfare of other workers and of employers.

Finally, income from wages is subject to income tax. If a worker is expected to increase his gross income as a result of being trained (and provided that this is not offset by a corresponding loss of income to someone else) the tax revenue of the government will be increased by the training of a worker. If we assume (as is conventional) that the government has a target level of tax revenue, the extra tax payments made by former trainees corresponds to a gain to other taxpayers (since the amount that the latter are called on to contribute thereby is reduced).

For concreteness, consider a training programme which is located in a particular region and which instructs unskilled workers in the skills of a particular 'training trade'. Suppose that in this region there is a persistent excess supply of unskilled labour (that is, there is involuntary unemployment) while in the training trade there is no unemployment and wages are determined by market forces.

Suppose for the present that the training programme is a small one and has no significant effects on wage rates. Given this assumption we can deduce immediately that the welfare of the members of a number of groups of people will be unaffected.

Consider first those people, other than the trainees themselves, who work in the training trade. Both before and after the training programme, these workers are free to sell their labour at the market wage. Since the programme does not change this wage, it does not affect the welfare of these workers.

A similar argument can be made concerning employers of both training-trade labour and unskilled labour. Both before and after the training programme, these employers are free to hire as much labour as they wish at the relevant wage rates. Since we have assumed that neither wage rate is affected by the training programme, employers are made neither better off nor worse off.

The one group of people involved in labour markets, apart from the trainees themselves, who are affected by the programme consists of those unskilled workers who do not receive training. This group gains from the introduction of the programme, even though the wage rate for unskilled workers remains unchanged. The crucial difference between the economic situation of this group and that of employers and training-trade workers is that in this case the prevailing wage does not represent a price at which an individual worker can trade freely. Since there is an excess supply of unskilled workers, a worker may be unemployed even though he would prefer to work at the prevailing wage rate. The training programme, by taking some workers out of the unskilled labour market, reduces the degree of competition for unskilled jobs and thus improves the employment prospects of unemployed workers.

For the purposes of analysis it is convenient to consider simultaneously the effects of the labour-training programme on trainees and on unskilled workers. The *net* effect of the programme may then be stated simply. During the training period the number of unemployed unskilled workers falls by the number of trainees, while the number of employed unskilled workers remains constant. It is, of course, irrelevant whether the trainees themselves were employed or unemployed before training, for if originally they were employed, their leaving their jobs will have created vacancies to be filled by other, previously unemployed, workers. After the training period, some proportion of the trainees (the 'successful trainees') will find jobs in the training trade. The remainder—and evidence suggests that this remainder may be a significant proportion—will either find unskilled jobs or will become unemployed. The net effect, then, is that the number of unemployed workers falls (below its level before the programme began) by the number of successful trainees. Taking our group of workers as a whole, the net effect of the programme on their money incomes is an increase equal to the total net-of-tax wages of the successful trainees *minus* the reduction in the net income of the group from transfer payments (social security benefits and allowances received while training). If we now expand the range of our accounting to include effects on taxpayers, transfer payments can be excluded. The net effect of the programme is a social benefit equal to the total gross-of-tax wages of the successful trainees.

In this calculation we have considered only the *money* incomes of workers. In effect we have assumed that workers are indifferent between the four states of 'working in an unskilled job', 'working in the training trade', 'receiving training' and 'being unemployed'—indifferent except insofar as these states have implications for their present or future money incomes. The assumption that workers are indifferent between the first three states is perhaps fairly plausible. That workers are indifferent between working and not working may seem less plausible, although this assumption is often made by practical cost-benefit analysts. If we are to avoid making this assumption we can deduce only that workers who become employed do not value the benefits of leisure more highly than the wage rate at which they choose to work. Hence a range of values could be calculated within which would lie the social cost imposed by the training programme through the reduction in the amount of leisure enjoyed by unemployed workers.

Of course, to complete the cost-benefit analysis we must substract from the social benefits so far calculated any elements of the costs of running the training programme that have not yet been counted. In considering all the effects of the programme on trainees and on unskilled workers we have already taken account of the opportunity costs to trainees of forgoing earning opportunities while training. And, in the 'netting out' of the benefits to trainees those that arise from transfer payments, we have taken account of the costs to taxpayers of paying allowances to trainees. (That is, we have taken account of this cost by cancelling it with an equal and opposite gain to trainees.) What remains are the operating costs of training centres—the wages of instructors, the rent of buildings, and so on. To sum up, then, given the assumption that workers are indifferent between working and not working, the net social benefit of the programme equals the present value of the gross future wages of successful trainees *minus* the operating costs of training centres.

Now let us introduce a new complication. Suppose that the programme is sufficiently large to induce a fall in the wage for training-trade labour. We shall continue to assume that the wage for unskilled labour is fixed and that unemployment persists in this market even after the training programme is completed. We need, therefore, to take account of the effects of the programme on two additional groups of people—employers and workers in the training-trade labour market.

Figure 9.8 illustrates the effects of the programme on this market. The curve D, relating the demand for labour to the wage, is unchanged by the programme. The supply curve of labour is shifted to the right by the number of successful trainees $(n' - n)$. The effect of this is to reduce the wage from w to w' and to increase the number of workers employed from n to n'. The original supply curve S may be interpeted as the supply curve of labour from workers other than trainees. It is assumed that, in the range of wage rates with which we are concerned, the supply of labour is completely unresponsive to changes in the wage rate. This assumption is symmetrical, in a sense, with the assumption that unskilled workers are indifferent between working and not working.

Using the arguments of Section 9.3, employers of labour gain an increase in

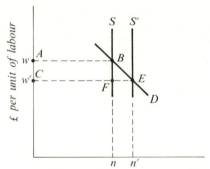

Quantity of labour per period

Fig. 9.8

producers' surplus equal to the area $ABEC$. If the change in the wage is a relatively small one it is convenient to approximate and to assume that supply curves and demand curves are straight lines in this range. Thus the gain to employers is

$$n(w - w') + \frac{1}{2}(n' - n)(w - w').$$ 9.1

(In speaking of 'employers' we are referring to the owners of capital, the supply of which is assumed to be fixed in quantity; and we are assuming that other prices in the economy are unaffected. It will be shown in Chapter 10 that if these assumptions do not hold, some of this gain may accrue ultimately to other people than owners of capital—to consumers, for example.) Training-trade workers, other than the trainees themselves, lose producers' surplus equal to the area $ABFC$, or

$$n(w - w').$$ 9.2

The net gain to employers and workers taken together is the area BEF, or approximately

$$\frac{1}{2}(n' - n)(w - w').$$ 9.3

In words, the net gain is approximately one-half of the product of the number of successful trainees and the fall in the training-trade wage. This should be added to the net benefits of the training programme that have already been calculated. In calculating the benefits of the programme to trainees we are, of course, concerned only with the training-trade wage *after* the programme is completed, for the original wage has no significance to trainees. The net benefits of the programme, excluding the costs of running training centres, were previously shown to equal the total wages of successful trainees. In symbols, this is

$$(n' - n)w'.$$ 9.4

The sum of the net benefits of the programme, excluding training centre costs, is thus

$$\frac{1}{2}(n' - n)(w + w').$$ 9.5

—that is, the product of the number of successful trainees and the average of the training-trade wages before and after the programme.

The above discussion of the effects of the programme on the training-trade market skated over one difficulty—that arising from the existence of income tax.

Implicitly it was assumed that there was no such tax. Fortunately, however, introducing income taxes into the problem does not require any major changes in the analysis. Suppose that, at the margin, incomes are subject to tax at the rate t. w and w' are gross-of-tax wages. Since employers are directly concerned only with the gross wage rate, our original calculation of their gain from the fall in the gross wage is correct. Employees, however, are concerned with the net wage. From their point of view, net wages fall as a result of the training programme by $(w - w')(1 - t)$. The loss of producers' surplus borne by training-trade workers is thus

$$n(w - w')(1 - t). \qquad 9.6$$

There also is a net loss to the government from the resulting reduction in its receipts of income tax. This loss is

$$n(w - w')t \qquad 9.7$$

and so the sum of the loss to workers and the loss to the government is

$$n(w - w'). \qquad 9.8$$

This is exactly equal to the loss originally calculated for workers alone, in the absence of income tax. The original conclusion about the total net benefit of the programme is therefore unaffected.

Before we leave this example, a point that will be made later in this book ought to be anticipated. In our financial appraisal of a labour-training programme (Section 5.6) the problem of uncertainty was central. Yet in this cost-benefit analysis, uncertainty has not even been mentioned. We have avoided the problem of uncertainty because we have been able to assume that the *aggregate* effects of the programme, measured, for example, by the increase in the number of workers in the training trade or by the decrease in the number of unemployed workers, could be predicted with certainty. This does not, of course, imply that individual workers do not face uncertainty. The individual trainee may not know whether, after training, he will find a job in the training trade or even whether he will find any job at all. In a sense, then, in our cost-benefit analysis we are cancelling one man's uncertainty against another's. How far this is legitimate will be discussed in Section 12.2 below. The argument of that section will be that the procedure of using aggregates is the equivalent of using the expected value criterion for evaluating uncertain costs and benefits to individuals.

Appendix: Income effects

In Section 9.2, which explained the concept of consumers' surplus, it was mentioned as an aside that the arguments being presented were based on the 'assumption of zero income effect', and that this assumption was to be adopted as a working rule throughout this book. In this appendix we shall consider in a little more detail just what this assumption implies and how its use can be justified. To do this we shall return to the problem of evaluating the effects of a price change on the welfare of a consumer, and analyse the problem in a rather more formal way. (Although the arguments in this appendix will all be made in relation to demand curves, the same arguments may be made in relation to supply curves.)

Consider a particular consumer, who has a money income of y_a, and who is able to buy and consume as much as he chooses of a particular good at the price p_1. He chooses to consume the quantity q_1. Our problem is to discover the sum of money that would exactly compensate him for an increase in the price to p_2.

In Figure 9.9 the line $D(y_a)$ represents the consumer's demand for the good *if his income is* y_a. If his income were to change, we should expect this demand

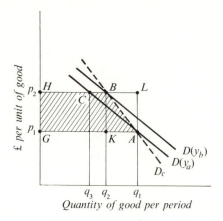

Fig. 9.9

curve to shift. The normal assumption is that, other things being equal, a consumer demands more of a good the higher is his income, and thus that an increase in income induces an outward (north-easterly) shift in the demand curve. This is the assumption that we shall use in this appendix. (The analysis of the opposite case of an 'inferior' good, the demand for which decreases as income increases, is very similar.) If the price of our good were to increase to p_2 while the consumer's income remained at y_a, the quantity consumed would decrease to q_3. However, the act of compensating the consumer for this price increase would produce an increase in his income and thus induce an outward shift of the demand curve. If he receives compensation, and if y_b is his income after compensation, he will consume the quantity q_2 (*not* q_3). The difference between q_2 and q_3 is the *income effect* of the price change.

Now consider the following four 'states of the world' (A, B, K and L). State A corresponds to the consumer's initial position, with an income of y_A, facing the price p_1 and choosing to consume the quantity q_1. State B corresponds to his final position *if he is exactly compensated for the price increase*. He has the income y_B, faces the price p_2, and chooses to consume the quantity q_2. The increase in his income $(y_B - y_A)$ is such as to ensure that he is indifferent between these two states. In other words, the sum $(y_B - y_A)$ is the sum that just compensates him for the price increase. Our problem is to find the value of this sum. States K and L are hypothetical ones. In state K the consumer faces the price p_1 but is compelled to buy the quantity q_2. His income, y_K, is such as to make him indifferent between this state and either of states A or B. In state L the consumer faces the price p_2 but is compelled to buy the quantity q_1. Again, his income, y_L, is such as to make him indifferent between this state and any of the others.

Compare states A and K. In state A the consumer faces the price p_1 and has the option to consume q_2. He chooses instead to consume q_1. In state K he faces the same price p_1 but is compelled to consume q_2. It is inconceivable that he would be indifferent between A and K—as we know he is—if he also had less income in state K than in state A. Thus we must deduce that

$$y_K \geqslant y_A. \qquad\qquad 9.9$$

By a completely symmetrical argument, we can compare states B and L and deduce that

$$y_L \geqslant y_B. \qquad\qquad 9.10$$

Now compare states A and L. In each state the consumer consumes q_1 (in the first state, by choice, in the second state, by compulsion). If he is indifferent between the two states—as he is—it can only be because what remains of his money income, after deducting his expenditure on buying q_1 of our good, is the same in each case. In other words, his income in state L must exceed his income in state A by an amount equal to the additional cost of q_1 at the higher rather than at the lower price. That is,

$$y_L - y_A = (p_2 - p_1)q_1. \qquad \qquad 9.11$$

By a completely symmetrical argument, a comparison of states B and K leads to the deduction that

$$y_B - y_K = (p_2 - p_1)q_2. \qquad \qquad 9.12$$

Using Equations 9.9 and 9.12,

$$y_B - y_A = (y_B - y_K) + (y_K - y_A) \geqslant (p_2 - p_1)q_2. \qquad 9.13$$

And using Equations 9.10 and 9.11,

$$y_B - y_A = (y_B - y_L) + (y_L - y_A) \leqslant (p_2 - p_1)q_1. \qquad 9.14$$

In terms of Figure 9.9, the sum that would just compensate the consumer for an increase in the price from p_1 to p_2—that is, the sum $(y_B - y_A)$—is *not less than* the area $GHBK$ and *not more than* the area $GHLA$. By considering the price increase as a succession of many small increases, it can be shown that the amount of compensation required by our consumer is equal to the area of the shaded strip to the left of the *compensated demand curve* D_C in Figure 9.9.

A compensated demand curve, like the more conventional 'constant money income' demand curve, shows how the quantity of a good consumed by an individual changes as its price changes, while other things are held equal. The difference concerns the 'other things'. A conventional demand curve (such as $D(y_a)$ or $D(y_b)$ in Figure 9.9) is constructed by holding constant the consumer's money income and allowing his level of welfare to change as the price changes. In contrast, a compensated demand curve is constructed by varying the consumer's money income in such a way as to hold his level of welfare constant at all points on the curve.

From the viewpoint of a practical cost-benefit analyst, there is one simple but crippling problem about the use of compensated demand curves: they are extremely difficult to trace. The reason is simple. Welfare, unlike money income, is not directly observable, and so statistical techniques—multiple regression analysis, for example—that allow an analyst to investigate the relationship between two variables while holding others constant cannot easily be used to estimate compensated demand curves. Thus although measures of the effects of price changes on consumers' welfare are properly defined in relation to compensated demand curves, the information that an analyst typically has is information about conventional constant-money-income demand curves.

A further complication is that the correct measure of a consumer's loss from a price increase from p_1 to p_2 is not necessarily the same as the correct measure of his gain from a reversal of the same price increase. Consider Figure 9.10, which repeats the relevant features of Figure 9.9. The initial price of some good is p_1. The consumer's income is y_a. The sum of money that would exactly compensate the consumer for an increase in the price from p_1 to p_2 is the area $GHBA$—the area of a strip to the left of the compensated demand curve D_c. This compensated curve is constructed by holding the consumer's welfare constant at its initial level (that is, at the level that he could attain with his initial income,

y_a, and with the initial price, p_1). But suppose that the price is increased but that the consumer is not compensated. He thus retains his initial income y_a and consumes the quantity q_3. Since he has not been compensated he is worse off than he was initially; he is on a new compensated demand curve, D'_c. The area GHCM to the left of *this* curve measures the sum of money that the consumer now would just be willing to pay in return for a reduction in the price from p_2 to p_1.

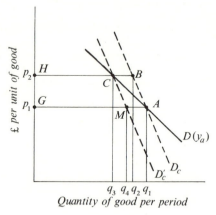

Fig. 9.10

The difference between the sum of money that would just compensate an individual for an adverse effect of a project and the sum that he would just be willing to pay to reverse this effect can be the source of a paradox (the *Scitovsky paradox*). To give a simple example, suppose that two consumers (Messrs. X and Y) have identical incomes (y_a in each case) and identical preferences; Figure 9.10 represents the demand for a particular good by either of the consumers. Suppose that a choice is to be made about which of the two is to be given the opportunity to buy the good at a concessionary price. The lucky one will be allowed to buy at the price p_1 while the other will face the higher price p_2. As far as the supplier of the good is concerned, it is a matter of complete indifference which of the two is given the concession, since in either case he will sell q_1 to one consumer and q_3 to the other. Let us compare the two alternatives in the light of the potential Pareto improvement criterion. Suppose, for the sake of argument, that the concession is given to Mr. X. Applying the potential Pareto improvement criterion, it is easy to show that it is better that X should keep the concession rather than that it be transferred to Y. For Y would be willing to pay, at most, only the area GHCM to get the concession while X would require the area GHBA as compensation for giving it up. But an exactly symmetrical argument shows that if Y has the concession, it is better that he should keep it. The potential Pareto improvement criterion has failed to produce an unambiguous ranking of two alternative 'states of the world'.

The approach used in this book is to cut through this knot of complications by adopting, as a working rule, the assumption that income effects are zero. It is assumed that the act of compensating a consumer for a change in the price of a good has no significant effect on the quantity of that good that he consumes. In terms of Figures 9.9 and 9.10 the quantities q_2 and q_3 are assumed to be equal. (Similarly, the quantities q_1 and q_4 are equal.) Consequently the two constant-money-income demand curves ($D(y_a)$ and $D(y_b)$) and the two compensated demand curves (D_c and D'_c) all coincide as a single curve (known as a *Marshallian demand curve* after the economist Alfred Marshall (1842–1924)). Given this assumption, the constant-money-income demand curve that can be traced from observations of consumers' behaviour is also a compensated demand curve, and so areas of strips to the left of it are correct measures of consumers' gains and losses from price changes. And the version of the Scitovsky paradox that was explained above cannot occur.

The justification for the assumption of zero income effects is that, in most cases dealt with in cost-benefit analysis, the actual magnitude of income effects is likely to be very small in relation to the margins of error present in all the information used by the analyst. The benefits of taking account of the possibility of non-zero income effects are usually far outweighed by the costs. (In a very few cases, income effects are particularly significant and the analyst must investigate their magnitude; but such cases are exceptional.)

Problems

For the purpose of these and subsequent problems, assume that all income effects are zero. Where necessary, estimate changes in producers' and consumers' surplus by assuming that supply curves and demand curves are straight lines in the relevant ranges.

1. As a result of investment incentives provided as part of the government's regional policy, a firm is opening a new factory in a coal-mining town. This factory will employ 1000 unskilled women workers, each working a 40-hour week. The government wishes to encourage developments of this kind because in mining areas the opportunities for women to find work are limited. There is not, however, any significant amount of involuntary unemployment amongst women, for they are weakly unionized and wages are determined by market forces.

It is predicted that, in this particular town, the opening of the new factory will have the following effects:

(*i*) The wage rate for unskilled women will rise, as a result of the increase in the demand for labour, from £25 per week to £27 per week.

(*ii*) Employers other than the owners of the new factory will react to the wage increase by reducing from 3200 to 3000 the number of women they employ. (Virtually all of these workers work 40-hour weeks.)

(*iii*) The net increase of 800 in the number of jobs will be filled by women induced to work by the increase in the wage.

The wage rates given are gross of tax. For an average worker, a gross wage of £25 per week is equivalent to £21 per week net of tax. A gross wage of £27 per week is equivalent of a net wage of £22·30.

What weekly benefit or loss is borne, as a result of the opening of the new factory, by (i) unskilled women workers, (ii) employers other than the owners of the new factory and (iii) the government in its role as collector of taxes?

2. A local authority owns and operates a bus company. It is considering reducing the fares charged on peak-hour services as a means of encouraging people to travel to work by bus rather than by car.

At present the average fare is 4p per passenger kilometre, and during peak hours 120 million passenger kilometres are travelled each year, giving an annual revenue of £4·8 m. It is proposed to reduce the average fare to 3p per passenger kilometre. This, it is predicted, would lead to an increase in the use of peak hour services to 135 m passenger kilometres per year. Peak-hour revenue would fall to £4·05 m per year.

The increase in the use of peak-hour services would lead to an increase of £0·235 m per year in the costs of operating the bus company. Adding to this the company's loss of revenue, the proposed reduction in the fare would involve a financial cost to the authority of £0·985 m per year.

A cost-benefit analysis would take account, not only of these financial costs, but also of the benefits accruing to bus users. If the number of passenger kilometres travelled during the year increases as much as is predicted, will the experiment result in a net social benefit or a net social loss?

(An important element of the benefit of reducing peak-hour fares cannot be considered at this stage. The benefit arises from the fact that an increase in the use of bus services at peak hours will be associated with a reduction in the use of private cars and hence with a reduction in the amount of traffic congestion on the roads. How such a benefit can be evaluated will be considered in Chapter 11.)

3. In the U.K., central and local government jointly run a scheme by which the owners of houses may claim grants to cover part of the costs of improving their houses in specific ways (such as by installing baths and indoor WCs). The following problem illustrates one approach to evaluating such a scheme.

Consider the stock of pre-1914 terrace houses in a city. For the sake of simplicity, let us assume that all such houses can be put into one of two classes—'improved' and 'unimproved' houses. As far as house buyers are concerned, all houses in each class are identical with each other. Any owner of an unimproved house can convert it into an improved house by spending a given sum of money —the 'cost of an improvement'. This cost is £2000.

Since all unimproved houses are identical, there will emerge a single market price for this type of house; and similarly for improved houses. The excess of the latter price over the former is the premium that must be paid to own an improved rather than an unimproved house. We may call this the 'market value of an improvement'. If the market value of an improvement exceeds the cost of improving a house, there will be financial gains to be made by improving houses. However, the greater is the number of improved houses relative to the number of unimproved ones, the less will the market value of an improvement tend to be. (This can be deduced from the plausible assumption that the demand curve for improvements is downward sloping.) Thus there will be a tendency for the market value of an improvement to move to a level no greater than the cost of an improvement. Let us suppose that, up to the present, no government grants have been given, the prices of improved and unimproved houses are respectively £10 000 and £8000, and virtually no more improvement is taking place. Of the 20 000 pre-1914 terrace houses in the city, only 2000 have been improved.

The government then considers introducing a system of grants, such that any house owner who subsequently improves his house will have some fixed proportion of the £2000 cost reimbursed. The government is prepared to consider giving grants of up to 50 per cent. Table (i) gives predictions of the number of houses in the city that would be improved, given each of a set of different rates of grant.

It is expected that the introduction of grants would not affect the prices of any type of house except improved houses. Thus the price of unimproved houses is expected to remain at £8000. (In a later problem this assumption will be relaxed—see Problem 2, Chapter 10.)

What would be the net social benefit or cost of introducing a scheme of 50 per cent improvement grants?

(*Note*: the key to tackling this problem is to consider 'an improvement' as a good with a demand curve and a market price. An improved house can be thought of as a combination of two goods sold jointly—an unimproved house and an improvement. The price of an improved house is thus the sum of the prices of its two components.)

Table (i)

Rate of grant (% of costs of improvement that is reimbursed)	Number of improved houses in city (including those improved before introduction of grant)	Total sum reimbursed by government (£'000)
0	2000	0
10	2200	40
20	2500	200
30	2900	540
40	3400	1120
50	4000	2000

Note: no part of the costs of improving the 2000 houses improved before the introduction of grants will be reimbursed.

Further reading

The analysis in this chapter derives from the classic work of Marshall. See Marshall (1920), Chapter 4 of Book 2, Chapter 6 of Book 3, and Appendix K.

For a fuller treatment of consumers' and producers' surpluses, and in particular of the problems discussed in the appendix to this chapter, see Mishan (1960), Nath (1969), Winch (1971), and Currie, Murphy and Schmitz (1971). The classic statement of the ambiguity of the concept of consumers' surplus when income effects are not zero is by Hicks (1944). A problem of a rather different nature, but which is also associated with non-zero income effects, has been pointed out by Boadway (1974).

For a thorough treatment of the theory of public enterprise pricing, see Millward (1971), Chapters 7 and 8.

For a general introduction to the economics of education and training, see Blaug (1970). For a cost-benefit study of investment in education, see Blaug (1967). A good sample of North American work on the cost-benefit analysis of labour-training programmes can be found in Somers and Wood (1969). For similar work in a British context, see Ziderman (1969 and 1975) and the general survey by Hughes (1970).

10. The Indirect Effects of Price Changes

10.1. Introduction

In a market economy a project that directly impinges only on one or a small number of markets can have indirect effects which are much more widespread. An initial impact can be dispersed through the economy as a whole by passing from market to market.

For example, if a branch-line railway service is closed there will be changes in the demands for other goods. There might be increases in the demand for motor cars, bicycles and local bus services, and decreases in the demand for houses near the former railway stations. Any of these changes might in turn induce changes in market prices. A decrease in the demand for houses near railway stations, for example, would cause a fall in their prices.

These indirect effects cause great problems for cost-benefit analysis. To begin with, it is often difficult to predict what indirect effects a project will have, or even to identify them after a project has been undertaken. If this problem is overcome, a second must be faced: how should indirect effects be evaluated?

In dealing with indirect effects, the cost-benefit analyst constantly faces the danger of *double counting*—that is, of counting a single element of benefit or cost more than once in his analysis. It is not at all easy to decide when an indirect effect is a benefit or cost which is independent of the direct effects of a project and when it is merely another manifestation of a direct benefit.

10.2. Indirect effects: quantity changes without price changes

Let us continue with the example of the closure of a rural railway service. Suppose that the closure of the railway leads to an increase in the demand for bus journeys but there is no change in their price.

This situation is represented in Figures 10.1a and 10.1b. In Figure 10.1a the line $D_r(p_b)$ is the demand for rail trips, given that the price of bus trips is p_b. The initial price of rail trips is p_r and the number of trips made is q_r. To close the rail service is equivalent to increasing the price of rail trips to p'_r (since at this price no one would choose to travel by train and so everyone would be indifferent to whether the service existed or not). The area ABC in Figure 10.1a is the loss of consumers' surplus as a result of this 'price increase'.

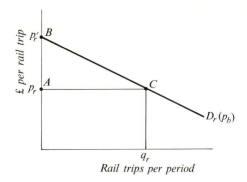

Fig. 10.1a

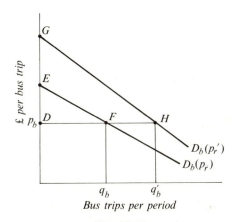

Fig. 10.1b

Figure 10.1b shows the demand for bus trips. $D_b(p_r)$ is the demand for bus trips if the price of rail trips is the original one of p_r. Closing the rail service—or increasing the price of rail trips to p'_r—increases the demand for bus trips to $D_b(p'_r)$ and the number of bus trips made increases from q_b to q'_b. The consumers' surplus from bus trips has increased as a result of the rail closure from area DEF to area DGH. It is tempting, but wrong, to interpret this increase as a social benefit attributable to the rail closure in the same sense that area ABC measures a social loss.

Consumers' surplus measures what consumers are willing to pay, in excess of what they actually are called on to pay, to consume a good. It thus measures the loss that would be borne by consumers if they lost the opportunity to buy that good. In our example, only one good, rail trips, has been withdrawn from the market, and the consumers' surplus that rail users have lost is the area ABC in Figure 10.1a. This is the only element of social loss to consumers. The areas

of consumers' surplus in Figure 10.1b certainly have economic meanings, but these meanings are irrelevant to our present problem. That
the consumers' surplus from bus trips has increased indicates that the
closure of the rail service increases consumers' willingness to pay for
bus trips. Or, in other words, the social loss that would be caused by
closing the bus service would be greater if there were no alternative
rail service than if there were one. This, of course, is to be expected.

Consider first those people who travelled by bus before the rail
closure. At that time, the amount they would have been willing to
pay to travel by bus was limited by their knowledge that a partial
substitute, travel by rail, was available. After the closure they are
more dependent on the bus service and thus it is more valuable to
them. This extra value forms a part of the increase in consumers'
surplus (the whole of which is the area $EGHF$). Clearly, however,
these people cannot be said to have been made any better off by the
rail closure.

Now consider those people who formerly travelled by train. When
they were able to use the train, they were not willing to pay even as
much as the price, p_b, to travel by bus. After the closure, they are
willing to pay at least this price for some of their trips (for $q'_b - q_b$
extra bus trips are made by displaced rail users). They may be willing
to pay more than this price for some of their trips, and if so, this is a
further element of the increase in the consumers' surplus from bus
trips. But, again, there is no reason to interpret this new dependence
on the bus service as a benefit of closing the railway. The amount of
consumers' surplus gained from bus trips merely measures how much
more worse off consumers would be if the bus service were closed
too.

To sum up, a change in the consumers' surplus associated with a
particular good measures a change in consumers' welfare only if the
change in surplus is caused by a change in the price of that good.
Changes in consumers' surplus caused in other ways (for example,
by changes in the price of *other* goods) have no similar interpretation.

So far we have measured the whole of the loss borne by rail users
(the area ABC in Figure 10.1a). We have said nothing of the gain or
loss to the other economic agents who are affected by the increase in
the demand for bus trips. These are the bus operators who 'produce'
bus trips. (If bus services are run by a private company, it is the
company's shareholders who are affected; if they are run by a public
agency, the producers are the taxpayers.)

These producers gain, as increased revenue, the product of the
increase in the number of trips $(q'_b - q_b)$ and the bus fare (p_b).
They also bear any additional costs involved in producing the
increased number of trips.

If, as we assumed as a working rule at the beginning of Chapter 8, price is a measure of marginal cost, then the increase in revenue and the increase in cost will just cancel each other out. The fact that the price of bus trips did not change as the number of trips changed indicates that in this range marginal cost is constant and equal to p_b. Thus there is no element of net social cost or benefit arising out of the indirect effects of the rail closure on the market for bus trips. There was no need to have investigated these indirect effects at all.

Unfortunately, however, prices are not always equal to marginal social costs, as was shown in Chapter 8. In practice, it is unlikely that the price of rural bus trips would equal their marginal social cost. Rural transport services typically are provided not by competitive firms but by local monopolies which are operated or regulated by government agencies.

Suppose, for example, that bus fares are set by a government agency and will not be changed as a result of the railway closure. Suppose, too, that the additional bus passengers can be carried without any increase in operating costs at all—that is, the marginal social cost of bus trips is zero in the relevant range. In this case bus operators make a net gain equal to the increase in their revenue and this must be counted as an element of social benefit to be set against the losses borne by rail users.

10.3.   Indirect effects: Induced price changes (pecuniary external effects)

Things become more complex if the price change whose effects are being evaluated itself causes, as an indirect effect, a change in some other price. Such indirect effects arise out of relationships of complementarity or substitutability between the demand or supply of one good and the demand or supply of another. (Two goods are *complementary in demand* if a reduction in the price of one good causes an increase in the demand for the other—consider butter and bread. Two goods are *substitutes in demand* if a reduction in the price of one causes a decrease in the demand for the other—consider margarine and butter.)

At the beginning of this chapter, an example of an indirect effect of this kind was mentioned—the closure of a rail service causing a reduction in the prices of houses near railway stations. Here, essentially, there are two goods, rail trips and houses, which are complementary in demand. In this section we shall consider this case in more detail and investigate how such a combination of direct and indirect effects should be evaluated.

For convenience, we shall consider an example where the initial change is not the complete withdrawal of a good from the market but simply a price increase. Instead of considering the closure of a railway service we shall consider an increase in the price of rail trips (following which, some trips, at least, continue to be made). If rail trips and houses are complementary in demand, this price increase will induce a fall in the price of houses (provided only that the supply of houses is not infinitely price-elastic).

Our first task is to investigate exactly why this occurs. In the interests of clarity, we shall make a number of simplifications. We shall suppose that there is only one type of rail trip and one type of house. Houses are let by 'landlords' to 'tenants' at market-determined rents—we shall speak of a market for, and a price of, 'tenancies'. (Although it may be helpful to think of landlords and tenants as two separate and non-overlapping sets of people, there is no need to rule out the possibility that a particular individual might simultaneously play both roles. An owner-occupier, for example, can be regarded as someone who is both landlord and tenant of the same property.)

The markets for rail trips and for tenancies are represented by Figures 10.2a and 10.2b. Suppose that initially the price of rail trips is, as an act of policy, set at p_r. Given this price of rail trips, the demand for tenancies is $D_t(p_r)$. The supply of tenancies, as a function of their price, is S_t; thus the market price of tenancies (or market rent) is p_t. Given that tenancies can be bought at this price, the demand for rail trips is $D_r(p_t)$. Since the price of rail trips is p_r, the quantity demand is q_r.

Now consider the effects of raising the price of rail trips to p'_r. Since tenancies and trips are complements, the demand for tenancies falls to $D_t(p'_r)$. This in turn implies a reduction in the price of tenancies to p'_t. The combined effect is to reduce the number of tenancies demanded (and supplied) to q'_t. The fall in the price of tenancies implies an increase in the demand for trips, from $D_r(p_t)$ to $D_r(p'_t)$; the number of trips demanded after the two price changes is q'_r.

It should be noted that, in normal circumstances, only one point on each of the demand curves for trips, $D_r(p_t)$ and $D_r(p'_t)$, can be observed. If, for example, the price of trips is p_r, we may observe that the price of tenancies is p_t and that the number of trips demanded is q_r. This identifies one point on $D_r(p_t)$. But the effect of changing the price of trips is to change the price of tenancies and thus the combination of price and quantity that results from the price change will lie on a different demand curve. This means that, although demand curves like $D_r(p_t)$ are useful theoretical constructs, it is extremely difficult to trace their positions. The relationship between price and quantity that can be traced directly is the *observed demand curve* $D_r{}^*$, which joins the combinations of prices and

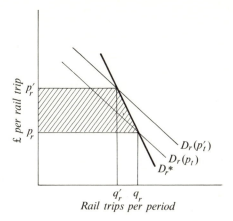

Fig. 10.2a

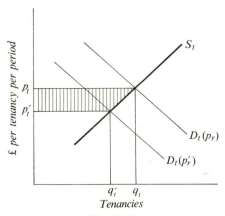

Fig. 10.2b

quantities that are actually observed in the market. Like other types of demand curves, this curve shows how the quantity demanded of one good (trips) changes as the price of that good changes, *other things being equal*. But in this case, the 'other things' that are being held equal are all those factors (other than the price of rail trips) that influence the prices of other goods in the economy. (In contrast, a demand curve like $D_r(p_t)$ is plotted by holding constant all other prices in the economy.) It will emerge that knowledge of the position of the observed demand curve is sufficient to allow an analyst to evaluate the net social costs or benefits of a price change.

To show why this is so, all that is required is a slight extension of the analysis used in Sections 9.2 and 9.3 to demonstrate the meaning and significance of consumers' and producers' surpluses. (As before, it is assumed that all income effects are zero—see the appendix to Chapter 9).

Consider the complex of price changes examined above and its effects on a single consumer. Suppose that when the prices of rail trips and of tenancies are p_r and p_t, this consumer demands the quantities Q_r and Q_t. When the price of trips has risen to p'_r and the price of tenancies has fallen to p'_t, he demands the quantities Q'_r and Q'_t. How much has he gained or lost as a result of the two price changes?

Let us consider four conceivable states. State A is that the prices are p_r and p_t and that our individual consumes Q_r and Q_t. State B has prices p'_r and p'_t and quantities consumed Q'_r and Q'_t. State C has prices p_r and p_t and quantities consumed Q'_r and Q'_t. State D has prices p'_r and p'_t and quantities consumed Q_r and Q_t. States A and B correspond to the consumer's actual positions before and after the price changes. State C is one that the consumer could have attained before the price changes—had he chosen to, he could have bought and consumed Q'_r and Q'_t at the old prices. State D is one that he could have attained after the price changes—he could have bought and consumed Q_r and Q_t at the new prices. Since state A was chosen in preference to state C, we can deduce that in moving from state A to state B, as the consumer actually does, he loses at least as much as he would have done in moving from C to B. Similarly, since B was chosen in preference to D, in moving from A to B the consumer loses no more than he would have done in moving from A to D.

It is quite easy to evaluate the net loss that our consumer would have incurred in moving from C to B, since in both states the same quantities $(Q'_r$ and $Q'_t)$ of the two goods are consumed. His loss is the net increase, resulting from the price changes, in the total cost of buying these quantities; it equals

$$Q'_r(p'_r - p_r) - Q'_t(p_t - p'_t). \qquad \textbf{10.1}$$

This provides a *lower estimate* of the loss the consumer actually incurs in moving from A to B; the actual loss is at least as great as this estimate. Similarly, the net loss that the consumer would have incurred in moving from A to D is

$$Q_r(p'_r - p_r) - Q_t(p_t - p'_t). \qquad \textbf{10.2}$$

This is the net increase in the total cost of buying the quantities Q_r and Q_t. This provides an *upper estimate* of the consumer's actual loss from moving from A to B; the actual loss is no greater than this estimate.

To produce upper and lower estimates of the total losses borne by all consumers taken together, all that is required is to add together the estimates for individuals. Thus if (as in Figures 10.2a and 10.2b) the total quantities of the two goods demanded by all consumers are

q_r and q_t before the price changes and q'_r and q'_t after them, it immediately follows that the total loss to consumers as a whole is no less than

$$q'_r(p'_r - p_r) - q'_t(p_t - p'_t).$$ 10.3

and no greater than

$$q_r(p'_r - p_r) - q_t(p_t - p'_t).$$ 10.4

To repeat yet again a very familiar argument, a large price change can be considered as a succession of small ones, and the smaller that these 'small' changes are made, the less significant becomes the difference between upper and lower estimates of consumers' gains or losses. It is easy to show that, in our example, the net loss to consumers as a whole is equal to the shaded area in Figure 10.2a *minus* the shaded area in Figure 10.2b. Both these areas are strips to the left of curves that join observed combinations of price and quantity consumed. In the market for rail trips the relevant curve is the observed demand curve. We are considering a price increase and thus the area of the shaded strip measures an element of net loss to consumers. In the market for tenancies the relevant curve is the supply curve. Here there is a price fall and so the shaded area measures an element of net gain to consumers.

It may be helpful here to consolidate ideas with a simple numerical example. Suppose that it is observed that when the price of rail trips is £1 per trip and when the price of tenancies is £10 per week, 10 000 rail trips per week are made and 1000 tenancies are held. An increase in the price of trips to £1·20 leads to a fall in the number of rail trips made to 9000 per week, a fall in the number of tenancies held to 950, and a fall in the price of tenancies to £9·50 per week. If, as an approximation, we take the observed demand curve for trips and the supply curve of tenancies to be straight lines in the relevant ranges, we can calculate that the net loss to consumers is approximately

$$\frac{(1\cdot20 - 1\cdot00)(10\ 000 + 9000)}{2} - \frac{(10\cdot00 - 9\cdot50)(1000 + 980)}{2} = 1900 - 495$$

$$= £1405 \, per \, week.$$

So far we have not considered the effects of the price changes on landlords, who will suffer losses as a result of the fall in the price of tenancies. Evaluating this loss is extremely simple, for we do not have to consider any relationships of complementarity or substitutability. The *relationship* between the price of tenancies and the quantity supplied is unaffected by the change in the price of rail trips. As far as landlords are concerned, all that has happened is that the price of tenancies has fallen. The shaded area in Figure 10.2b (the area of a strip to the left of the supply curve) measures the loss of producers' surplus.

The interesting point here is that this area has been used already in the evaluation of the net loss to consumers that results from the price changes. For consumers, however, this area was an element of gain (to be set against a larger element of loss, measured by the shaded area in Figure 10.2a). The shaded area in Figure 10.2b, then, measures a gain on the part of consumers and an exactly equal and opposite loss on the part of landlords. If we are concerned solely with evaluating the aggregate net loss to consumers and landlords taken together, these gains and losses simply cancel out. There is no need to know how much the price of tenancies or the quantity of them demanded changes; the shaded area in Figure 10.2a (the area of a strip to the left of the observed demand curve for trips) measures the *net* loss borne by consumers and landlords. (In the numerical example, the net weekly loss is £1900; consumers lose £1405 per week and landlords lose £495 per week.)

In this example, the initial price change (a change in the price of trips) has had an indirect effect on the welfare of landlords, and this effect has been transmitted through the interactions of competitive markets. Such an indirect effect is often called a *pecuniary external effect*. The effect is *external* to the market in which the initial price change takes place, since it affects individuals (landlords in this example) who need not be parties to transactions in that market. The word 'pecuniary' is used to imply that the effect concerns the *distribution* between individuals of changes in the community's real income, but does not concern the magnitude of that change. The aggregate change in the welfare of consumers and landlords is measured by reference to the observed demand curve in the market that was directly affected by the initial price change. The additional information that can be extracted from a knowledge of the magnitudes of induced changes in prices and in quantities traded in other markets concerns how this aggregate welfare change is divided between different groups of individuals.

The particular problem considered above is an example of a problem that is very common in cost-benefit analysis, and the solution given to the particular problem is of very general application. To illustrate this point we shall consider very briefly another problem, which seems at first sight to be very different from the one concerning rail trips and tenancies.

Consider an industry in which capital-owning producers hire specialized labour (along with other inputs) and manufacture some product which they then sell to consumers. There is a relationship between the producers' demand for labour and their supply of the product that is analogous to that between the demand for rail trips and the demand for tenancies. In our present example, an increase in the price of labour—the wage rate—will imply a contraction in the supply of the product—that is, an upward shift in the supply curve. (This reflects the fact that the marginal cost of producing any quantity of the product will be greater, the greater the wage rate.) Conversely, an increase in the price at which the product can be sold will imply an increase in the demand for labour.

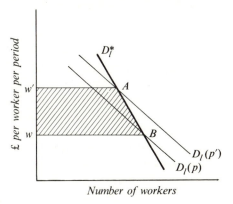

Fig. 10.3a

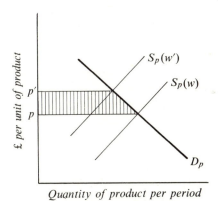

Fig. 10.3b

Now consider the effects of a change in the wage rate—let us say, an increase decided on by a monopoly labour union. Producers simply take as given the wage rate set by the union and are free to hire as much labour as they wish at this rate. The effects of an increase in the wage from w to w' are illustrated in Figures 10.3a and 10.3b. The supply of the product contracts from $S_p(w)$ to $S_p(w')$. D_p being the demand for the product, the price of the product increases from p to p'. This implies that the demand for labour increases from $D_l(p)$ to $D_l(p')$. The two observed combinations of wage rate and number of workers demanded are the points A and B which lie on the observed demand curve for labour D_l^*.

Using arguments analogous to those used in the analysis of the 'rail trips and tenancies' problem, it can be shown that the net loss imposed on producers equals the shaded area in Figure 10.3a *minus* the shaded area in Figure 10.3b. (The first area is associated with a price increase that it unfavourable to producers, since producers are buyers in the labour market; the second area is associated with a price increase that is in their favour.) The shaded area in Figure 10.3b also measures an exactly equal and opposite loss of consumers' surplus by the consumers of the product. The net loss to producers and consumers taken together is the shaded area in Figure 10.3a, the area of a strip to the left of the observed demand curve in the market directly affected by the initial price change (the labour market).

In general, whenever an initial price change induces other price changes in competitive markets, an analysis can be made that is broadly similar to our treatment of the two examples above. The net change in the welfare of all individuals affected directly by the initial price change, or affected by the induced price changes, is measured by the area of a strip to the left of the observed demand curve for the good whose price initially changed. (In cases where the initial price change directly affects sellers rather than buyers, an observed supply curve rather than an observed demand curve is used to evaluate welfare changes.)

If a cost-benefit analyst is using the potential Pareto improvement criterion he needs to evaluate only the *net* effect of a project on the community as a whole. One person's gain of £1 exactly offsets another person's loss of £1. Thus there is no need for him to examine the magnitude of pecuniary external effects; he needs information only about changes in prices and in quantities traded in markets *directly* affected by a project. This, then, is one important way in which the criterion is a convenient one.

In subsequent chapters we shall be discussing alternative approaches to cost-benefit analysis, some of which imply that gains and losses received by or borne by different individuals ought to be weighted differently. If such weighting systems are to be used, the analyst must investigate all the significant pecuniary external effects that projects induce.

Problems

1. Two theatres in a city are supported by subsidies from the government. Each theatre specializes in a particular type of production. Theatre-goers regard tickets for performances at the two theatres as (imperfect) substitutes for each other; thus if one theatre were to close while the other remained open, the demand for the tickets of the surviving theatre would increase. This is shown

diagramatically in Figures (i) and (ii). D_X is the demand for tickets for theatre X, given that theatre Y is open and is charging the price p_Y. D'_X is the demand for tickets for theatre X if theatre Y is closed. Similarly D_Y is the demand for tickets for theatre Y if theatre X charges p_X; D'_Y is the demand for tickets for theatre Y is theatre X is closed.

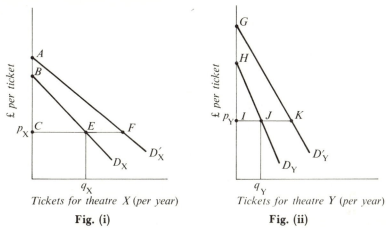

Tickets for theatre X (per year)   Tickets for theatre Y (per year)

Fig. (i)   **Fig. (ii)**

Currently the prices charged are p_X and p_Y and the number of tickets sold per year are q_X and q_Y. Suppose that the government were to withdraw its subsidies and that, as a result, both theatres closed. Which area or areas in the diagram measure(s) the loss of consumers' surplus that would be borne by theatre-goers?

2. Reconsider Problem 3 of Chapter 9 (p. 132) which concerned the evaluation of a scheme of giving grants for the improvement of houses.

It was argued that, whatever the rate of grant offered, the number of improved houses would tend to the number at which the market value of an improvement (the excess of the price of an improved house over the price of an unimproved one) was just equal to the cost to a house owner of improving his house (that is, the cost net of the government grant). In the original presentation of the problem it was assumed that the introduction of grants would affect only the price of improved houses; the price of unimproved houses would remain constant.

Such an assumption probably would be unrealistic. One might expect the introduction of grants not only to lead to a fall in the price of improved houses but also to lead to an increase in the price of unimproved houses. (The difference between the prices would, of course, still equal the cost of an improvement.) Suppose that it is predicted that the effects of introducing grants would be those shown in Table (i). What would be the net social benefit or cost of introducing a scheme of 50 per cent improvement grants?

(*Note*: the original problem was analysed by considering there to be two goods, 'unimproved houses' and 'improvements', each of which had a market price. An improved house was treated as the combination of one unit of each of these two goods, bought and sold jointly. The price of an improved house was the sum of the prices of the two goods. Given our definition of the good 'unimproved houses', the stock of this good that is supplied is the total number of pre-1914 terraced houses in the city; this is so, whatever the price of an unimproved house. In the present problem, the government's policy implies a change in the price of improvements. This, in turn, induces a change in the price of unimproved houses.)

Table (i)

Rate of grant (% of costs of improvement that is reimbursed)	Number of improved houses in city	Market price of unimproved house (£)	Market price of improved house (£)
0	2000	8000	10 000
10	2200	8050	9850
20	2500	8100	9700
30	2900	8150	9550
40	3400	8200	9400
50	4000	8250	9250

3. In Section 9.3 it was argued that areas of strips to the left of market supply curves for goods measured changes in producers' surplus to firms or, strictly, to owners of capital. Suppose, for example, that some product can be sold at a world-market price of £20 per unit. At this price, firms in some region produce at the rate of 20 000 units per week. The price then rises to £25 per unit and production increases to 24 000 units per week. According to the argument of Section 9.3, the shaded area in Figure (iii), to the left of a supply curve joining observed combinations of price and output, measures the resulting increase in producers' surplus to owners of capital. (This increase is of approximately £110 000 per week.) To reach this conclusion, however, it is necessary to assume that the price of other inputs used in the process of production remain constant.

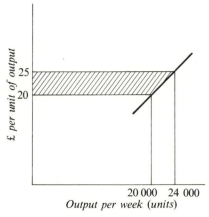

Fig. (iii)

Suppose, however, that investigation shows that the increase in the price of output has induced an increase in the price of one particular input, skilled labour. (The prices of all other inputs have remained constant.) Before the price of output increased, 200 000 man hours of labour were employed per week by firms in the region. (Not all of these firms were engaged in producing the particular output whose price increased.) The wage rate was £1·50 per man hour. The increase in the price of output led to an increase in the demand for skilled labour by producers of this output. As a result, the wage rate increased to £1·70 per man hour and the total quantity of labour employed in the region increased to 225 000 man hours per week.

How much is gained by (*i*) owners of capital and (*ii*) suppliers of labour as a result of the changes in the price of output and in the wage rate? What is the significance of the shaded area in Figure (iii)?

(Assume that the wage rate is determined in a competitive market and that there is no income tax.)

Further reading

The analysis of induced price changes which was presented in Section 10.3 derives from Hicks (1946) (quoted by Little (1957), p. 177). The main conclusions of this analysis have since been restated a number of times in technical literature, and have been derived in various ways. See Harberger (1971) and Burns (1973). There is a close relationship between the conclusion that changes in consumers' welfare can be measured by the areas of strips to the left of observed demand curves and the 'theorem of the symmetry of substitution effects' or 'reciprocity theorem' of demand theory; see Hicks (1956), Chapters 12 and 13.

It was shown in Section 10.3 that changes in producers' surplus when price changes were induced could be evaluated in a way very similar to that used for evaluating changes in consumers' surplus. This conclusion is in opposition to Mishan's assertion that 'the area above the long-period industry supply curve . . . carries no welfare significance'. See Mishan (1968) and Mishan (1971*a*), Chapter 9, and compare with our treatment of Problem 3 in this chapter of this book.

An empirical study of the relationship between the price of houses and the cost of travel by public transport is reported by Wabe (1971).

11. Individuals' Valuations of Unmarketed Goods

11.1. The problem of unmarketed goods

Market prices are useful to the cost-benefit analyst because they convey information. In a competitive market the price of a good carries information both about the marginal cost of producing the good and about its marginal value to consumers: price equals marginal cost and price equals marginal valuation. Because prices in competitive markets have these two properties it is often possible to use market prices in cost-benefit analysis just as they are used in financial appraisal. In previous chapters it has been shown that, for the purposes of cost-benefit analysis, market prices sometimes need to be adjusted to take account of the influences of price and quantity constraints and of taxes. Where a project causes market prices to change, further problems were shown to arise, requiring the use of measures of producers' and consumers' surplus.

But so far we have always dealt with goods which had clearly observable market prices. However accurately or inaccurately these prices measured marginal costs and marginal valuations, there was always *some* market price which conveyed *some* information that could be adapted for use in a cost-benefit analysis. But one of the most pervasive of the problems faced by cost-benefit analysts is that many goods are not directly bought and sold and so do not have obvious market prices.

A decision-maker in a public agency, choosing the location for a hospital or a school, would want to take account of the relative convenience of alternative locations for patients and visitors or schoolchildren and parents. Amongst other things, he would want to take account of the amount of time that people would spend travelling to and from the alternative sites. But although it seems clear that people value savings in travelling time, there is no obvious market in which travelling time is bought and sold.

Similarly, public roads provide services which have value to road users. A cost-benefit analysis of a proposal to build a new road would need information about how the road would be valued by its users. But it is rare for the use of individual roads to be priced.

Again, quietness is a good which people value. Undertaking a particular project may make more or less quietness available. Building a new airport will make less quietness available in the area around the airport, but might make more available around other airports if flights were diverted. But there is no obvious market in quietness.

The cost-benefit analyst, using the potential Pareto improvement criterion, needs to know how much people would be willing to pay for additional units of such goods as time saving, road use and quietness—just as he needs to know how much they would be willing to pay for additional units of electricity or for additional bus journeys. Although the existence of markets makes the job of discovering how much people are willing to pay for goods a much easier one, the idea of 'willingness to pay' does not require there to be markets in which people actually pay for goods. Where there is no market, the analyst must try to deduce, from whatever evidence he can find, how people would behave if there were one. This chapter will consider some of the ways in which such deductions can be made.

11.2. Opportunity cost prices

So far our conception of prices has been a very literal one. It has been that of sums of money paid, say over a shop counter, by the buyer of a good to its seller. Many goods, it is now clear, do not have prices in this sense.

Insofar as the cost-benefit analyst is interested in inferring the marginal value of a good to a consumer, prices are useful because they show how much money the consumer must give up to get more of the good. It does not matter where the money goes to, once the consumer pays it. All that matters is that the consumer must give up money. A good that does not have a price in the literal or over-the-counter sense may nevertheless have a price in the sense that consumers must give up something of value in order to get more of the good. A measurement of the cost that a consumer must bear to be able to consume more of a good may be called an *opportunity cost price*.

Consider, for example, the allocation of health care when, as under the British National Health Service, very low or even zero money prices are charged for using health care services. The fact that a patient does not have to pay his G.P. for a consultation does not mean that consultations are costless to the patient. Visiting a surgery requires the patient to sacrifice time—travelling to and from the surgery, waiting to see the G.P., and the time spent in the consultation itself. For most people, time is a scarce good; giving up time means giving up something that is valued. If someone prefers spending an evening watching television to spending it travelling to and from his G.P.'s surgery, then consulting his G.P. is costly to him. (If he travels to the surgery by car or by public transport, or if he has to take time off work, the consultation may also involve outlays of money.)

Or consider the allocation of road space. Road space is a good, and it is one which is often scarce relative to the demand for it. Yet typically there is no charge for using public roads. (A driver may have to buy a licence before he can go on *any* roads; but road space is scarce relative to the demands of licensed drivers.) Although there is no explicit price for using road space, using it is nonetheless costly. Ignoring the use of roads as parking space, it is not very useful to think of road space as being a final consumption good. The good that car users desire is the trip, the act of moving from one place to another. Trips are far from costless, requiring outlays both of money —for fuel, oil, and so on—and of time. These costs fulfil—to some extent at least—the function of a price in rationing scarce road space. Where the demand for road space is greatest in relation to the supply of it, trips are slowest and hence most costly.

Knowledge of what an individual has to forgo to consume more of a good—that is, knowledge of its opportunity cost price—allows an analyst to make inferences about the value to the individual of additional consumption. However, there is a problem to be faced. Opportunity cost prices, as we have seen, are not necessarily expressed in money units (while, in a modern economy, over-the-counter prices almost invariably are). Since the cost-benefit analyst is concerned with valuing costs and benefits in money units, he must be able to convert opportunity cost prices into these units. Because 'time spent travelling' so frequently occurs as an element in the opportunity cost prices of goods, we shall consider how one might convert units of travelling time into equivalent units of money. The general principles that we shall use can be applied to the evaluation of many other kinds of opportunity cost price.

Since the cost-benefit analyst uses information about opportunity cost prices to make inferences about how individuals value changes in their consumption of goods, he must convert units of travelling time into units of money according to the individuals' own valuations. His objective, then, must be to discover the money outlays that, in the consumers' own scales of preference, are the equivalents of particular 'expenditures' of travelling time. The most obvious line of approach is to seek out situations in which individuals have to choose between spending money and spending time and then to study the choices that they make. Such situations often occur when people can make a particular journey between two places by more than one mode of transport.

Suppose, for simplicity, that for some trips there are two alternative modes of transport. We shall assume that travellers' choices about how to travel are influenced only by the relative money costs and relative travelling times of the two modes of transport, and that, other things being equal, travellers prefer lower money costs and faster travel. If one mode is both faster and cheaper than the other, the choice problem faced by travellers is not particularly interesting: the faster and cheaper mode will necessarily be chosen. But if one mode is the cheaper while the other is the faster, there is a real problem of choice. Someone who has decided to make a trip must then choose whether to pay the extra money cost of the faster mode in order to have the saving in travelling time that this mode offers. In other words, time saving is a good which can be bought at a money cost or opportunity cost price. The choice that a traveller makes reveals something of his willingness to pay for time saving. If, for example, one mode of transport is 30 minutes faster than the other but costs 20p more, anyone who uses it must value time saving as at least 40p per hour. Conversely, anyone who uses the slower mode must value time saving at no more than 40p per hour.

By collecting and analysing a large number of such observations it is possible to deduce the average value of time saving to people with particular characteristics making particular types of trip. The statistical techniques usually used to make these deductions are beyond the scope of this book. But the first attempt (made by Beesley)[1] to derive a value of time saving from information of this kind used a method which is quite easy to understand. It illustrates well the principles underlying more involved methods.

Beesley began by selecting a group of people (civil servants in a particular income bracket) and a type of trip (journeys to work at a particular office in London). He then tried to find the value of time saving that best explained the choices that these people made between alternative modes of transport for their trips.

Each person was asked to say how he travelled to work and what was the best alternative way of making the trip. The difference in travelling time and the difference in money cost between the preferred and alternative modes of transport were then calculated. Each reply can be plotted as a point on a graph such as that shown in Figure 11.1. This shows in two dimensions the net saving of time and the net saving of money by using the preferred rather than the alternative mode.

Now suppose that the money value of a unit of time saving is the same for everyone in the sample. A line can then be drawn through the origin of the graph joining together all those combinations of time saving and money saving that would lead to a traveller being indifferent between the two modes. This is shown in Figure 11.1 as the straight line through Q and O. A saving of OP travelling time is just worth a sacrifice of PQ money; the value of a unit of time saving is thus PQ/OP.

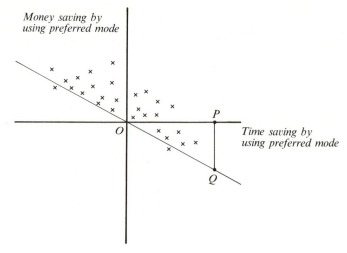

Fig. 11.1

If all travellers attach this value to time saving, then each of their replies should imply a point which lies on or to the north-east of this line. (A point south-west of the line implies a contradiction. It implies that the time saving achieved by using the preferred mode is not worth its money cost, or that the money saving is not worth its cost in extra travelling time. In other words, the 'preferred' mode ought not to have been preferred.)

Beesley's method was to find the straight line through the origin that had the smallest number of observations at the wrong side of it. The slope of this line represents an estimate of the value of time saving to people with characteristics similar to those of the people in the sample.

This general approach has many possible applications. One might, for example, find useful information about how people value changes in various characteristics of publicly provided health care serves by studying the choices they make between public and private health care. In Britain, for example, greater promptness of treatment can sometimes be secured by paying the extra costs of being treated outside the National Health Service.

11.3.   An example: alleviating traffic congestion in cities

The current trend towards the greater use of private cars has produced increasingly severe traffic congestion in cities. There has been much controversy about what governments should do about this problem. Typically, governments are closely involved in determining the form of urban transport systems; both the building and upkeep of roads and the operation of public transport services are usually responsibilities of public agencies.

Two different strategies for tackling the problem of traffic congestion are frequently suggested.

One strategy is a simple one, to provide more road space. The other is to reduce the costs to passengers of using public transport. (This could be done by reducing fares or by increasing the frequency or the speed of services.) This, it is hoped, would induce people to substitute trips by public transport for trips by car and thus reduce traffic congestion. (These two strategies are not, of course, mutually exclusive. Nor do they exhaust the possibilities open to governments; other possibilities include doing nothing and introducing prices for the use of road space.)

In this section we shall consider how specific policies of providing more road space and of reducing the costs of using public transport can be evaluated. The example we shall use is a very simple one, which illustrates the fundamental principles involved in evaluating such policies. The analysis of urban transport systems is now a highly developed specialism with its own jargon and its own set of techniques, which often involve quite complex mathematics. However, the underlying economic principles are quite straightforward and are those common to all cost-benefit analysis.

Consider a simple and self-contained transport system, consisting of two places (A and B) and two modes of passenger transport between them. One mode is the use of private cars on the single road between the two places; the other is the use of public transport, which does not use the road at all (it is, let us say, a rail service).

From the viewpoint of the potential traveller, or consumer, there are two relevant opportunity cost prices, one for each mode of transport. The opportunity cost price measures the money value of the costs of travel to the traveller; it includes both money outlays and a valuation of the time taken to make a trip. For simplicity, we shall assume that the opportunity cost price of a mode is the same for all consumers (for example, everyone has the same valuation of travelling time). One exception to this assumption may be permitted, and is common in cost-benefit analyses of transport projects. Consumers may be divided into two groups, one of which has access to trips by car at the common opportunity cost price, the other of which has no access to trips by car at any price.

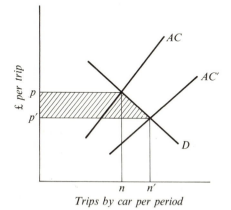

Fig. 11.2

We may now construct a demand curve for trips by car, relating the number of trips demanded (say, per week) to their opportunity cost price. Such a curve is shown as D in Figure 11.2. (It is constructed for a given opportunity cost price of public transport.) The cost of a trip by car itself depends upon the total number of trips that are made. Traffic engineers have shown that, beyond a certain point, as the flow of traffic on a given stretch of road increases, the speed falls in a predictable way. Since to an economist, travelling time is an element of the cost of trips, a 'speed/flow relationship' can be reinterpreted as a relationship between the *quantities* produced of the good, 'trips by car', and the *average cost* of the good. For a given type of road between our two places A and B, the relationship between the number of trips made and the average cost at which they can be made is shown as the curve AC in Figure 11.2.

The number of trips actually made (n in this case) and their average cost (p) is determined by the intersection of these two curves. This is the only outcome that is consistent both with consumers' preferences—represented by the demand curve—and what is technically feasible—represented by the average cost curve.

Now consider a proposal to improve the road between A and B so as to increase its ability to handle large volumes of traffic. At volumes of traffic at which the existing road is congested, the proposed road will be less congested and thus trips will be less costly. The proposal, then, can be represented as a downward shift of the average cost curve to AC'. This has two effects; it reduces the opportunity cost price of trips from p to p' and it induces the number of trips made to increase from n to n'.

If these magnitudes can be predicted accurately, evaluating the benefits of the road improvement to consumers is very simple. The benefit is a gain of consumers' surplus equal to the shaded area in the diagram, or approximately

$$n(p - p') + \tfrac{1}{2}(n' - n)(p - p').\qquad\qquad\textbf{11.1}$$

Reducing the price of public transport trips

Now consider an alternative policy, to reduce the opportunity cost price of trips by public transport. To analyse and evaluate the effects of this policy we must consider the interrelationships between the demands for two goods, trips by car and trips by public transport. The theoretical framework in which this problem can best be handled is that introduced in Section 10.3. The application of this framework to our present problem is shown in Figures 11.3a and 11.3b.

Initially the opportunity cost price ('price' for short) of public transport trips is p_p. Given this 'price', the demand for car trips is $D_c(p_p)$. Since the relationship between the number of car trips and their average cost is AC, the number of car trips made is n_c and the 'price' of car trips is p_c. This in turn implies that the demand for public transport trips is $D_p(p_c)$ and so the number of these trips made is n_p.

Then, as an act of policy, the government reduces the 'price' of public transport trips to p'_p. Since the two kinds of trip are substitues for each other, the effect of this is to reduce the demand for car trips to $D_c(p'_p)$. This in turn reduces the amount of traffic congestion; the number of car trips falls to n'_c and the 'price' to p'_c. With this lower 'price' of car trips, the demand for public transport trips is $D_p(p'_c)$ and the number of trips made is n'_p.

Analytically, this problem is very similar to that presented in Section 10.3 concerning the interrelationships between a market for rail trips and a market for tenancies. In the earlier problem, the price of one good (rail trips) was increased as an act of policy; this induced a fall in the price of a complementary good (tenancies). In the present problem, the price of one good (public transport trips) is reduced as an act of policy and this induces a fall in the price of a substitute good (car trips). Using the method explained in relation to the earlier problem, the net gain to 'consumers'—that is, to public transport users and car

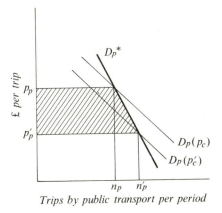

Fig. 11.3a

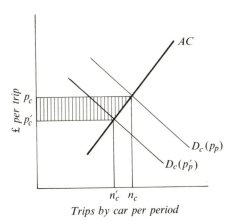

Fig. 11.3b

users—is the sum of the area of the shaded strip in Figure 11.3a to the left of the observed demand curve for public transport trips and the area of the shaded strip in Figure 11.3b to the left of the average cost curve for car trips. Approximating, this may be written as a

$$\text{net gain to consumers} = n_p(p_p - p'_p) + \tfrac{1}{2}(n'_p - n_p)(p_p - p'_p) + n'_c(p_c - p'_c)$$

$$+ \tfrac{1}{2}(n_c - n'_c)(p_c - p'_c). \qquad\qquad 11.2$$

Provided, then, that it is possible to predict the effects of the policy of reducing the price of public transport trips on the average cost of car trips and on the number of trips made by each mode, it is not difficult to evaluate the benefits that accrue to public transport users and to car users.

(The reader may be puzzled by a difference between the present example and the example, presented in Chapter 10, involving rail trips and tenancies. In the present example, the shaded area in Figure 11.3b measures an element of gain to consumers but does not also measure an exactly equal and opposite loss to any other party. The equivalent area in the earlier example (the shaded area in Figure 10.2b, p. 139) simultaneously measured an element of gain to consumers and a loss borne by the suppliers of tenancies (landlords). The difference between these two examples stems from the difference between an over-the-counter price and an opportunity cost price. In the present example, the 'price of car trips' is an opportunity cost price. *As far as consumers are concerned*, the two kinds of price are exactly equivalent to one another, and thus we can analyse the problem *as if* the price were an over-the-counter price. But if we are considering the supply side of a market the two kinds of price are very different, for the simple reason that over-the-counter prices are payments of money made to individuals who supply goods while opportunity cost prices need not be received by anyone (consider the 'expenditure' of time). Thus areas of strips to the left of the curve *AC* in Figure 11.3b cannot be interpreted as measuring changes in any form of producers' surplus.)

11.4.   Identifying a complete demand curve: the Clawson method

Where a service, such as that provided by a hospital or a theatre or a supermarket, is provided at a geographically fixed point, one of the costs of using the service is the cost of travelling to it. Travel cost, seen as an opportunity cost price of using a service, has a property which typically is not shared by over-the-counter prices. This is that the price of a good faced by one group of individuals can differ greatly from the price faced by another group. This provides the cost-benefit analyst with a means of observing simultaneously a large number of points on the demand curve for a good. The method by which this can be done is named after Clawson, who first introduced it to cost-benefit analysis.[2]

Consider a theatre in a large urban area, which happens to be the area's only theatre. Our aim is to calculate the consumers' surplus that would be lost if the theatre were closed.

The opportunity cost price of attending the theatre comprises the price of a ticket and the cost of travelling between the theatre and—we shall assume—the theatre-goer's home. Different people will face different prices, according to where they live, whether or not they own a car, and so on.

Now consider all those people for whom the opportunity cost price is some given value, say OC_1 in Figure 11.4. For these people we can conceive of a demand curve, drawn as D in the diagram, showing how they would respond to hypothetical changes in the opportunity cost price. We shall use as our unit of quantity 'visits per person per year'.

The consumers' surplus that would be lost by the group of people we are considering if the theatre were closed is measured by the area C_1PX_1. (Because of our choice of unit, this is the average loss per person per year.)

This is fine in principle. But there is the practical problem that only one point on the demand curve can be observed directly. This is the point X_1, which represents the number of trips actually made at the price actually faced. Without more information it would be impossible to say how large the area C_1PX_1 is.

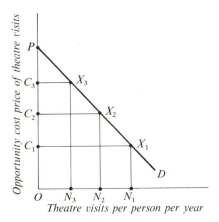

Fig. 11.4

We can repeat this analysis for any other group of individuals, identified by their sharing a common opportunity cost price of theatre visits. For each group we can conceive of a demand curve and we can observe only a single point on the curve.

We now make the crucial assumption that the demand curves of all such groups of individuals are identical. This implies, for example, that if the opportunity cost price for all those people currently facing a price of OC_1 were raised from OC_1 to OC_2, they would respond by adopting the same rate of theatre-visiting as is characteristic of those people who already face a price of OC_2.

If we observe that the rate of theatre-visiting is ON_1 for people facing a price of OC_1, ON_2 for people facing a price of OC_2, and so on, we can locate sufficient points on the demand curve to enable us to calculate reasonably accurately the area C_1PX_1. Similarly we can calculate the area C_2PX_2, the average loss for those people currently facing a price of OC_2, and so on.

The assumption that all of the groups of individuals have the same demand curve is convenient, but in some circumstances it might also be unrealistic. Making it might lead to significant errors in the estimation of the consumers' surplus gained from theatre visits. The resulting difficulties can be overcome, although at the cost of additional complexity.

First, it is clear that different individuals will have different preferences. Some will have much stronger preferences for visiting the theatre than will others. The underlying assumption is that such differences will tend to cancel each other out when large groups of people are dealt with; although Mr. A's demand function may be very different from Mr. B's, the demand function for all the inhabitants of one town taken together might be expected to be very similar to that for all the inhabitants of another town of equal size.

Second, a more serious difficulty is that there are variables other than the opportunity cost price of theatre visits that can be expected to affect the demand for visits. We should expect a typical individual's demand to be a function, not only of this price, but also of the prices of goods that are complementary to, or substitutes for, theatre visits, and of his income. Problems arise if there is a tendency for individuals who are more accessible to the theatre to have higher (or lower) values for any of these significant variables than do individuals who are less accessible.

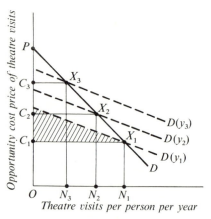

Fig. 11.5

One such example is illustrated in Figure 11.5. As before, we consider three groups of theatre-goers facing, respectively, opportunity cost prices of OC_1, OC_2 and OC_3. But suppose that those people who face the lower prices are, on average, poorer than those who face the higher ones. (For example, the theatre might be in the centre of a city and there might be a tendency for richer people to live further from the city centre.) Suppose that the average income of these three groups are y_1 (the lowest), y_2 and y_3 (the highest). The demand curve appropriate to the first group is drawn as $D(y_1)$ in the diagram. Since this group in fact faces an opportunity cost price of OC_1, the consumers' surplus enjoyed by these people is measured by the area shaded in the diagram. If the demand for theatre visits increases as income increases (other things being equal), the demand curves for the other two (richer) groups—$D(y_2)$ and $D(y_3)$—will lie above and to the right of $D(y_1)$. Consequently the shaded area will be less than the area C_1PX_1 which originally we took to be a measure of the consumers' surplus enjoyed by those people who faced the price OC_1. The original 'measurement' of consumers' surplus is thus an overestimate of the true surplus.

In a case such as this, the analyst must be able to estimate separately each of the relevant demand curves. Or, more formally, he must be able to estimate the demand *function* which relates the quantity of the good demanded by the members of a group not only to the opportunity cost price of the good but also to other significant variables. How this can best be done is a problem of statistical method and, as such, is beyond the scope of this book.

11.5. Public goods and external effects

The goods we have considered so far have all been of a particular kind: individuals are able to choose how much of them to consume. These choices are made in relation to prices—whether literal, over-the-counter prices, or less obvious opportunity cost prices. By observing people's choices, the cost-benefit analyst is able to infer how they value the goods they consume.

There is, however, an important class of goods, known as *public goods*, for which it is impossible for individuals to choose independently of each other how much they will consume. The essential property of a public good is that if more of it is provided for one member of a group of people, more is necessarily provided for all members. (The above describes a public good in its pure or idealized form. In practice, as we shall see, goods are often partly public goods and partly not—a fact which helps the cost-benefit analyst.)

As an example, consider street lighting in an estate of houses. Each resident has an interest not simply in the lighting of the roadway outside his own house but also in the lighting of the estate as a whole, since he must use the estate's road system to get access to his house. Suppose that the cost of lighting must be paid by the householders of the estate, and that the cost is divided equally between them.

A higher standard of lighting is more costly than a lower standard, and so in this sense standards of lighting have prices. Each householder will have his own preference as to which standard he would like to see provided (given that he will have to pay his share of the costs). But if different householders have different preferences, all cannot be completely satisfied. They must reach a collective decision about the standard which will be provided for, and paid for by, all. Their collective decision will not necessarily represent the preference of any particular individual.

So if a cost-benefit analyst needs to know what social benefit is provided by a street lighting system, he cannot discover the value that individuals place on lighting by studying choices made by them about how much lighting to consume. The nature of a public good does not allow this sort of choice to be made—or, at least, choices can be made only in a rather indirect way.

This problem does not arise only where public goods are provided as a result of a deliberate, collective decision (as street lighting is). Often a project, designed for some other purpose, has the incidental effect of changing the supply of a public good.

Consider the good 'clean air'. Clean air is a public good (at least outside buildings; the interiors of buildings can be air-conditioned independently). Whatever degree of air cleanliness is enjoyed by one householder is also enjoyed by his immediate neighbours; each cannot choose independently of the others what kind of air he will breathe. A project designed by a private firm or a public agency may affect, incidentally, the supply of this good. The building of a chemical works, for example, will reduce the supply of clean air in the surrounding area. As there is no market in clean air, the owners of the works do not have to pay for the clean air they destroy. No account would be taken of this effect in a financial appraisal made on behalf of the owners. But a cost-benefit analysis must take account of it, since clean air is something that people value.

Effects of this kind are known as *external effects* or, sometimes, externalities, spillover effects, or neighbourhood effects. (These external effects, which physically affect the conditions under which goods are supplied or consumed, are essentially different from the pecuniary external effects discussed in Chapter 10 above. Pecuniary external effects affect only the market prices of goods. To distinguish the two sorts of effect, the non-pecuniary sort is sometimes called a *technological external effect*.)

In trying to discover how highly people value additional consumption of goods, the cost-benefit analyst tries to find situations in which individuals are confronted with choices between consuming more of a good at a higher cost and less at a lower cost. To say, as we did above, that such choices cannot exist for public goods, is an oversimplification. For the pure public good of economic theory, this would be true. But few goods are so public as to completely eliminate the opportunity for independent individual choice.

Market prices of access to public goods: property values

Consider again the street lighting example. In our discussion of this case we implicitly assumed that each house was occupied by a particular householder, who would continue to live there for ever.

But houses can be bought and sold. Consider the problem from the viewpoint of a house buyer, who can choose between many

houses offered for sale. Each house buyer will have his own preferences about street lighting and each, other things being equal, will
presumably be willing to pay more for a house the higher is the
standard of lighting associated with it. Because of this, houses on
better-lit estates will command higher prices. Each buyer is free to
make an independent choice about what standard of lighting to buy,
given the prices at which different standards can be bought. In this
sense street lighting is not a public good. The extra price that a house
on a well-lit estate can command over and above the price of a similar
house on a poorly-lit estate is a measure of the marginal value to
house buyers of the extra lighting.

The key to the apparent contradiction here is that, although
lighting is a good which is supplied simultaneously to a group of
people (householders), *access to* the group is bought and sold on a
market. It is as if lighting were one of the benefits of membership of
a club, whose membership is limited to those willing to pay the
membership fee. The marginal social value of street lighting is
measured by the market price of access to it. If it were not for the
fact that ownership of the right of access to our street lighting scheme
is divided amongst a number of householders, financial appraisal of
lighting projects would be appropriate. A speculative builder, for
example, building a complete estate of houses for sale, would compare
the costs of different standards of lighting with the financial returns
they offered him. Since returns are determined by the prices at
which houses can be sold, financial returns and social benefits would
be identical (provided that the number of houses built was not so
large as to affect the relative market values of houses enjoying different standards of lighting).

It often is possible to find the value to individuals of additional
consumption of (apparent) public goods by identifying markets in
which access to public goods is bought and sold.

One problem for which this approach has proved useful is that of
valuing the social costs of aircraft noise—an external effect of air
travel. Much of the nuisance of aircraft noise affects people in the
role of householder; they suffer in and around their homes. In the
same way that street lighting is a public good, aircraft noise is a
public bad. It affects simultaneously a number of individuals; if one
householder suffers, so do his neighbours. But the effects are localized, and house buyers are free to choose between affected and
unaffected houses. There is a market in access to quietness. The
difference between the market prices of affected houses and unaffected (but otherwise identical) houses measures the marginal value
to householders of freedom from aircraft noise.

The range of possible applications of this approach is extremely wide. In principle, it could be used to uncover the values of all forms of localized 'amenity' and 'disamenity' that affect householders, from corner shops to diesel fumes. The main difficulty with the approach is statistical: it is not always easy to identify the relationship between property values and amenities or disamenities. So far, such relationships have been identified successfully only for quite extreme disamenities, such as high levels of aircraft noise.

Not all public goods and bads can be valued in this way, however. Some are too diffuse in their effects for people to have genuine choices between enjoying them (or putting up with them, in the case of public bads) and not enjoying them. A man who is willing to pay for a suitably located house can buy freedom from high levels of aircraft noise but it is far more difficult to buy freedom from exposure to radioactive material in the atmosphere. Access to the enjoyment of street lightning on small housing estates is far more restricted than is access to the enjoyment of lighting on public highways between cities.

The approach of measuring the social values of public goods through their effects on the market value of property confronts a number of problems of principle.

The approach is, in effect, to identify market prices—for example, the market price of freedom from noise. The argument that the fall in the market value of houses as a result of a localized increase in noise is a measure of the social cost of this extra noise depends upon the assumption that the price of freedom from noise remains constant. In other words, the difference between the prices of quiet and noisy houses is unchanged. This would be the case if the increase in noise affected only a small number of houses, 'small' being measured relative to the number of houses which buyers regarded as close substitutes for one another. If, on the other hand, a project affected a large part of a housing market, the price of freedom from noise would probably change. If, for example, a new airport subjected most of an isolated town to noise nuisance, the resulting scarcity of quiet houses would bring about an increase in the price of freedom from noise. In such cases the analysis becomes more complicated and must use measures of consumers' surplus. (Analytically, the issues involved here are very similar to those raised by Problem 2 in Chapter 10 (p. 145), concerning the valuation of a programme of improvements to houses.)

As a further problem of principle, it is strictly correct to use changes in the market values of houses to measure social costs and benefits only if moving house does not involve significant costs. The price of freedom from noise is a *marginal* value. It measures the value of this freedom to someone who is on the margin of choice between living in a quiet house and living in a noisy one. In other words, it measures the value of freedom from noise to the household which, of all households living in quiet houses, values it least. But suppose that a project inflicts noise on a small number of the quiet houses of a town. It would be sheer coincidence if the houses affected happened, at the time, to be occupied by those households which valued quiet the least. Over time, however, there will be a process of adjustment. Suppose, for example, that Mr. A is willing to pay £300 for freedom from noise while the market price of it is only £100. Naturally he will live in a quiet house. If the quietness of his home is destroyed, he would do better to accept a loss of £100 in the value of his house and buy a quiet house somewhere else, than to stay on and bear a loss of £300. Ultimately, then, noisy houses *will* be occupied by those who value quiet least. But the process of reaching this state involves 'transaction costs' such as the costs of searching out alternatives and of the labour of removal men. If these costs are significant, they should be taken account of in a cost-benefit analysis.

It may seem that the method of valuing technological external effects by reference to changes in property values is inconsistent with the treatment of pecuniary external effects in Chapter 10. In that chapter, we considered an example in which the closure of a railway service led to a fall in the market value of houses (Section 10.3, pp. 137–42), and argued that in a cost-benefit analysis no account need be taken of this pecuniary external effect. Yet now it is argued that a fall in the market values of houses that results from a technological external effect ought to be taken account of. Why the difference?

If we chose, we could regard the price of houses near a railway station as including a payment for access to the station. By doing this, we should be treating the station as a kind of public good, like quietness. To the extent that people can benefit from a railway service only by living near railway stations, the social loss from closing the service can be measured by the fall in the value of houses that it brings about. But this would be an *alternative* to valuing the social loss by considering people's willingness to pay for individual trips by train. In practice, this latter method is usually far more convenient. The argument of Chapter 10 was that it is wrong to add together two alternative measures of the same social loss.

Opportunity cost prices of access to public goods: the Clawson approach

The key to finding how highly individuals value increases in their consumption of public goods is, as we have seen, the identification of situations where individuals have to pay for access to public goods. Property markets are a straightforward example, for in these markets rights of access to localized public goods are bought and sold. However, as was argued in Section 11.2, it is not necessary for a good to be sold in the conventional over-the-counter sense for the analyst to be able to infer its value to individuals. It is enough for there to be a measurable opportunity cost attached to consuming the good.

This argument can be applied to the case of access to a public good, access itself being a good. Often access, although not sold on any market, has an opportunity cost price. An important example is the cost of travelling to a public good that can be consumed only in a specific place.

Consider the services for consumption by ramblers provided by an expanse of open moorland. Provided that the moor is not so well-used as to be in the eyes of ramblers congested, it is a classic example of a public good. The more moorland there is for one rambler to walk on, the more there is for all. If the moor is common land, access to it is not restricted to particular individuals, nor to the residents of particular localities. It is open to all who are willing to incur the costs of travelling to it.

Here is another application for the Clawson method of identifying the demand curve for a good. The problem of valuing the services provided by a stretch of moorland, or the services of any other public recreation facility is essentially the same as that of valuing the services of the theatre discussed in Section 11.4.

Problems

1. Two small country towns, A and B, lie on an important express railway line. At present, some through trains stop at A while none stop at B. A local passenger service, operating by diesel multiple-unit trains, runs between A and B. There are no intermediate stations. The service runs at a financial loss and is subsidized by the government.

It is proposed to stop running this service and to close the station at B. To do this would, it is estimated, reduce the total costs of operating the railway system by £67 000 per year. 250 000 single trips between A and B are made on the service each year. The average fare paid is 20p per trip. The total revenue of the service is thus £50 000 per year and it makes a financial loss of £17 000 per year.

If the railway were closed, it would be replaced by a new bus service between A and B, which would be run by a public agency. The fare charged would be 20p per trip, the same as the present rail fare. The trip would, however, take considerably longer by bus than by train—30 minutes instead of 15 minutes. The best estimate that can be made is that 150 000 trips would be made on this service each year. The total cost of operating the bus service would be £32 000 per year and so the agency running the service would incur a small financial loss of £2000 per year. This would be covered by a grant from the government.

Of the 100 000 trips per year that would be made by train if the railway were open but would not be made by bus, it is estimated that 50 000 would be made by private car and 50 000 would not be made at all. A trip by car between the two towns takes 14 minutes and involves marginal money costs of 18p. (Marginal costs are relevant here because it is assumed that no one chooses to buy a car as a result of the closure of the rail service.) These figures suggest that car trips are both faster and cheaper than train trips, which raises the question of why any-one who had access to a car should have travelled by train in the first place. The most likely explanation is that in car-owning households in which there are more people than cars, one person's using a car may have an opportunity cost (some-one else's not being able to use it) in addition to the money costs of running the car. There is, unfortunately, no practical way of discovering *directly* how great these opportunity costs are.

Make a cost-benefit analysis of the proposal to close the railway service. (Since all costs and benefits can be expressed as steady flows of £ per year, it is sufficient to evaluate social costs and benefits per year. Take the value of savings of travelling time to be 36p per hour. Assume where necessary that prices other than those for bus and train trips are equal to marginal social costs.)

2. A public agency is responsible for a large reservoir which is situated close to a densely populated area. For many years the agency did not allow the general public to have access to the reservoir but recently it decided, as an experiment, to change this policy. Motorists were allowed, on payment of a charge of 10p per person, to use a private road around the reservoir and to park their cars in certain areas. This experiment was monitored over a period of 12 months. A sample survey was made of visitors to the reservoir to discover how far people travelled to reach it. The results of this survey are shown in Table (i), which gives estimates of the total numbers of people travelling to the reservoir during the year from each of 6 zones. (Each zone is defined by the average distance of its inhabitants from the reservoir.) It is estimated that the financial costs to the agency of opening the reservoir to the public are £13 000 per year. (These costs include the labour of wardens and the additional costs of maintaining roads and parking areas to cope with the increased traffic.) There were 97 400 visits during the year, bringing a total financial revenue of £9740.

Table (i)

Zone	Average distance of zone's population from reservoir (km)	Average cost of travel to reservoir (£ per return trip per person)	Population of zone ('000)	Visits per year ('000)	Visits per person per year
A	5	0·26	90	13·1	0·1456
B	15	0·52	930	45·2	0·0486
C	25	0·78	1040	18·3	0·0176
D	35	1·04	2000	16·2	0·0081
E	45	1·30	1520	4·6	0·0030
F	55	1·56	1760	negligible	negligible

Note: 'Cost of travel' does not include the entrance charge of £0·10.

The agency is now considering whether to make the experimental policy per-manent or whether to abandon the policy altogether and again not to allow motorists any access to the reservoir. A further option that is open to the agency is to attempt to cover the costs of opening the reservoir roads to motorists by raising the charge from 10p per person. (If fewer motorists visited the reservoir, following an increase in the charge, there would be a small but significant reduc-tion in the costs of providing access. It is estimated that these costs, which were

£13 000 during the year of the experiment, would be £12 000 per year if there were only 75 000 visitors per year and £11 000 per year if there were only 50 000 visitors per year. Decreases in the number of visitors below the level of 50 000 per year would have no significant effect on costs.)

(*i*) Make a cost-benefit analysis of the policy of allowing access to the reservoir at a charge of 10p per person, relative to the alternative policy of prohibiting access altogether.

(*ii*) Predict whether the agency would make a financial profit from allowing access to the reservoir if it charged 36p per person.

(Assume that the average incomes of the inhabitants of each zone are the same and that other recreational facilities, which might be substitutes for the reservoir are not, on average, more accessible to the inhabitants of some zones than they are to those of others.)

3. Reconsider the previous problem. The consumers' surplus enjoyed by visitors to the reservoir was estimated from the information given in Table (i), on the assumption that 'other recreational facilities, which might be substitutes for the reservoir are not, on average, more accessible to the inhabitants of some zones than they are to those of others'.

Suppose that this assumption is at variance with the facts. The reservoir is located in an expanse of upland open space in the centre of an otherwise flat, built-up and industrial region. Most of the region's beauty spots (visits to which are substitutes for visits to the reservoir) are also in this upland area. Does the original estimate of consumers' surplus understate or overstate the true benefit accruing to visitors from their being allowed access to the reservoir?

4. A certain town lies under the flight paths of planes landing at and taking off from a major airport. Until recently, 17 per cent of the houses in the town were affected by noise nuisance from planes. Then, following the construction of a new runway at the airport, the number of houses affected by noise increased to 50 per cent of the total in the town.

A study is made of the prices of houses before and after the building of the runway. (The earlier observations of prices were made before it was widely known that the runway would be built.) By using appropriate price indices it is possible to make estimates of what the prices of houses would have been, in the year the new runway actually came into use, had the new runway not been built. These estimates can then be compared with the actual prices of houses in that year. These comparisons are shown in Table (ii). For the purposes of the study, the town is divided into three areas. Area A was not affected by noise either before or after the new runway was built. Area B was not affected before the runway was built but was affected after. Area C was affected both before and after. The houses of the town are almost all of a common type (3-bedroomed semi-detached houses between 10 and 30 years old). In the last 10 years no new houses have

Table (ii)

Area	Number of houses in area	Average price of houses if runway not built (£ per house)	Average price of houses if runway built (£ per house)
A	18 000	12 000	12 250
B	12 000	12 000	11 050
C	6000	11 250	11 050

been built because of a green-belt policy followed by the local planning authority. It is not expected that more houses will be built in the forseeable future.

What is the net social loss imposed on householders and property owners by the increase in the size of the area affected by aircraft noise?

(*Note*: analytically, this problem is very similar to Problem 2 of Chapter 10. The present problem can most usefully be analysed as one involving two goods, 'houses' and 'freedom from noise'. A house in an area affected by aircraft noise is one unit of the good 'houses'; a house in a quiet area is a combination of one unit of 'houses' and one unit of 'freedom from noise'. The difference between the prices of houses in affected and in unaffected areas is the price of 'freedom from noise'. It may be assumed that the *degree* of noise nuisance is the same for all houses affected by it; building the new runway does not increase the degree of nuisance but only the number of houses affected by this nuisance.)

Notes

[1] See Beesley (1965).
[2] See Clawson (1959).

Further reading

A comprehensive survey of work aimed at finding individuals' valuations of savings of travelling time is given by Harrison and Quarmby (1972).

The classic cost-benefit analyses of transport projects are the studies of the London-Birmingham motorway (Coburn, Beesley and Reynolds (1960)) and of the Victoria Line underground railway in London (Foster and Beesley (1963) and Beesley and Foster (1965)). A cost-benefit analysis of a proposal to close a railway service in Wales is reported in Ministry of Transport (1969); the Ministry's methodology is criticized by one of the present authors in Sugden (1972). A cost-benefit analysis of a proposed urban motorway is described in Pearce and Nash (1973). For a book-length discussion of the problems involved in appraising transport projects, see Harrison (1974). The methods currently used by the British Government to appraise investments in the transport sector are described in Department of the Environment (1976), Vol. 2, Paper 5.

The classic work on the Clawson method of identifying a demand curve is Clawson (1959). This method has been applied to the valuation of recreation facilities in Britain by Mansfield (1971) and by Smith (1971).

For a full discussion of the economic theory of public goods, see Buchanan (1968). For a theoretical treatment of the relationship between property values and the public good, 'freedom from noise', see Walters (1975). The Roskill Commission's cost-benefit analysis of alternative sites for a third London airport included an attempt to find individuals' valuations of freedom from aircraft noise by studying property values; see Roskill (1970) or the brief summary of the Commission's cost-benefit analysis given in Flowerdew (1972). Attempts to find, from studies of property values, how highly individuals value the absence of various environmental disamenities have been made by Ridker and Henning (1967), by Anderson and Crocker (1971) and by Wabe (1971). A brief survey of work in this field is given in Ball (1973).

12. Uncertainty and Cost-benefit Analysis

12.1. Introduction

The implications of uncertainty for financial appraisal were discussed in Chapter 5 above. The arguments developed in that chapter were equally applicable to cost-benefit analysis and the present chapter should be considered as a supplement to the earlier one. The differences between the two kinds of appraisal do not concern their ways of treating uncertainty in the abstract, but rather concern the kinds of uncertainty that have to be taken account of. In a financial appraisal the only uncertainty that is relevant is uncertainty about the financial costs and returns of a project. In a cost-benefit analysis uncertainty about any effect of a project on any member of the community is relevant. This broader scope of cost-benefit analysis leads to some problems in the treatment of uncertainty that do not arise, or arise to much less an extent, in financial appraisal. It is these problems that we must now consider.

12.2. Subjective probabilities and expected values in cost-benefit analysis

In Chapter 5 we considered the role of subjective probability judgements in financial appraisal. These judgements, we argued, were ultimately the responsibility of the decision-maker, who acted as the agent of less well-informed members of the general public (see Section 5.2). This argument is equally valid for cost-benefit analysis, given the decision-making approach. In the Paretian interpretation of cost-benefit analysis, however, the analyst makes recommendations independently of any decision-maker. It is then debatable whether a Paretian cost-benefit analysis of a project should rest on the probability judgements of the analyst or on the judgements of those members of the general public who are affected by the project. For the most part, our discussion of uncertainty is based on the proposition that probability judgements for cost-benefit analysis are supplied by the decision-maker or by the analyst; they are not supplied by the general public.

In Section 5.3 we defined the *expected value criterion* for financial appraisal under uncertainty. This criterion was that a project should be undertaken if, and only if, the expected present value of its financial returns exceeded the expected present value of its financial costs. This criterion was shown to be consistent with our initial interpretation of the financial objectives of firms and public agencies, provided that two conditions were satisfied. First, each individual affected by a project should risk only small changes in his wealth. Second, the risks involved in the project should be independent of other risks borne by these individuals.

If we redefine the expected value criterion in terms of social benefits and social costs, rather than financial returns and financial costs, this argument may equally well be applied to cost-benefit analysis. We should therefore consider whether these two conditions are likely to be satisfied in cases where cost-benefit analysis is being used.

There is little useful to be said about the condition of independent risks. We can concede that the risks of projects might sometimes not be independent. For example, a public investment in a manufacturing industry might be expected to produce large benefits if there was a rapid rate of economic growth but smaller benefits if the rate of growth was slower. In this case, the project would produce most benefit in a state of the world in which people, on the whole, would in any case be relatively rich. Where an effect of this kind is very significant, the expected value criterion cannot necessarily be justified.

The other condition is that risks should be 'small' in the sense that individuals should risk only small changes in their wealth. This condition can normally be assumed to hold for the financial risks that are taken account of in a public agency's financial appraisal. The tax system is a very effective risk-spreading institution. To the extent that the costs and benefits of a project affect individuals only via the tax system, a project will not impose significant risks on any individuals (unless the costs and benefits of the project as a whole are huge, or unless the section of the community that is taxed is very small).

But when projects impose uncertain *direct* costs, or confer uncertain *direct* benefits, on particular individuals, there is no similar presumption that risks will be small. Suppose, for example, that a public agency plans a project to supply, at the taxpayers' expense, irrigation water to a number of family-owned farms. If there is uncertainty about the project's capital costs, these risks will be spread amongst many taxpayers. But if there is uncertainty about the amount of additional agricultural produce that will result from using the irrigation water, and hence there is uncertainty about the project's contribution to the profits of farms, these risks will be borne by farmers. Unless farmers are able to insure against risks of this kind—and typically they are not—these risks will be spread no further.

Where a project imposes large risks on individuals, calculations of expected values can be used only to establish upper or lower bounds to the range in which the social benefits or costs of the project lie. In the example of the irrigation project, for instance, the expected value of the increased profits of farmers is the upper bound of the range. (It is assumed that farmers are risk-averse. For a discussion of the implications of risk aversion, see Section 5.3 above.)

This leads on to a further problem. So far we have discussed uncertainty as if all that was involved was uncertainty about the *total* costs and benefits of a project; but often there also is uncertainty about how such totals will be distributed between individuals. When this is the case, and if the individuals affected by a project do not value uncertain prospects of benefit or cost at their expected values, the end result of an appraisal may depend on how benefits and costs are aggregated.

It is quite common for events that are highly predictable in the aggregate to be uncertain at the level of the individual instance. Take, for example, investment in retraining labour. It may be possible to predict with a fair degree of certainty what *proportion* of a large number of trainees will find jobs that make use of their skills. Yet for the individual trainee, whether *he* will find such a job may be highly uncertain. Thus the total money gains that will accrue to a group of trainees is known by the analyst with virtual certainty, while each individual is uncertain about what gain will accrue to him.

How this kind of uncertainty should be handled is debatable.

One possible argument[1] is that, if the total benefits of a project are known with certainty, there is no risk to society. All that society is uncertain about is the distribution of these benefits between individuals and, if we adopt the potential Pareto improvement criterion, cost-benefit analysis is not concerned about the distribution of costs and benefits. It is enough to know what the total of benefits will be; no special treatment is required because individuals face uncertainty. The hallmark of this approach is that it looks at uncertainty from a viewpoint 'after the event'. After a group of trainees has returned to the labour market, we can identify who has gained what from training. The total of these gains is a measure of how much ex-trainees, with the benefit of hindsight, will *then* believe their training *was worth*. This, we have assumed, can be predicted with certainty.

An alternative approach is to look at uncertainty from a viewpoint 'before the event'. The analyst asks how much trainees believe their training *will be worth* when they decide to enrol. At this stage trainees face uncertainty. If the risks they face are small, and so they value their training at the expected value of the net gains it will produce for them, this before-the-event measure will be identical to the average gain measured after the event. But if they face large risks, the two measures will not be the same. The before-the-event value will be the smaller of the two because it will include some element of risk aversion.

The before-the-event approach seems the more satisfactory, for some of the implications of the other approach are distinctly unappealing. For example, using the after-the-event approach we should be forced to conclude that the activities of insurance companies produce only a massive social waste. They use valuable resources of office space and labour and yet produce only transfers of income between individuals (from the lucky, who do not claim on their policies, to the unlucky, who do). According to the potential Pareto improvement criterion, transfer payments have no significance for social welfare. Yet the customers of insurance companies enter into insurance contracts willingly and without imposing external costs on others. It would be very odd to conclude that by doing so they are contributing to a loss to society.

Given the position that uncertainty should be viewed from before the event, using after-the-event totals of costs and benefits as measures of social costs and benefits is equivalent to applying the expected value criterion. It is correct to do this only if the individuals concerned risk only small changes in their wealth.

12.3. The direct valuation of uncertain prospects

It has been argued in section 12.2 that the expected value criterion is appropriate only where individuals do not risk large changes in wealth. When large changes are at risk some alternative means of handling uncertainty is required.

The expected value approach is essentially an indirect way of inferring individuals' preferences in situations of uncertainty. The aim of the analyst is to find the value to an individual of an uncertain prospect of cost or benefit. The expected value approach is to use a process of theoretical deductions. If an individual's preferences have certain plausible properties, it is argued, then, under certain conditions, the value to him of an uncertain prospect will equal its expected value.

An obvious alternative is to avoid the need for these deductions by trying to infer directly, from observations of individuals' choices under uncertainty, how much they are willing to pay for uncertain prospects of benefit (or to avoid uncertain prospects of cost). For example, in choosing whether or not to insure against the financial consequences of damage to his own car in road accidents, a motorist reveals something of his willingness to pay to avoid a particular uncertain prospect of financial loss. This brings us back to the kind of problems of inferring individuals' valuations that we discussed in Chapter 11.

One particular characteristic of this approach is important. Individuals make their own choices in the light of their own subjective assessments of probabilities, and these assessments may be different from those of experts. For example, a motorist who chooses not to insure against damage to his car may do so partly because he has more confidence in his ability to avoid accidents than insurance companies have. Thus if the analyst is to infer individuals' degrees of risk aversion from observations of their choices, he must feel confident that he knows what these individuals judge the relevant probabilities to be. In practice, this usually means that he must feel justified in assuming that the judgements of experts are widely known and accepted.

A good example of the usefulness of this approach is its use in the evaluation of changes in risks of death and injury. In the following section this particular problem will be considered in some detail.

12.4.   The 'value of life'

Public decision-makers regularly have to make choices that have implications for the risks of death faced by individuals. Should there be more investment in hospitals, which would reduce the risk of death for everyone who is a potential patient but which would impose costs on taxpayers? Should there be more spending on the fire service? Should manually operated railway level crossings be replaced with automatic barriers, which are more dangerous but which reduce delays for road users? Somehow or other, decision-makers must decide how much it is worth paying to reduce risks by particular amounts.

In each of these cases the total effect of a decision could, in principle at least, probably be predicted fairly accurately. Thus, for example, we might know the number of lives that would be saved each year by an additional £1m of spending on a particular type of medical equipment. It is tempting to use the after-the-event veiwpoint (see Section 12.2) and to attach a value to each life saved. Many economists have adopted this approach and talk in terms of 'the value of a life' or 'the value of a prevented death'.

This way of looking at the problem leads to great difficulties. To begin with, there is a moral problem. The taking of life is an act of immense moral significance and to suggest that there is some money saving that can outweigh the loss to society of one of its members is, to put it mildly, unpleasant. There is also a technical problem. What, in terms of the potential Pareto improvement criterion, is the social value of preventing a death? One might argue that it is the maximum sum of money that an individual would be willing to pay to prevent his own premature death. This sum clearly is finite since it is limited by the individual's own wealth. Alternatively, one might argue that it is the minimum sum of money that an individual would accept as compensation for his own death (the compensation being added to his estate and so to the wealth of his heirs). It is quite conceivable—indeed, highly probable—that no finite sum of money would be acceptable to someone as compensation. That there should be two, probably vastly different, 'individual valuations' of preventing death is inconvenient. (Formally, this is an example of the problem of income effects that was introduced in the appendix to Chapter 9. The potential Pareto improvement criterion can be ambiguous when projects involve large changes in individuals' real incomes; and dying is hardly a small change.)

Those economists who have tried to derive a single value of a 'prevented death' have been compelled to drop the potential Pareto improvement criterion and to assume other social objectives.

Some writers have argued that the value of preventing a man's death is the present value of his expected future earnings.[2] This measures the value of the extra consumption that he and others would enjoy as a result of his surviving. The social objective that justifies this measure is the objective of maximizing gross national product. The unpleasantness of this objective can be judged from one of its implications: that it is not worth bearing any costs, however small, to prolong the lives of people once they have retired from the workforce. (The fact that a retired person may be living on a pension that he has in the past paid for makes no difference. If a pensioner dies, other people—deserving or undeserving—will benefit from the ending of the obligation to pay the pension.)

Another and even more cold-blooded suggestion is that the value of one man's life is the financial loss that would be imposed *on others* if he died.[3] In a world of selfish individuals this approach can be justified by one very simple revision of the potential Pareto improvement criterion. We simply define 'the community' to exclude the person whose death is in question—after all, one could argue, he will not be part of the community when he is dead. This social objective can, however, hardly be taken seriously. It would imply that it would be positively beneficial to society that retired people be exterminated.

Having rejected the idea of using a 'social value of a prevented death', let us investigate the possibilities of inferring directly how much individuals are willing to pay for reductions in *risks* of death.

Many of the problems raised by the previous approaches immediately evaporate. While 'taking life' and 'saving life'—taking and saving *known* lives—raise deep moral issues, all of us regularly and casually take decisions that affect the *risks* of our dying. We choose whether or not to cross busy roads, whether or not to smoke, whether to travel by car or by train. Most of us do not think of such choices as involving important ethical problems. And the problem of income effects no longer troubles the analysis. Changes in risks of death of the magnitude dealt with in most cost-benefit analyses are not valued very highly by individuals; they represent only very small changes in individuals' wealth. (If this were not so, there would be few private cars on the road.)

The problem for the analyst is largely a practical one—of inferring from observation of people's behaviour how highly reductions in risks of death are valued.

The most obvious approach is to identify situations where individuals are faced with choices between reductions in risks of death and increases in money income—in other words, situations where reductions in risk can be bought at an opportunity cost price. Such situations certainly exist. Men take on dangerous jobs such as soldiering or steeplejacking or working on North Sea oil rigs in return for money payments. Similarly, safety can sometimes be bought by making sacrifices other than of money. By making a long-distance journey by bus rather than by car a traveller normally gains both safety and money but at the expense of travelling time. If the value that people put on saving travelling time is itself known, the choice between bus and car can be expressed as one between safety and money. In principle, the problem of inferring from choices of this kind how changes in risks of death are valued is very similar to that of inferring the value of savings in travelling time (discussed in Section 11.2).

An alternative approach is to resort to a method more akin to the experiments of the laboratory sciences. Systematically selected individuals may be asked to imagine having to make particular choices between safety and money gain (or risk and money loss) and their hypothetical choices can be recorded and analysed. This has the disadvantage that there is little incentive for reflection on the part of participants. It has the compensating advantage that the choice problem can be very carefully specified so that the participants' responses are of maximum value to the analyst. In particular, respondents can be told exactly how great are the hypothetical risks involved in their choices; whilst the typical potential oil rig worker or air traveller may be only vaguely aware of the sizes of the risks he is considering taking on.

In some cases, the *principle* of using individuals' valuations of changes in risks of death has implications for cost-benefit analysis that can be followed without knowing the money value of these changes.

In Section 11.5 it was argued that the noise nuisance to householders as a result of the building of an airport could be evaluated by using information about the differences between the prices of houses in areas with different amounts of noise nuisance. An airport not only creates nuisance for people living under its flight paths, but also imposes on these people the risk of being killed or injured if a plane crashes. In principle this effect, too, could be evaluated by using information about the differences in house prices between more and less safe areas. In practice, however, it might be very difficult statistically to disentangle the effects on house prices of noise nuisance and danger. The more frequently and the lower planes fly overhead, the greater, presumably, is both the noise nuisance and the danger. Fortunately, however, there may be no need to estimate separately householders' valuations of these two 'bads'. If house prices are found to be related in a systematic way to some index of the extent to which planes fly low overhead, this provides a way of inferring the value of 'freedom from low-flying planes'. How far this is valued because it implies freedom from noise and how far it is valued because it implies freedom from danger is irrelevant to a decision about the siting of an airport (provided, of course, that the *relative* quantities of noise nuisance and danger are the same at all airports and airport sites).

Problems

1. The river that flows through a certain local authority area occasionally overflows its banks and floods areas of houses. At present 1500 houses are subject to some risk of flooding. (This amounts to only a small part of the total stock of houses in the local authority area.) The authority is considering a small civil engineering project which, if undertaken, would virtually eliminate the risk of flooding for 150 of the 1500 houses presently affected by floods but would not affect the other houses.

The local authority's engineers attach probabilities to the occurrence of different rates of river flow, and hence to different levels of flooding that would occur if the flood relief scheme were not built. These probabilities represent the engineers' judgements, which are based on studies of past instances of flooding on this and other rivers. The probabilities are expressed in the form of statements about mathematical expectation—for example, 'the expected number of instances of flooding to a depth of 1 metre or more in any given year is 0·1', which is equivalent to the statement 'floods of this depth occur, on average, once every 10 years'.

The authority wishes to evaluate the social benefits that would result from building the flood relief scheme. It investigates what effects on the 150 relevant houses could be expected to follow from each possible depth of flooding and then attempts to put money values on those effects. In the case of damage to property this is relatively simple; the cost of damage to property is taken to be measured by the sums paid out by insurance companies in response to claims by householders and house owners. (Virtually all householders and house owners are insured against damage to their property.) Other elements of social cost imposed by flooding are more difficult to value. There is the time that householders have to spend cleaning and repairing their houses after flooding, and there is the less tangible but equally real discomfort and inconvenience of the experience of flooding itself. The local authority calculates that the expected value of flood damage to property (in the absence of the flood relief scheme) is £8 per house per year. (This is an average for the 150 affected houses. Expected values are calculated from the engineers' judgements of probabilities.) With less confidence, it estimates that the expected number of hours spent by house-holders repairing the effects of flood damage is 8 person hours per house per year. It is not clear how this time should be valued, but the authority decides to value it as if it were time spent travelling (since a good deal is known about how people value such time; the average value of savings in travelling time is 30p per hour for people with income similar to those of the people affected by floods). At 30p per hour, the expected value of this item of the social costs of flooding is £2·40 per house per year. The authority does not attempt to put a money value on the intangible items of discomfort and inconvenience.

The authority also attempts to predict how much the value of the 150 houses would increase if the flood relief scheme were built. It finds that, on average, flood-affected houses sell for £250 less than unaffected, but otherwise similar, houses. (This average applies both to the 150 houses affected by the flood relief scheme and to the whole 1500 houses subject to the risk of flooding.) It is not expected that the size of the premium paid on house prices for freedom from the risk of flooding would change if the flood relief scheme were built (since only a relatively small number of houses are affected by the scheme). Thus it is predicted that the 150 houses would increase in value by an average of £250 per house if the scheme were built.

(*i*) What is the value of the social benefits that would be created by the flood relief scheme? If it is not possible to give a precise figure, give an upper or lower boundary to the range in which the benefit lies. (The market interest rate is 6 per cent, and local authorities are instructed by the central government to use this rate as a discount rate when appraising projects. A time horizon of 50 years after the completion of the flood relief scheme may be used. It may be assumed that insurance companies do not charge higher premiums to householders in areas affected by flooding than they do to others (the administrative costs of such fine discrimination being prohibitive). It may also be assumed that, at the time that it was observed that flood-affected houses sold for £250 less than other houses, house buyers were unaware that any flood-relief schemes were being considered by the local authority.)

(*ii*) How would your conclusions be altered if, at the time that the difference between the prices of flood-affected houses and those of other houses was observed, it had been widely known that the local authority was seriously con-sidering a major flood-relief project? This project would have greatly reduced the risk of flooding for most of the 1500 flood-affected houses. In the event, how-ever, this project was not undertaken; the project currently being considered, which affects only 150 houses, is a much less ambitious one.

2. The government is considering improving a major road between two large towns. It makes a cost-benefit analysis of the project.

The main benefit of the project is that it increases the speed of traffic between the two towns. The average time taken to make a trip by car between the towns would be reduced by 10 minutes. (The marginal money outlay required to make a trip would remain unchanged.) This reduction in the opportunity cost of trips would induce an increase in the number made, from 6·9m per year to 8·5m per year. Car users are known to value savings in travelling time at the rate of 30p per hour. Using this value, it is easy to calculate that the road improvement confers benefits (in the form of an increase in consumers' surplus) on car users which have a value of approximately £385 000 per year.

The improvement of the road will also lead to changes in the expected numbers of people killed and injured in road accidents. These changes are summarized in Tables (i) and (ii). People killed or injured are divided into two categories, car users who are people in the process of making the trip between the two towns, and pedestrians. Casualty rates are expressed in terms of the expected number of deaths or serious injuries per million trips made by car. Multiplying these rates by the number of trips made per year gives the expected number of deaths or serious injuries per year.

Table (i)
Deaths in road accidents

	Trips per year (millions)	Deaths per million car trips			Deaths per year		
		Car users	Pedestrians	Total	Car users	Pedestrians	Total
If road not improved	6·9	0·11	0·05	0·16	0·759	0·345	1·104
If road improved	8·5	0·10	0·04	0·14	0·850	0·340	1·190

Table (ii)
Serious injuries in road accidents

	Trips per year (millions)	Injuries per million car trips			Injuries per year		
		Car users	Pedestrians	Total	Car users	Pedestrians	Total
If road not improved	6·9	0·40	0·20	0·60	2·760	1·380	4·140
If road improved	8·5	0·33	0·15	0·48	2·805	1·275	4·080

Is it possible to say whether taking account of these changes in casualty rates would make the total benefits of the road improvement greater or less than £385 000 per year?

3. A cost-benefit analysis is to be made of a proposal to close a racecourse. One of the effects of closing the course would be that the opportunities for people to bet on horse races would be reduced. It is predicted that the net effect would be to reduce by £65 000 per year the total sum of money staked by punters. The total sum paid by punters to bookmakers would fall by £50 000 per year (the other £15 000 representing the stakes on bets won by punters). The total sum paid by bookmakers to punters (that is, punters' winnings) would fall by £30 000 per year. Thus the revenue of bookmakers (that is, the net flow to them from punters) would fall by £20 000 per year. The costs of the betting

industry (labour, rent of property, and so forth) would fall by £12 000 per year. These figures have been given as if they were known with certainty, even though the betting industry exists only because events are not known with certainty. The justification for assuming certainty is the 'law of large numbers': while the outcome of individual bets are uncertain, the total outcome of all the bets made over a year with any bookmaker can (it is assumed) be predicted with confidence.

What is the net social benefit or cost that results from the reduction in betting? (Assume that the transactions involved in the betting industry have no external effects—for example, there is no tax on betting. Use the potential Pareto improvement criterion. If it is not possible to give a precise figure for the net social benefit or cost, give an upper or a lower value for the range in which this benefit or cost lies.)

Notes

[1] This after-the-event approach is used by Hirshleifer (1966) in his discussion by the implications of uncertainty for public decision-making. That the alternative before-the-event approach is preferable is one of the criticisms of this paper that are made by Arrow and Lind (1970).

[2] This approach is used, for example, by Weisbrod (1971).

[3] This approach is used by Dawson (1967) and, as an alternative to the previous approach, by Weisbrod (1971). Layard (1972, p. 28) seems to advocate this approach: 'As far as the individual who may die is concerned . . . fear of death is in fact the only element that enters the calculation, since he will feel nothing once he is dead'.

Further reading

Reading on the general problem of uncertainty is given at the end of Chapter 5.

On the implications of uncertainty for the appraisal of public investment decisions, two papers are of particular importance—Arrow and Lind (1970) and Hirshleifer (1966). (The latter paper is a continuation of an earlier one—Hirshleifer (1965). These two should be read as one.) Arrow and Lind present formally the arguments given in our Section 12.2 for the use of the expected value criterion. Hirshleifer seems to reach a very different conclusion—that risky projects should be appraised by using the discount rate that is used by private sector firms when appraising projects with similar risks. This, in effect, is a recommendation for the use of 'risk premia'. The key to Hirschleifer's argument is an heroic assumption that insurance markets are 'perfect' and thus that *all* risks, private as well as public, can be spread. From this it follows that private sector firms will use the expected value criterion to appraise projects whenever projects' risks are 'independent' and, according to Hirshleifer's recommendation, public agencies should do likewise. This is consistent with Arrow and Lind's result.

For a very perceptive essay on the valuation of changes in risks of death, see Schelling (1968). The case for using individuals' valuations is made very forcefully by Mishan (1971*b*). For a more formal discussion of individuals' valuations of changes in risks of death, see Jones-Lee (1976). Attempts to value 'lives' or 'prevented deaths' without taking account of the uncertainty that is faced by the individuals who may die can be found in Dawson (1967) and Weisbrod (1971).

13. Decision-makers' Valuations

13.1. Introduction

So far our discussion of cost-benefit analysis has consisted of an exploration of the implications of the potential Pareto improvement criterion. The effect of a project on social welfare (or, at least, on 'economic efficiency', regarded as one dimension of social welfare) has been measured by the sum of its effects on the welfare of individuals. An individual's loss or gain as a result of a project has been measured by the increase or decrease in his money income that, in combination with the project, would leave him just as well off—in his own estimation—as he would have been in the absence of the project. In other words, we have used *individuals' valuations.*

In some cases, market prices provide good measures of individuals' valuations of changes in their consumption of goods. Thus the effects of a project may often be valued, for the purposes of a cost-benefit analysis, by using market prices. (See Section 7.5.) In other cases, market prices do not *directly* reveal individuals' marginal valuations of goods. The cost-benefit analyst must then deduce these valuations from whatever evidence is available. As we have seen, there are many varied and often ingenious ways in which such deductions can be made; the resulting estimates of marginal valuations may have no obvious relationship to any conventional market prices. (See Chapter 11.) Nonetheless, the underlying principle of valuation is a 'market' one; we are valuing how much people *would be willing to pay* for goods if, by some means or other, they were called upon to pay for what they consume.

Now clearly this is not the only principle upon which social valuations could be made. Valuations are expressed, or revealed, not only by people acting as private individuals but also through the political system, both directly (for example, through people's voting behaviour) and indirectly, through the agency of decision-makers. So far our approach has been to use the values expressed by private individuals to *prescribe* how collective decisions *ought to be made.*

In this chapter we shall explore the significance of valuations expressed through the political system and, in particular, valuations expressed by decision-makers. We shall investigate how these valuations might be inferred, and how they might be incorporated into a cost-benefit analysis.

13.2.   The limitations of the potential Pareto improvement criterion

In principle, cost-benefit analysis *could* be more and no less than the application of the potential Pareto improvement criterion. The desired end-product of a cost-benefit analysis would be a measure of the sum by which the total gains made by individuals as a result of a project exceeded or fell short of the total losses. 'Gains' and 'losses' would be measured in money terms and by reference to the preferences of the individuals affected. This approach to cost-benefit analysis does, however, involve some important difficulties.

Should individuals' valuations be accepted by society?

Governments may feel that in certain circumstances individuals' valuations ought not to be taken account of in public decision-making; and this judgement may reflect deep-seated beliefs in the community as a whole. The benefits that some good confers on society are argued to be something different in principle from the benefits that individuals perceive themselves to receive from it. (Goods with this alleged property are sometimes called *merit goods*.)

For example, many people assert that the consumption of education has a 'merit' that its consumers are not able to perceive. Or, in reverse, the non-medical consumption of narcotic drugs has 'demerit'. Most people would probably agree that for someone to begin to consume heroin for fun is not in that person's best interests; and this judgement would be unaltered by the known fact that some people *choose* to consume heroin. It would be absurd, one might then argue, to value an increase in the consumption of heroin by reference to its (black) market price.

The analyst should not, however, be too ready to conclude that governments subscribe to 'merit good' arguments. Often what on first hearing seem to be assertions that individuals' valuations ought not to be taken account of turn out to be arguments about the existence of external effects, or about the distribution of income.

For example, a policy-maker may maintain that the social value of university education ought not to be measured by the willingness of students to pay for it.

Further discussion may reveal that what he has in mind is the idea that university education confers benefits on people other than the students themselves. Taxpayers will benefit if university education increases the future money incomes, and hence tax payments, of students. Less easily quantifiable is the proposition that 'educated' people contribute to national political and cultural life in a way that other people value. These are not arguments for overruling individual valuations but only for seeking information about how individuals value these external effects.

Or it may be that the policy-maker is arguing that society ought to take account of the effects of university education on the distribution of income. Because a rich person is willing to pay more than a poor person for education, it should not be inferred that educating the rich is socially more valuable than educating the poor. This is an issue that we shall return to in Chapter 14. It will be argued in that chapter that there is an important difference between a belief that the distribution of income ought to be changed and a belief that people's preferences do not always correspond to their best interests. (This latter belief is the merit good case.)

But despite these reservations, it is undeniable that in some circumstances governments do decide that individuals' valuations ought not to be taken account of in public decision-making.

The practical limits of analysis

In principle, provided that people are capable of making the relevant choices, for *any* (small) change in an individual's circumstances there is a money figure that measures his valuation of the change. But this is not to say that the analyst is always able to discover what this figure is. Chapter 11 showed that there are many ways of setting out to discover individuals' valuations, but these are not always successful. Discovering facts requires time, effort and ingenuity as well as more material resources, all of which are scarce, and therefore costly, goods. Very often the analyst is forced to conclude that he does not know how individuals value some of the effects of a project. Perhaps he knows a way to find out, but it is too costly to be worthwhile. Or perhaps at present no one knows of a satisfactory way. A cost-benefit analysis that uses only the potential Pareto improvement criterion will often end with some gaps in its coverage of costs and benefits.

Responses to these difficulties: the Paretian approach

The most enthusiastic advocates of what we have called the 'Paretian approach' (see Section 7.4) deny that these difficulties are real ones.[1]

Cost benefit analysis, they argue, is about the application of the potential Pareto improvement criterion, or the measurement of changes in economic efficiency. There can, therefore, be no question of 'replacing' or 'overruling' individuals' valuations *within a cost-benefit analysis* on the grounds that economic efficiency is not desirable. A politician or a citizen might legitimately judge say, that the merit good characteristics of an education project outweighed its unfavourable effect on economic efficiency. But, it is argued, cost-benefit analysis is not the proper framework for taking account of judgements of this kind.

An analyst's lack of knowledge of individuals' valuations presents a rather more serious problem, for it means that a complete cost-benefit analysis, according to the potential Pareto improvement criterion, cannot be produced. The purist would argue that the analyst should leave matters at this point and report that he is unable to discharge his task.[2] He should value those effects that he is able to and then simply report which of the costs and benefits of a project he has been unable to value.

Responses to these difficulties: the decision-making approach

The exponents of the Paretian approach argue that projects may have effects that are important to society but which the analyst should not put money values on—either because these effects concern dimensions of social welfare other than economic efficiency or because the analyst does not know how individuals value them. But although the analyst may leave matters here, the decision-maker cannot. The decision-maker cannot refuse to express judgements about the relative importance of economic efficiency and merit good arguments. Nor can be refuse to judge the social values of goods on the grounds of lack of information. It is his job to choose between alternatives. Just as choice by an individual reveals some-thing about his preferences, so choice by a decision-maker implies some judgement about social values. If cost-benefit analysis is viewed as part of a decision-making process, the analyst may be called on to assist the decision-maker in making these judgements or, at least, to clarify the implications of alternative judgements.

13.3.   Inferring decision-makers' valuations

In previous chapters it has been shown how individuals' valuations of changes in their consumption of goods may be inferred from observations of the choices they make. In an analogous way, it is possible to infer decision-makers' valuations of changes in social cirmumstances from the choices they make between alternative courses of public action.

Before considering how to infer decision-makers' valuations, let us recall how cost-benefit analysts have set about inferring individuals' valuations. Investigators have begun by identifying situations in which individuals make choices (for example, choices between alternative modes of transport—see Section 11.2). They have then made assump-tions about which entities involved in the choice problem were 'goods' or 'bads'—to which individuals attach values, positive or negative; and which entities had no such significance. (Choices between modes of transport were assumed to be determined only by relative travelling times and relative money outlays, with travelling time having a constant, though unknown, money value.) Finally, analysis of individuals' choices within the framework imposed by the assumptions has produced estimates of individuals' valuations of the goods and bads in the problem (in our example, the money value of travelling time).

Decision-makers' valuations can be investigated in a similar way. One needs to identify situations in which decision-makers must choose between alternatives and then to make suitable assumptions about the objectives that guide these choices.

To clarify ideas, consider valuations of medical care services made by public decision-makers.

This example is chosen because the method of using individuals' valuations to guide social choice runs into particular difficulties when choices have to be made about the supply of medical care. First, it is often alleged that the provision of medical care generates important external effects of a sort that is very difficult to measure—*interpersonal external effects*. Such an external effect exists when one person considers himself to be better off (or worse off) simply from knowing that someone else is consuming some good, even though this consumption has no physical effect on the first person. Charitable propensities—the willingness to incur personal costs so as to confer benefits on others—are a manifestation of interpersonal external effects. Although such effects are not peculiar to the case of medical care, it is a historical fact that helping others to consume medical care has been a particularly common form of charitable activity. The problems involved in attaching individuals' valuations to this external effect can easily be imagined. Further, many people argue that medical care has merit good characteristics; individuals' valuations are not necessarily relevant for guiding social choices. (Since very little is known about the magnitude of interpersonal external effects, the dividing line between 'merit good' arguments and 'external effects' arguments, though clear in principle, is far from easy to draw in practice.)

If one wishes to deduce how decision-makers value different aspects of medical care, one must identify situations in which they have to make choices. One such situation is that faced by physicians and hospital administrators when they have to allocate the scarce resources of hospitals (beds, physicians' time, nurses' time and so on) between the competing demands of patients with different medical conditions. No health care service is able to provide as much care as people are capable of benefiting from, nor is it likely that any service ever will. Medical conditions that are unpleasant or uncomfortable but not dangerous are not always treated immediately or even at all. Let us consider the way in which health service decision-makers allocate resources between the treatment of two such conditions, which we may call conditions 1 and 2.

The next stage is to make some assumptions about decision-makers' perceptions of the problem. It seems plausible to assume that a decision-maker (the singular noun is used for convenience) sees his role as being to maximize the social value of the medical care provided by that part of the health service for which he is responsible, subject to a constraint on the amount of resources available to him. This constraint is imposed by higher level decision-makers (the government) who take decisions about the allocation of resources to the health service as a whole and, within the service, between its constituent sectors.

The phrase 'the social value of medical care' is rather vague. If we are to proceed we must make some assumptions about what 'outputs' of the medical care industry are regarded by the decision-maker as having social value. It is tempting to identify the outputs of a health service with its *activities*—so many surgical operations of different kinds, so many consultations between patients and general practitioners, and so on. It is more appropriate, however, to think of these activities as the means by which the true outputs of a health service are produced. Ultimately, the outputs that have social value are improvements in people's states of health. Thus a natural way to measure the outputs of those activities which are concerned with a particular medical condition is the number of patients cured (that is, the number of people who do not suffer from the condition but who, if they had not received medical care, would have). This, of course, is a very crude measure, and one which would be appropriate only to certain medical conditions. For some medical care activities, for example, the ultimate objective is not to cure but to reduce the pain and discomfort caused by an illness. For the purpose of exposition, let us take our two medical conditions, 1 and 2, to be ones that are curable. The outputs of medical care activities concerned with these conditions can be measured in two units—the number of cases of condition 1 that are cured (q_1) and the number of cases of condition 2 that are cured (q_2). We shall assume that our decision-maker regards every case of a given condition that is cured as having the same social value as every other case cured. Thus his objective is to maximize the 'social value of medical care', V, the value of which is given by the expression

$$V = a_1q_1 + a_2q_2. \qquad 13.1$$

a_1 is the (constant) social value of each 'condition 1' cure; a_2 is the (constant) social value of each 'condition 2' cure.

It is convenient to rewrite this expression as

$$V = a_1 \left(q_1 + \frac{a_2}{a_1} q_2 \right).$$ 13.2

The expression within the brackets is a measure of the social value of the output of our sector of the health service, measured in units of 'condition 1' cures. It is an *index* of output which is based on judgements about the *relative* social values of the two outputs q_1 and q_2 but which contains no judgement about the social value of medical care relative to that of other goods. (If a_1 and a_2 were both multiplied by the same constant, the value of this index of output would be unchanged.) It is convenient to write the decision-maker's objective in this way because to maximize the social value of output (V) is to maximize the 'quantity' of output (as measured by the index)—and vice versa. Thus the decision-maker's choices will not be affected by his absolute, or money, valuations of the two outputs. They will be affected only by his relative valuation of them.

The decision-maker's problem is to allocate a fixed budget (given to him by the government) between various activities concerned with the treatment of conditions 1 and 2. The information that he needs if he is to make a rational decision can be summarized in two *cost functions*, one for each condition. The cost function for a condition is a statement of the minimum cost that must be incurred to produce each possible rate of 'output' of cures of that condition. It is plausible to suppose that this function will be one of increasing marginal cost. Cures can be produced in various ways, some of which are more costly than others, but the least costly ways are not necessarily suitable for all cases. For example, some cases may be suitable for treatment with drugs, while others may require surgery of varying degrees of complexity. For some conditions it is possible to increase the number of cures produced per year by running screening programmes. A rational decision-maker (given that he subscribes to the objectives we have attributed to him) would use whatever money he allocated to the treatment of a particular condition on those activities that produced the maximum number of cures. The more money that has already been allocated to producing one kind of cure, the greater (we assume) is the additional cost of producing an additional cure. For every amount of money allocated to producing cures for a given condition, there is a *marginal cost of cures*—the additional cost of an additional cure, or the cost-saving that could be achieved by producing one fewer cure.

A rational decision-maker would allocate his budget between the treatment of the conditions in such a way that the additional social value that could be generated by spending an extra £1 on the treatment of condition 1 was just equal to the additional social value that could be generated by spending an extra £1 on the treatment of condition 2. (This is equivalent to using a shadow price for the constrained input, money.) If the marginal cost of cures is MC_1 for condition 1 and MC_2 for condition 2, an extra £1 spent on treating condition 1 would yield a_1/MC_1 in additional social value while an extra £1 spent on treating condition 2 would yield a_2/MC_2. Rationality requires that

$$\frac{a_1}{MC_1} = \frac{a_2}{MC_2}$$

or

$$\frac{a_2}{a_1} = \frac{MC_2}{MC_1}. \qquad\qquad 13.3$$

For any allocation of his budget that the decision-maker chooses, the values of MC_1 and MC_2 can be calculated. Thus the value of a_2/a_1 can be inferred. The decision-maker's choice has revealed his implicit relative valuation of the two outputs.

To put this another way, the decision-maker has revealed his judgement about the most appropriate index of the output of the medical care services for which he is responsible. This index, it will be remembered, is

$$q_1 + \frac{a_2}{a_1}q_2.$$

He has not revealed any judgement about the absolute social value of the outputs—that is, about their social value relative to that of other goods. The reason is that this decision-maker is not required to choose whether the community should have more medical care and higher taxes or less care and less taxes. This, we assumed at the outset, was the job of the government.

The government reveals its valuation of medical care in its decisions about how much money to allocate to the health service. In our present illustrative example we have assumed that the government decides how much money should be spent on the treatment of conditions 1 and 2 and then delegates to the decision-maker the task of spending this money in the way that maximizes the social value of the treatments. Since the government has, implicitly, delegated to the decision-maker the job of judging the relative social values of the two outputs, we may infer that the government is willing to subscribe to these judgements. That is, the government is willing to regard the decision-maker's index of the output of medical care services as appropriate.

The government's objective, in choosing how much money to allocate to the decision-maker, is (presumably) to maximize the amount by which the social value of medical care exceeds the costs of producing it. We may assume that the social costs of medical care services are accurately measured by their financial costs. All this implies that the government should allocate a sum of money to the decision-maker such that the social value of the additional output that he could produce with an additional £1 is just equal to £1. If, given the budget the decision-maker has been allocated by the government, the marginal cost of a 'condition 1' cure is MC_1, an additional £1 could produce additional output worth a_1/MC_1, where a_1 is the social value of a cure. The government's decision thus implies that $a_1/MC_1 = 1$ or that $a_1 = MC_1$. It has revealed an implicit judgement about the value of medical care services relative to the value of other goods.

13.4. Postulated values

In principle there is no reason why an analyst should not seek to discover decision-makers' valuations by a much more direct method— by simply asking. Decision-makers' valuations derived in this direct way, rather than by inference from a study of their decisions, are sometimes known as *postulated values.* In practice it is not at all easy for anyone to think in totally abstract terms about the relative social values of different goods, and it is unlikely that a decision-maker would be completely confident about the appropriateness of a valuation he had postulated until he had some idea of its implications for policy. But on the other hand people typically do have some ability to think of values independently of policies. We shall argue shortly that the best way to arrive at decision-makers' considered judgements about the values of goods is by an iterative chain of thought, involving successively the postulation of values and the working out of the implications of these values for policy. For the present, however, it is sufficient to recognize the existence of this direct source of valuations.

This source is such an obvious one that the reader may wonder why a similarly direct approach was not considered in our discussion of the problems of inferring individuals' valuations (in Chapter 11). If the analyst does not know how individuals value particular goods, why does he not simply ask them? The problem with this approach is that normally, private individuals have little incentive to reflect or to seek relevant information before answering questions of this kind; according to how the respondent believes his answers will be used, there may even be an incentive for him to answer dishonestly. This problem is virtually inevitable, since people are being asked to express preferences without committing themselves to act according to these preferences.[3] In a literal sense, then, the analyst is being given *irresponsible* answers to his questions.

Valuations postulated by decision-makers, however, are responsible ones. Valuations are used in cost-benefit analysis to guide choices made by governments and public agencies. A decision-maker's postulated valuation of a good for whose production he is responsible implies a commitment to act in accordance with this valuation.

Consider again the example discussed in Section 13.3 of the problem of allocating resources to, and between, the treatment of two medical conditions. It was shown that any decision by the government about how much money to allocate to the treatment of these conditions implied a judgement about the social value of 'cures'. If, given the government's decision, the marginal cost of producing an additional cure of condition 1 was MC_1, the government implicitly was judging the social value of each cure to be MC_1. Now suppose that the government were to assert that the true social value of a cure was rather higher than this. This would imply a judgement that the budget allowed for the treatment of our two conditions ought to be increased (up to the point where the marginal cost of cures rose to a level equal to the government's postulated value of them). If the government were not prepared to act in this way it would be admitting its own inconsistency.

13.5. Consistency

The analysis of decision-makers' valuations may reveal inconsistencies. The postulated values asserted by a decision-maker may be inconsistent with the values implied by the choices he makes in practice. Or the valuations implied by one decision may be inconsistent with those implied by another.

We cannot assume, as a matter of fact, that decision-makers always will be consistent or rational in the sense that their decisions will always be in favour of the best available means of achieving the social objectives to which they are committed. As was argued at the very beginning of this book, project appraisal is concerned with prescribing procedures that will ensure that public decisions are 'rational' in this sense. There would be no purpose in doing this unless one believed that, without such procedures, public decisions might be irrational. Inconsistencies arise in practice because public decisions are often too complex for the decision-maker, without the aid of analysis, to be clear about the implications of alternative choices. It should be remembered, too, that the single 'decision-maker' is only a convenient fiction. Most public decisions are taken by groups of people. Even if each member of a group is himself always consistent in the social valuations he uses to appraise alternative courses of action, if different members use different valuations the group's joint decisions may be inconsistent with each other. (The 'paradox of voting' is one very simple and well-known example of this problem.)[4]

The revelation of inconsistencies is a prime function of the analysis of decision-makers' valuations. It might seem that, since decision-makers' valuations are in a sense arbitrary (there is no external standard against which their rightness or wrongness may be judged), consistency is of doubtful merit. But a strong case can be made to the contrary.

Consider first the possibility of inconsistency between the valuations implied by decisions and the valuations postualted directly by decision-makers. The elucidation of decision-makers' valuations may be seen as part of a dialogue between decision-maker and analyst, through which the former clarifies his own judgements. On the one hand, decisions may have been made in the past without a full awareness of their implications. On realizing that these decisions imply social valuations to which he does not subscribe, the decision-maker may wish to revise his policies for the future. On the other hand, a statement in the abstract, postulating a social valuation, may be made without a full understanding of its implications for policy. On realizing what these implications are, a decision-maker may wish to revise the values he has postulated. So the search for consistency is to be seen as a thought process on the part of the decision-maker, with the aim of making his decisions and his objectives mutually consistent.

Now consider the possibility of inconsistencies between the valuations implied by different decisions.

To make the discussion concrete, let us return to the example introduced in Section 13.3. In that example, a decision-maker was responsible for allocating a given budget between various activities, each of which led to the production of one of two outputs, q_1 and q_2. (These were numbers of cures of two medical conditions.) We considered a single decision-maker who, we assumed, sought to maximize the social value of medical care. This social value, V, was (in his judgement) given by the equation

$$V = a_1 \left(q_1 + \frac{a_2}{a_1} q_2 \right). \qquad 13.4$$

Now suppose instead that the health service is organized in such a way that *two* decision-makers are responsible for determining how much is spent on producing these two outputs. One decision-maker, X, is responsible for one geographical area; the other, X', is responsible for another. Each is allocated a budget by the government which he must spend on treating the two conditions within his area. Suppose that decision-maker X subscribes to the judgements represented in Expression 13.4; the social value of a cure of a case of condition 2, relative to that of a cure of condition 1, is a_2/a_1. He believes that this judgement is the right one, not only for his own area, but also for the area for which X' is responsible.

X' however, disagrees. He believes that the social value, V', of the two outputs is given by the equation

$$V' = a'_1 \left(q_1 + \frac{a'_2}{a'_1} q_2 \right).$$ 13.5

His relative valuation of the two outputs, a'_2/a'_1, is not the same as X's. X', let us say, has the lower relative valuation of cures of condition 2. That is,

$$\frac{a_2}{a_1} > \frac{a'_2}{a'_1}.$$ 13.6

Like X, X' believes that his own judgement is the right one for both areas.

Each decision-maker will, in his own area, allocate his budget between the production of the two outputs so that the ratio of the marginal cost of a 'condition 2' cure to that of a 'condition 1' cure is equal to the relative value of the two outputs. That is, so that

$$\frac{MC_2}{MC_1} = \frac{a_2}{a_1} \text{ and } \frac{MC'_2}{MC'_1} = \frac{a'_2}{a'_1}$$ 13.7

(see pp. 184–5 and Expression 13.3 above). MC_1 and MC'_1 are the marginal costs of 'condition 1' cures in the respective areas; MC_2 and MC'_2 are defined similarly. Combining these deductions with Expression 13.6, it follows that

$$\frac{MC_2}{MC_1} > \frac{MC'_2}{MC'_1}$$ 13.8

We know that this outcome is inconsistent in the sense that the allocation of money between the production of the two outputs is based on one set of judgements about social values in one area and on another set in the other area. It might seem that this conclusion is unhelpful. Each decision-maker has acted consistently with his own judgements; each is convinced he is right and the other is wrong; and there is no way in which a third party can determine objectively which of the two is right (if, indeed, either is).

But, nonetheless, the outcome of this inconsistency is inefficient in an unambiguous sense. It would be possible to reallocate resources in a way that *both* decision-makers would agree to be an improvement. Decision-maker X', it will be remembered, attached the lower relative value to 'condition 2' cures. Suppose that he were induced to produce one more such cure, at a financial cost of MC'_2. Given that he has a fixed budget, the opportunity cost would be that MC'_2/MC'_1 fewer 'condition 1' cures would be produced in his area. Suppose that, at the same time, X were induced to produce one less 'condition 2' cure. This would allow him to produce MC_2/MC_1 more 'condition 1' cures. In the two areas together, the number of 'condition 2' cures produced would remain the same; there would be a net change in the number of 'condition 1' cures of

$$\frac{MC_2}{MC_1} - \frac{MC'_2}{MC'_1}. \qquad\qquad 13.9$$

A glance at Expression 13.8 shows that this net change must be an increase. Both decision-makers, and indeed anyone who believes that cures have a positive social value, would judge that social welfare would be increased by such a reallocation.

In general, whenever different decisions are being taken by reference to different valuations of the same goods, there will be inefficiency. That is, it will be possible to produce unambiguous improvements in the allocation of resources. It is, then, more efficient for a number of independent decision-makers to take decisions by using a common, agreed set of valuations of goods than for each to use his own valuations. That inconsistency implies inefficiency is the essence of the case for consistency.

13.6.   Decision-makers' valuations, cost-effectiveness analysis, and cost-benefit analysis

Having considered what decision-makers' valuations are, and how they can be discovered, it is now time to consider how they can be used in cost-benefit analysis. This requires little more than a reinterpretation of the content of the preceding sections of this chapter. This should not be surprising, for there is a clear circularity in the idea of using decision-makers' valuations to determine decisions when these valuations are themselves implied by decisions. Ultimately, we can expect no more than that decisions are mutually consistent.

We may begin by examining a form of analysis which is often thought of as a halfway house on the road to cost-benefit analysis. This is *cost-effectiveness analysis*. Its underlying principle is that it is possible to make a clear separation between the costs of a project and its benefits (or effectiveness). 'Costs'—which may be purely financial costs or, more broadly, social costs—can be measured in money units, either by using market prices or, in the case of some social costs, by inferring individuals' valuations in other ways. 'Benefits' cannot, as a matter of practice, or should not, as a matter of principle, be measured in money by reference to individuals' valuations. Cost-effectiveness analysis tries to show how a given level of benefit can be achieved at the minimum cost, or to show how the maximum benefit can be achieved at some given level of cost. The keynote of both of these problems is that it is not necessary to attach any explicit money value to benefits.

One simple form of cost-effectiveness has been discussed in this book from the very beginning. This concerns choosing between mutually exclusive ways of achieving a particular, very clearly defined, benefit. A typical example was the choice between alternative locations for a hospital, where the objective was to achieve the benefits of a hospital of particular characteristics at the minimum financial cost. (See Problem 3, Chapter 3.) An example that has been the subject of a published study is the choice between hemodialysis (that is, treatment by artificial kidneys) and transplantation as means of prolonging the lives of people with chronic renal disease.[5]

Cost-effectiveness analysis becomes more difficult—and more illuminating—the less narrowly 'benefits' are defined and hence the wider the range of alternatives that can be subjected to analysis. Consider the example introduced in Section 13.3, of the problem faced by a decision-maker of allocating a fixed budget between a number of medical care activities. In the original discussion we worked backwards from the allocation chosen by the decision-maker to an inference about his valuations of outputs. If instead we look at the example as a decision problem, to be analysed on behalf of the decision-maker, it is a problem in cost-effectiveness analysis. The decision-maker can state his objective as being to maximize a particular index of output subject to a budget constraint. (See Expression 13.2 and the related discussion (pp. 183–4).) The index is a measure of 'benefit'; the problem is to achieve the maximum benefit at a given cost.

It was shown in Section 13.3 that the solution to this problem was independent of the decision-makers' judgements about the social values in money units of the outputs he produced (that is, of judgements about their social values relative to those of other goods). This underlines the point that the problem is one in cost-effectiveness analysis; benefits need not be valued in money units. It was also shown, however, that the decision (by 'the government') to impose a particular cost constraint on the decision-maker *did* imply a money valuation of the output he was producing—although the valuation was the government's and not his.

This way of looking at the problem treats the decision as to how much to produce of a number of socially valuable outputs in two distinct stages—the imposition of a cost constraint, which implies a money valuation of output, followed by a cost-effectiveness analysis.

An alternative approach, which would lead to precisely the same outcome, would be to compress these two stages into one. The government would state explicitly its money valuation of an output. (If, as in the original example, an index of output was required, the government might agree with the lower level decision-makers on an

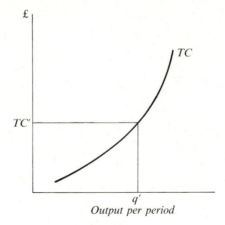

Fig. 13.1a

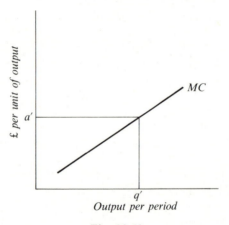

Fig. 13.1b

appropriate index.) Decision-makers would then be instructed to act consistently with this valuation. Figures 13.1a and 13.1b show why the two approaches are equivalent to one another. The curve TC in Figure 13.1a represents the total cost of producing each possible rate of output of some socially valuable good; the curve MC in Figure 13.1b represents the marginal cost of each rate of output (on the same horizontal scale). In a two-stage decision-making process, the government selects some level of total cost, TC', which is given as a budget allocation to a lower level decision-maker. His job is to maximize output subject to this budget constraint. The maximum output he can produce is q', which implies a marginal cost of a'. The decision-maker is acting *as if* he attached a value of a' to each unit of output and were seeking to maximize the surplus of benefits (valued in this way) over costs. Thus the same outcome—an output of q'

produced at a total cost of TC'—could be achieved by the government's postulating directly that output had a social value of a' per unit and then instructing the decision-maker to appraise all projects using this postulated value.

The appraisal of projects by using money valuations of benefits that have been postulated by the government or by decision-makers can be regarded as a form of cost-benefit analysis. This form of cost-benefit analysis is distinguished from the kind that has been discussed in previous chapters by the fact that it does not use individuals' valuations exclusively. For some (though not necessarily for all) entities in the appraisal, individuals' valuations are set aside and replaced by decision-makers' valuations. The effect of this is to change in a fundamental way the meanings of the words 'cost' and 'benefit'. The statement that the benefits of a project exceed its costs no longer implies that the project represents a potential Pareto improvement. Instead it implies that, in the judgement of the decision-maker, the project ought to be undertaken.

This kind of cost-benefit analysis has a number of pitfalls peculiar to itself, which the analyst must be careful if he is to avoid. Within the same cost-benefit analysis, two very different kinds of valuation are typically being used—individuals' valuations and decision-makers' valuations. (In principle, all the valuations are the decision-maker's. but for some goods he has judged that they should be valued as individuals value them.) Mixing together two different kinds of valuation leads to the dangers of inconsistency and double counting.

Each good which enters into a particular cost-benefit analysis must consistently be valued *either* by reference to individuals' valuations *or* by reference to the decision-maker's. It is surprisingly easy in practice to use one type of valuation for a particular good at one stage of an analysis and then to use the other type of valuation for the same good at another stage. It is also easy to double count by using *both* types of valuation for the same item of benefit as if there were two rather than one benefit to be counted. To give just one example of the sort of problem that can arise, consider the use of 'observed demand curves' to evaluate the effects of price changes. Areas to the left of such curves may measure individuals' valuations, not only of direct effects of price changes, but also of a whole array of 'induced' or 'indirect' effects. It is quite possible that a decision-maker would want to value some of these indirect effects according to his own valuations while using individuals' valuations for others. It is far from easy to disentangle a problem of this kind. The analyst, then, must always be on his guard against error when using different kinds of valuation in the same analysis.

Problems

1. An unwanted by-product of coal-fired electricity generating stations is the grit and dust which is carried in the waste gas produced by burning coal.[6] By installing equipment of various kinds it is possible to prevent greater or lesser quantities of this grit and dust being emitted to the atmosphere. It is relatively cheap to 'arrest' the largest particles of grit, but as the size of particle that is to be arrested decreases, costs rise very steeply. This can be expressed as a cost schedule, relating levels of efficiency to the cost of the equipment necessary to achieve each level. 'Efficiency' is defined by the proportion of the total mass of grit and dust produced that is arrested (the remainder passing to the atmosphere). By far the most important element of cost is the capital cost of the equipment, but there also are some recurrent costs associated with using it. Table (i) shows the total cost of installing and using, at a certain type of power station, equipment of a range of different levels of efficiency. These costs are expressed as 'annual equivalents', using a discount rate of 10 per cent and on the assumption that the life of equipment is 40 years. (Thus, for example, the stream of costs associated with 94·0 per cent efficient equipment has the same present value in year 0 (£278 000) as a stream of costs of £28 400 per year in each of years 1 to 40.)

Table (i)

Efficiency of equipment (% of grit and dust arrested)	Cost (annual equivalent: £'000 per year)
94·0	28·4
95·0	30·3
96·0	32·9
97·0	36·3
98·0	40·9
98·2	42·0
98·4	43·2
98·6	44·7
98·8	46·5
98·9	47·5
99·0	48·6
99·1	49·8
99·2	51·4
99·3	53·5
99·4	56·2
99·5	59·8

In a certain small area there are two power stations, A and B, each of which is of such a size that the costs shown in Table (i) apply to it. If station A had no grit-arresting equipment at all, it would produce and emit 8000 metric tons of grit and dust per year. Station B, which burns coal which has been mined at a different pit, would emit only 4000 metric tons per year. Both stations have only very primitive equipment for arresting grit and dust. The government department that is responsible for pollution control decides that both should install new and much more efficient equipment. It then has to decide precisely how efficient the new equipment should be. It is decided that a 'reasonable' level of efficiency for grit-arresting equipment is 98·8 per cent and the electricity generating authority is instructred to install equipment of this efficiency at each of the power stations.

The officials who were responsible for these decisions agree that the mass of grit and dust emitted to the atmosphere per period of time is a good unit in which to measure the quantity of the 'public bad' of air pollution caused by power stations. They also agree that the marginal social value of a reduction in the quantity of this 'bad' is, for any given locality, constant (that is, independent of the current quantity of air pollution). The two power stations are so close together that they can be regarded as being in the same locality.

(*i*) Is the decision that power station A should install 98·8 per cent efficient equipment consistent with the decision that station B should install equipment with the same level of efficiency?

(*ii*) What marginal social value of preventing the emission of grit and dust is implied by each of the two decisions?

(*iii*) Suggest a pair of decisions about the levels of efficiency of the equipment to be installed at the two power stations that, according to the officials' own judgements, is clearly to be preferred to the decisions they actually took.

2. Among the projects currently being considered by a highway authority are the following three projects. Each is designed with the sole aim of reducing the number of people killed in road accidents. (For simplicity, only fatal accidents will be considered; accidents involving injuries but not deaths will be ignored.)

Project A is to build a set of pedestrian subways at a busy road junction. This project has a capital cost of £100 000 (to be borne in year 0) and would reduce the expected number of deaths in road accidents by 0·6 per year from year 1 onwards. It would have no significant effects on the time taken by people to make trips (whether on foot or in vehicles).

Project B and project A are mutually exclusive. Project B is to install pedestrian crossings at the same road junction. The capital cost would be only £5000 (to be borne in year 0). It would reduce the expected number of deaths in road accidents by 0·4 per year from year 1 onwards. It would have the undesirable side-effect of imposing delays on road traffic. The money value of the resulting increase in the total amount of time spent by people travelling would be £3500 per year. (There would be no significant effect on the total number of trips made by road users.)

Project C is completely independent of the other two. It is to build a length of crash barrier along the central reservation of a dual carriageway road. Its capital cost is £150 000 (borne in year 0) and it would reduce the expected number of deaths in road accidents by 0·8 per year.

The highway authority does not want decisions about the allocation of resources to improve road safety to be made by reference to individuals' valuations of changes in their risks of death. Instead, it wishes to use decision-makers' own valuations of road safety. The authority's decision-makers assert that the social value of an increase in road safety is given by the reduction in the expected number of deaths multiplied by some constant (the value of a prevented death). The 'value of a prevented death' is a decision-makers' valuation, and is the same no matter whose lives are at risk.

(*i*) Suppose that the highway authority chooses to undertake project B but not to undertake project C. Is this policy consistent with what is known about the authority's objectives and, if so, with what range of decision-makers' valuations of prevented deaths is it consistent?

(*ii*) Suppose that the authority chooses to undertake projects A and C and repeat the above exercise.

(*iii*) Suppose that the authority chooses to undertake only project C and repeat the above exercise.

(Use a 50-year time horizon and a discount rate of 10 per cent. Assume that the 'value of a prevented death' is constant over time. Thus, for example, if one death prevented in year 0 has a social value of £x in that year, a death prevented in year 1 is equivalent to a social benefit of £x occurring in year 1; the present value in year 0 of this benefit is, of course, rather less than £x).

3. Problem 3 of Chapter 3 concerned a choice between two alternative locations for a hospital. (See p. 40.) This problem required a financial appraisal of the two alternatives. But at the very beginning of this book we questioned whether financial appraisal was appropriate for such a problem. (See p. 7). One of the two locations was more accessible than the other for patients and visitors; thus to choose the less accessible rather than the more accessible site would be to impose costs on members of the community. A health authority that is responsible to the community ought, it can be argued, to take account of these costs by basing its decision on a cost-benefit analysis.

It is fairly easy to take account of these costs if the number of trips made to and from the hospital by patients and visitors (per period of time) is independent of the location of the hospital. All that is needed is a valuation of the difference between the opportunity costs of trips made to the hospital if it were at one site and the equivalent costs for the other site.

But suppose that the number of trips made to hospital is greater, the more accessible the hospital is to potential patients. Consider a particular treatment, for some minor ailment, that is provided at hospitals to out-patients. Patients are referred to hospitals by their G.P.s. It may be assumed that all people who are capable of benefiting (in a medical sense) from the treatment are offered hospital treatment (provided, of course, that they have first consulted their G.P.s). Whether a patient takes advantage of this offer, however, is for him to choose. (People cannot be compelled to go to hospital.) Although, at the hospital, treatment is supplied free of charge, attending hospital can involve quite large costs for the patient. These are the costs of travelling to and from the hospital (direct money outlays and the value of time spent travelling) and the opportunity cost of the time spent waiting for and receiving treatment. Some patients choose not to incur these costs and not to receive the treatment they have been offered.

Suppose that, if the hospital were built in the more accessible location, the (average) cost to a patient of visiting the hospital for treatment would be £1·20 per visit. If the hospital were built in the less accessible location, this cost would be £1·50 per visit. In the former case, the number of visits made by people receiving the particular treatment we are considering would be 10 000 per year; in the latter case, the number would be 8500 per year. (It may be assumed that the number of people consulting G.P.s would be the same, whichever location were chosen.) The marginal cost to the health authority of providing the treatment is £2·00 per visit by a patient. (This marginal cost is constant in the range 8000–10 000 visits per year.)

A cost-benefit analysis is being made of the choice between the two locations for the hospital. One element in this analysis is the net social cost that would result from the opportunity cost to patients of receiving this treatment being £1·50 rather than £1·20, and from the number of visits per year being 8500 rather than 10 000.

Evaluate this net social loss, given (in turn) each of the following two alternative approaches to the valuation of health care:

(*i*) Individuals' valuations are to be used throughout the cost-benefit analysis. The analysis as a whole will rest on the potential Pareto improvement criterion alone.

(*ii*) The health authority's decision-makers do not believe that the consumers of medical care services are good judges of the 'true' value of these services to themselves (that is to the consumers). Valuations of medical care services used in the cost-benefit analysis are to be valuations postulated by the decision-makers. They postulate that the act of receiving treatment confers on the patients benefits whose gross social value is £3·80 per visit. (The word 'gross' is used because no deduction has been made either for the costs to the health authority of supplying treatment or for the costs incurred by the patient in getting access to the treatment.) The decision-makers believe, however, that individuals are the best judges of their own welfares in all relevant matters other than the consumption of medical care. Thus all goods in the cost-benefit analysis other than medical care are to be valued by using individuals' valuations.

Notes

[1] See Mishan (1971a), especially Chapters 45–47, and Mishan (1974).

[2] Mishan (1971a), p. 324.

[3] This problem can be overcome to some extent by getting the respondent to react to simulated choice problems. See, for example, Hoinville (1969).

[4] See, for example, the footnote on p. 135 of Nath (1969).

[5] Klarman, Francis and Rosenthal (1968).

[6] This problem is based on a study made by Martin Brookes when he was at the University of York.

Further reading

An attempt to infer decision-makers' valuations of forms of hospital treatment is reported in Lavers (1972). For a discussion of the problems involved in constructing indices of the outputs of a health service, see Culyer *et al* (1971). For a cost-effectiveness analysis of a particular problem of allocating resources within a health service, see Klarman *et al* (1968).

A general and introductory treatment of the application of economic analysis to decision-making in the social services is provided by Williams and Anderson (1975). More advanced are the papers collected in Cooper and Culyer (1973).

14. The Distribution of Income

14.1. Introduction

Most public projects that are subjected to cost-benefit analysis provide gains to some members of the community while imposing losses on others. If the government improves a road at the taxpayers' expense, those people who have a high demand for the road's services gain while other taxpayers lose. If a new airport is built in a remote and lightly populated area rather than in a more accessible and more densely populated one, householders in the latter area gain (noise is not inflicted on them) while air travellers lose. And so on.

Governments and public agencies do, of course, sometimes take decisions that do not require one person's gains to be weighed against another's losses. In our discussions of financial appraisal we considered many decision problems of this kind. If, for example, a public agency has to choose between two alternative methods of producing the same output, and if the financial costs of each method accurately measure the respective social costs, and if the financial costs are to be borne by taxpayers, then it is in the interests of all taxpayers that the less costly method be chosen. (Even in such simple cases, problems can arise if different taxpayers have different MTPRs—see Section 4.2.) But once we move away from the sort of problem that can be handled with the techniques of financial appraisal, we almost inevitably have to face the fact that alternative courses of action have different implications for the distribution of income between members of the community.

So far, we have handled this problem by using the potential Pareto improvement criterion. A project satisfies this criterion if *in principle it is possible* to redistribute money between individuals so that, as a result of the combination of the project and the redistribution of money, at least one member of the community is made better off and no one is made worse off. It does not matter whether these transfers of money take place *in fact*, for the purpose of the potential Pareto improvement criterion is to provide a rule by which one person's gains can be compared with another person's losses. The rule is a very simple one. If a project produces a gain of £1 for some individual, the implications of this for the admissibility of the project are the same whether the gainer is rich or poor, young or old, white or black. 'Social benefits' and 'social costs' are calculated simply by adding up benefits and costs to individuals. (See Section 7.2.)

It will be remembered that one interpretation of cost-benefit analysis, the *Paretian interpretation,* began from the value judgement—or definition—that a cost-benefit analysis was an application of the potential Pareto improvement criterion. (See Section 7.4.) Given this interpretation, there is little more to be said. The potential Pareto improvement criterion provides a means of making statements about a project's contribution to economic efficiency, but it cannot provide any guidance about the desirability or otherwise of a project's effects on the distribution of income. Since, in the framework of this criterion, £1 of additional income has the same significance whoever receives it, any project that simply transferred money between individuals would neither increase nor decrease economic efficiency—which is all that the criterion can measure changes in. There is, then, no way by which the criterion may be used to rank different distributions of the same total income. According to the exponents of the Paretian approach, it is not the job of the cost-benefit analyst to try to evaluate the merits of different distributions of income.

A decision-maker, however, cannot avoid the necessity of choosing between alternatives. If a project provides gains for one group of people at the cost of imposing losses on another, a person who is entrusted with the job of choosing whether or not to undertake the project *must* in some way weigh the one group's gains against the other group's losses. He must, that is, make some judgement about the relative desirability of different distributions of income. If we adopt the decision-making interpretation of cost-benefit analysis, the role of the analyst is to assist the decision-maker to make choices that are consistent with the latter's objectives (see Section 7.3). We cannot then say that the analyst may always ignore distributional issues. He may be called on to assist the decision-maker to take account, in a rational and consistent way, of the effects of projects on the distribution of income. In this chapter we shall consider how this might be done.

14.2. The case for the potential Pareto improvement criterion

To say that a cost-benefit analysis ought to take explicit account of decision-makers' judgements about the relative desirability of different distributions of income is not to say that the potential Pareto improvement criterion is necessarily inadequate. Seen as a rule for choosing whether or not to undertake projects (rather than merely as an indicator of changes in economic efficiency) the criterion implies a particular, and simple, set of distributional judgements. An extra £1 of income has the same significance for social welfare (that is, for what the decision-maker is trying to achieve) irrespective of who in the community receives it. And if any one person gains £1 while any other loses £1, there is no change in social welfare.

There is a strong prima facie case that a government, in choosing whether or not to undertake individual projects ought, if it is to be consistent, to make these particular judgements. (The outline of this case has been sketched out already, in Section 7.3). If a £1 gain by one person combined with a £1 loss by another has no effect on social welfare, it is clear that social welfare cannot be increased by transferring income between individuals. This implies that the existing distribution of income cannot be improved by any programme of transfers. It is contrary to common sense to suppose that a government would make this judgement about every conceivable distribution of income. (To do this would be for it to have no views about the relative desirability of different distributions.) But it is much more plausible to argue that a government would make this judgement about the particular distribution of income that currently exists.

In a nation with an efficient tax-collecting service, a government has in its own hands the means to change the distribution of income. If it wishes to make one group of people better off at the expense of another, it can reduce the tax liabilities of the first group and increase those of the second. (Alternatively, it can change the rates of subsidy and benefit payments.) If the government has the power to determine the distribution of income, we must conclude that whatever distribution exists has been *approved* by the government. The government must judge that the marginal social value of income is the same for all members of the community—if it does not, why has it not changed the distribution of income? So, if it is true that the government can transfer income costlessly between individuals, consistency requires it to accept, for the purposes of appraising individual projects, the distributional judgements implied by the potential Pareto improvement criterion.

The great weakness of this line of argument is that it rests on the assumption that 'costless' transfers of income are possible. That is, if the government chooses to make any person £1 better off, it can do this by changing taxes in a way that imposes a total loss on other people of just £1.Unfortunately, no system of taxation is as efficient as this assumption implies.[1] Tax systems require bureaucracies to organize them, and so transfers of income involve administrative costs. In addition, as was shown in Section 8.3, taxes levied on goods impose social costs because they restrict the responsiveness of markets to individuals' preferences. (Income taxes are no exception, since these taxes are levied on the supply of the good 'labour services' and distort the market for this good.) In reality, a transfer of an additional £1 to a relatively poor person might be achieved only by imposing losses totalling, say £1·10 on relatively rich people. (The additional £0·10 is the *excess burden* of tax imposed on the relatively rich.)

To the extent that direct transfers of income are costly, the prevailing distribution of income may not be the one that (in the government's judgement) maximizes social welfare. A gain of £1 by one member of the community may contribute more to social welfare than a similar gain by another. If this is the case, the distributional judgements implied by the potential Pareto improvement criterion are not consistent with the government's conception of social welfare.

(These arguments are analysed in more detail in an appendix to this chapter.)

14.3.   Distributional weights

A cost-benefit analysis can be seen as involving two separate stages. The first is to evaluate, in money units, the gains and losses accruing to or borne by each of the individuals affected by a project. The second is to combine these gains and losses into a single measure of 'changes in social welfare'. It is at this second stage that judgements about how income should be distributed are injected into the analysis. The potential Pareto improvement criterion, which implies that gains and losses should be combined by the simple operation of addition, is one such judgement. The decision-maker, however, may wish to inject a different set of distributional judgements.

The most convenient way to express these judgements is by using *distributional weights*. Suppose that the effect of a project is to produce net gains, measured in money units, of $dy_1, dy_2, \ldots, dy_n$ to each of the members of the community $1, 2, \ldots, n$. (Some of these net gains may, of course, be negative.) We now assert that the net change in social welfare, dW, is a *weighted* sum of these individual gains and losses:

$$dW = v_1 dy_1 + v_2 dy_2 + \ldots + v_n dy_n. \qquad 14.1$$

The v symbols in this expression are distributional weights. They express the relative social values of increases in the incomes of different individuals. A gain of £1 by individual 1, for example, has the same significance for social welfare as a gain of $£v_1/v_2$ by individual 2. (For convenience we may take as a numeraire, or standard of measurement, the social value of additional income to one particular individual—say, individual 1. Then his weight, v_1, would be given a value of unity.) In this framework, the potential Pareto improvement criterion implies merely a particular (though highly convenient) set of distributional weights:

$$v_1 = v_2 = \ldots = v_n = 1. \qquad 14.2$$

This may be called a set of *unitary weights*.

It is only with the decision-making interpretation of cost-benefit analysis that distributional judgements are required (see Section 14.1). The role of distributional weights, then, is to express decision-makers' judgements about the relative social values of increments of income accruing to different individuals. There are many similarities between the idea of distributional weights and the idea of using decision-makers' valuations of goods. Many of the issues involved in inferring and using these weights are similar to those already discussed in Chapter 13. In the following sections we shall consider various possible ways of inferring the distributional weights that are consistent with the judgements of decision-makers.

14.4.   The opportunity cost of redistributive transfers

When a decision-maker chooses between alternative courses of action that have different implications for the distribution of income, he is expressing a judgement about the relative desirabilities of different distributions. If we assert that the decision-maker believes that changes in social welfare are measured by weighted sums of changes in individuals' incomes, his choices will imply particular values for distributional weights. By examining the choices that governments make, it is possible to deduce the set of distributional weights that is consistent with these choices.

One way of setting about this task is to study the decisions taken by governments about the extent to which the system of taxes and social benefits should be used to redistribute income. (This is an approach that has been advocated by Musgrave).[2]

We may begin by classifying the population into groups, composed so that the distributional weight appropriate for any one member of a group is the same as the weight for every other member of the same group. In other words, all the members of a group are equally 'deserving' of additional income. This process requires us to make some assumptions about the government's objectives. For most purposes it is probably most appropriate to classify people by the size of their pre-tax incomes. Sometimes, however, governments may also hold judgements about the distribution of income along other dimensions—for example, between people of different races or between the inhabitants of different regions.

The next stage is to discover the opportunity costs of transferring money, by use of the system of taxes and social benefits, between different groups of people. As we have seen, such transfers are not always costless (see Section 14.2). The terms on which income can, at the margin, be transferred between groups reveal the implicit distributional weights being used by the government.

Suppose, for simplicity, that there are just two relevant groups, 'the rich' with high pre-tax incomes and 'the poor' with low pre-tax incomes. The rich pay income taxes while the poor receive various social benefits in the form of cash payments. By choosing the prevailing levels of taxes and benefits, rather than any other, the government has implicitly judged that social welfare would not be increased either by transferring more money from the rich to the poor, or by transferring less. But suppose that for some reason the government were to decide to increase the total income of the poor by £1, by increasing the taxes paid by the rich. If these taxes have excess burdens, the cost imposed on the rich would be greater than £1—let us say, £1·25. By choosing, as in fact it has done, not to make this additional transfer of income, the government has judged that the marginal social value of £1·25 enjoyed by the rich is at least as great as that of £1 enjoyed by the poor. Similarly, it would be possible for the government to transfer slightly less income from the rich to the poor. If the government chose that the poor should be £1 less well off than in fact they are, the rich could, we may assume, be made £1·25 better off. By rejecting this possibility, too, the government is judging that the marginal social value of £1·25 enjoyed by the rich is no greater than that of £1 enjoyed by the poor. Putting our two conclusions together, we must infer that these two marginal social values are equal. That is, the distributional weights for the rich and for the poor, given the prevailing distribution of income, should be in the ratio 1:1·25.

In general, if a change in the income of individual A by one unit can be achieved by securing a change in the income of individual B by $-y_B$ units, *or* by a change in the income of individual C by $-y_C$ units, and so on, the government's acceptance of the prevailing distribution of income implies a judgement that the distributional weights for A, B, C, . . . should be in the ratio $1:1/y_B:1/y_C: . . ..$

The case of 'costless transfers' is simply a special case of this general conclusion. If transfers can be made costlessly,

$$y_B = y_C = \ldots = 1 \qquad\qquad 14.3$$

and hence the implied distributional weights for all individuals are equal. In other words, the potential Pareto improvement criterion is appropriate for cost-benefit analysis.

(A more formal presentation of the above argument is given in an appendix to this chapter.)

14.5. Distributional weights implied by previous decisions about projects

Another source of information about the distributional judgements made by public decision-makers lies in observations of their past decisions about whether or not to undertake particular projects. This approach has been advocated and tried by Weisbrod.[3]

The method used by Weisbrod to infer distributional weights from past decisions is, in principle, very similar to the methods of inferring decision-makers' valuations that were discussed in Section 13.3. He used a form of cost-effectiveness analysis. In effect, he assumed that the objective of the government in selecting projects was to maximize benefit subject to a constraint on total cost. Benefits were weighted according to the identity of the recipient. (Dealing with the U.S., Weisbrod used four classes of recipients—poor whites, rich whites, poor blacks and rich blacks.) Starting from a knowledge of which projects had been undertaken and which had not, he deduced the set of distributional weights that was consistent with these decisions.

Just as in the case of decision-makers' valuations of goods, there is a very strong case for consistency in the use of distributional weights. If different decisions are made by using different sets of weights, the combined outcome will be inefficient. The set of weights implied by government decisions about whether or not to undertake particular projects, and the set of weights implied by government policy towards the redistribution of income, ought to be the same.

Suppose, for example, that a project is undertaken which involves a cost of £1·5 m to be borne by 'the rich' and which provides a benefit of £1 m to 'the poor'. This implies a ratio between the distributional weights of these two classes of at least 1·5:1 in favour of the poor. Suppose that at the same time the opportunity cost of redistributive tranfers is such that each additional £1 accruing to the poor requires a loss of £1·25 to the rich; the implied ratio of distributional weights is 1·25:1 in favour of the poor. This inconsistency indicates that it will be possible to find a course of action that will increase social welfare, whichever of the two sets of weights is used to identify changes in welfare. For example, by a programme of redistributive tranfers, the rich could be made £1·25 m worse off and the poor £1 m better off. By substituting this programme for the project, the rich save £0·25 m while the poor lose nothing. Any set of positive distributional weights would indicate that this substitution increased social welfare.

14.6. Postulated distributional weights

Just as decision-makers may directly postulate valuations of goods, so they may postulate the distributional weights that they judge to be appropriate for use in cost-benefit analysis.

For a decision-maker to postulate a set of distributional weights is for him to express an intention to act in accordance with these weights. It is because of the clear relationship between postulated objectives and actions that the decision-maker's statements about his objectives can be regarded as responsible ones (see Section 13.4).

This point is important because there is a great temptation for decision-makers, and even more so for economists giving advice to decision-makers, to postulate sets of distributional weights that have been derived from beliefs about what is right and wrong, just and unjust. This is valid only if decision-makers intend, when faced with the need to choose between alternative courses of action, to choose the alternative that is most consistent with a set of ethical principles. If in fact their choices will be influenced by other criteria—such as political expediency—then the distributional weights that they postulate should also reflect these criteria.

The set of ethical principles most commonly used by economists seeking to justify the use of distributional weights is that of *utilitarianism*. To sum up this ethical position very briefly, it is asserted that the process of consumption confers 'utility' on the consumer. Utility may, for our present purposes, be interpreted as something akin to 'happiness' or 'satisfaction'. Utilities enjoyed by different people are commensurable and may meaningfully be added together. The proper objective of a government is to maximize the sum of the utilities enjoyed by each member of the community.

This ethical system has the convenient implication that it is right to appraise projects by using distributional weights. Suppose that a project produces small net gains, measured in money units, of dy_1, $dy_2, \ldots, dy_n$ to each of individuals $1, 2, \ldots, n$. ('Net gains' may be negative.) Since money, or income, is a store of claims on consumption, it confers utility. We may talk of the 'marginal utility of income'—that is, the extra utility that is conferred on the recipient of an extra £1 of income. If for each of our individuals the marginal utility of income is $MU_1, MU_2, \ldots, MU_n$, then the net change dU, in the total utility enjoyed by the community as a result of the project is given by

$$dU = MU_1 dy_1 + MU_2 dy_2 + \ldots + MU_n dy_n. \qquad 14.4$$

In words, the net change in total utility, or social welfare, is a weighted sum of the changes in individuals' incomes; the weight for each individual is given by the marginal utility of income to him.

Marginal utilities cannot be observed; they are merely parts of a mental construct. But one can use introspection as a guide and assert what one believes to be the relative magnitudes of the marginal utilities of income for people in different circumstances. A commonly made and plausible assertion is that, other things being equal, the more income a person has, the lower will be the marginal utility of income to him. If a rich man and a poor man are alike in all circumstances other than their incomes, an extra £1 would give more extra satisfaction or utility to the poor man than it would to the rich man.

This implies that, if distributional weights are to be applied to groups of people classified by the size of their incomes, the lower the average income of a group, the higher its distributional weight should be.

As an ethical system, this may be appealing. (Or it may not; it has been powerfully criticized by many thinkers).[4] But, given our present standpoint of adopting the decision-making approach to cost-benefit analysis, it is more important to ask, 'would a government want to act on such a set of distributional weights?' We need to consider the implications of using lower weights for people with higher incomes. An obvious and very radical implication is that, if it is possible to redistribute income costlessly, it should be redistributed so that everyone has the same income. (Any costless transfer of income from someone with a low distributional weight to someone with a high one will increase social welfare; only when everyone has the same income and thus the same weight will welfare have been maximized.) If a government genuinely intends consistently to apply such a set of weights in determining all its policies, then the cost-benefit analyst should use them in his work. But if it is clear that the government is not prepared to act on these weights when choosing how far to redistribute income, the analyst should not encourage the government to be inconsistent by using them in cost-benefit analysis. Distributional weights are statements of the government's objectives, and 'objectives' should be interpreted as 'those principles that determine decisions'. Objectives and decisions must be consistent if the concept of an objective is to have any meaning.

14.7. Distributional weights in practice

In principle, the potential Pareto improvement criterion, which in most of this book we have used as the criterion for public decision-making, is simply a particular set of distributional weights—'unitary weights' (see Section 14.3). It might seem that to use instead some other set of weights would not introduce new difficulties for the practice of cost-benefit analysis. Unfortunately this is not the case. To use non-unitary weights is to make cost-benefit analysis a much more difficult and time-consuming exercise.

Cost-benefit analysis requires information. The bulk of the information normally used is generated by the workings of the market system. The prices at which goods change hands, and the total quantities in which they are traded, are relatively easy to discover. These pieces of information provide many of the main building-blocks of cost-benefit analysis. From information about market prices and about quantities of goods being bought and sold, it is possible to measure changes in consumers' surplus and in producers' surplus, and such measurements are used again and again in cost-benefit analysis.

The problem with this is that consumers' surplus and producers' surplus, measured from observable market demand-and-supply relationships, are themselves aggregates. Areas of strips to the left of market demand curves, for example, measure *total* gains or losses to consumers as a whole (see Section 9.2). In arriving at these totals, the use of unitary weights is implicit. To apply a different set of distributional weights requires the analyst to unscramble an omelette of market-generated information.

It is relatively easy to identify separately the effects of projects on different groups of people, *classified by their market roles.* To give one of many possible examples, in our analysis of a labour-training programme (Section 9.4) we were able to evaluate separately the programme's effects on sellers of labour and on owners of capital. It would be a simple matter to apply different distributional weights to different groups of people if groups were classified in this way. But it is doubtful whether this is the most appropriate way to classify people for the purpose of assigning distributional weights. If, for example, a decision-maker wishes to classify people by their incomes, measures of consumers' surplus and of producers' surplus may aggregate the gains or losses of people in different classes. Owners of capital, for example, may be very rich, or not at all rich. (Holders of life-assurance policies are, indirectly, owners of capital.) To apportion amongst income groups a benefit accruing to owners of capital it is necessary to know the proportions of shares in companies that are owned, directly or indirectly, by people with different levels of income. To collect and use such information is not impossible, but it adds to the complexity—and cost—of a cost-benefit analysis.

A further difficulty connected with the use of distributional weights was mentioned in Section 10.3 (p. 144). One piece of economic theory that is extremely useful for cost-benefit analysis is the theory of pecuniary external effects. It was shown in Section 10.3 that the net social benefits or costs of a change in the price of one good could be calculated solely from observations of the observed demand curve for that good—even though the initial price change might induce other price changes. But the analysis that produced this convenient conclusion was inextricably linked with the use of the potential Pareto improvement criterion—that is, with the use of unitary distributional weights. The key feature of a pecuniary external effect is that it consists of a gain to one party and an exactly equal and opposite loss to another. That such gains and losses may be cancelled out follows from the acceptance of the potential Pareto improvement criterion. But if the cost-benefit analyst is to weigh changes in income differently according to which individuals are involved he cannot take the short cut of ignoring pecuniary external effects.

Appendix: Social welfare functions and the distribution of income

The arguments of Sections 14.2 (the case for the potential Pareto improvement criterion) and 14.4 (deriving implicit distributional weights from observations of the opportunity costs of redistributive transfers) can be presented more consisely by using the concept of a *social welfare function*.

Consider a community made up of a number of individuals, which has a government which takes decisions on behalf of these individuals. The government's job, then, is to choose between alternative 'social states'. Its objective is to maximize 'social welfare'. This statement is, at this stage, a tautology: social welfare is that entity that the government, for whatever reasons, wishes to maximize. The government's ranking of social states, in order of the amount of social welfare they give rise to, is its *social welfare function*. Whatever criteria the government uses to compare social states are embodied in this function.

Now let us suppose that the government's social welfare function has three properties. Social welfare is a function solely of the welfare of the individuals who make up society. Social welfare is an increasing function of individuals' welfares—that is, if one person's welfare increases and no one else's decreases, then social welfare increases. And each individual is taken to be the best judge of his own welfare. A social welfare function with these three properties (a 'Paretian' social welfare function) embodies the judgement that an *actual* Pareto improvement necessarily increases social welfare (and thus embodies a rejection of the concept of merit goods).

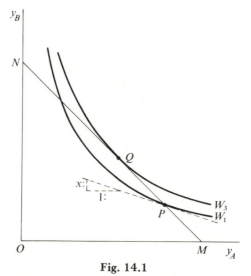

Fig. 14.1

For simplicity of presentation, let us consider a community made up of only two individuals, A and B. (The conclusions that will be reached are of much more general application.) And let us consider only one good, 'income'. Each individual always prefers more income to less. Then each possible pair of A's income (y_A) and B's income (y_B) is a social state. The government's social welfare function can be represented by a family of equal-welfare curves, such as W_1 and W_3 in a diagram like Figure 14.1. Each curve links pairs of y_A and y_B that produce equal levels of social welfare. The principle that any actual Pareto improvement increases social welfare implies that these curves slope down from left to right and that the more north-easterly curves correspond to higher levels of welfare. It is assumed in addition that these curves are convex to the origin. (A justification for this assumption will emerge shortly.)

Suppose that initially the combination of the incomes of our two individuals is that represented by point P in Figure 14.1. A is relatively rich; B is relatively poor. At this point, social welfare is at the level W_1. The slope of the equal-welfare curve at this point ($-x$) is the 'marginal rate of substitution' between y_B and y_A. That is, given this initial distribution of income, a small increase in B's income by x units, combined with a small decrease in A's by one unit, would leave social welfare unchanged. This implies that the distributional weights for A and for B should be in the ratio $x:1$. Unless x equals unity—and there is no reason to suppose that it should—this result is inconsistent with the distributional judgements implied by the potential Pareto improvement criterion.

But now suppose that the government is able to transfer, costlessly, income from one individual to the other. This implies that any point on the line MN, whose gradient is -1, can be reached by redistributing the initial incomes of A and B. The government will choose to redistribute income in the way that maximizes social welfare; it will select point Q. (Convexity of the equal-welfare curves implies that the chosen point will be one at which both A and B have positive incomes. Concave curves would imply that the government would choose that either A or B should have an income of zero—which is clearly unrealistic.) At the chosen distribution of income, Q, the marginal rate of substitution between y_B and y_A is -1 (equal to the slope of MN). Thus the distributional weights for the two individuals are equal; a small increase in the income of one, combined with an equal and opposite small decrease in the income of the other, would leave social welfare unchanged. This is consistent with the distributional judgements implied by the potential Pareto improvement criterion.

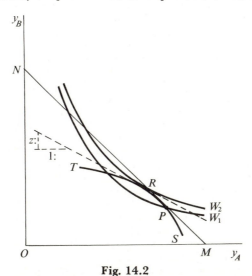

Fig. 14.2

Now consider the possibility that income can be transferred between individuals, but not necessarily costlessly. This case is shown in Figure 14.2. The initial distribution of income is P. The distributions that can be attained by redistributing this income are bounded by the line $TRPS$. That, except at P, this line lies below and to the left of the line MN (whose gradient is -1) represents the assumption that redistributive transfers are not costless. Amongst the distributions of income that are feasible, the one that gives most social welfare is that represented by point R. Here the marginal rate of substitution between y_B and y_A $(-z)$ is equal to the rate at which, at the margin, income may be transferred between B and A. (For each extra unit of income given up by A, B receives an additional z units.) The distributional weights for A and for B should be in the ratio $z:1$. Thus, in general, the potential Pareto improvement criterion is not appropriate. Distributional weights should be used in cost-benefit analysis and the relative values of these weights can be inferred from obervations of the costs incurred in transferring income between individuals.

Notes

[1] Estimates of the excess burdens of certain taxes in the U.S. are given by Harberger (1964 and 1966).

[2] See Musgrave (1969).

[3] See Weisbrod (1968).

[4] A different concept of justice is offered by Rawls (1971).

Further reading

The argument presented in Section 14.2 that, when appraising projects, a public decision-maker should act on the assumption that the distribution of income that exists at the time has been chosen by the government, derives from Musgrave (1959). In Chapter 1 of this book, Musgrave argues that the functions of government can be divided into three branches, dealing respectively with 'allocation', 'distribution' and 'stabilization'. Project appraisal is the responsibility of the allocation branch. According to Musgrave, each branch should work 'on the assumption that the other two branches will perform their respective functions properly' (p. 5).

Harberger (1971) argues that the distributional judgements implied by the potential Pareto improvement criterion should be adopted as one of the basic postulates of all applied welfare economics (of which cost-benefit analysis is a branch).

The classic attempt to infer distributional weights from government decisions in the past is by Weisbrod (1968). A plea for the use of postulated distributional weights is made by Maass (1966). McGuire and Garn (1969) attempt to construct a set of such weights after 'seeking out administrators' preferences'.

Some writers argue that the government's distributional judgements can be inferred from the degree of progressiveness in the set of income tax rates that it chooses. Mera (1969) derives a set of distributional weights from a study of federal income tax rates in the U.S. His analysis rests on the assumptions that the decisions of the U.S. Congress are consistent with a utilitarian conception of justice and that the excess burdens of income taxes are zero; it is only by sleight of hand that he avoids the implication of these assumptions, that Congress would seek to make everyone's income equal to everyone else's.

For an attempt to discover, in practice, the distributional effects of a particular public programme, see Bonnen (1968).

For a statement and defence of utilitarianism as an ethical system, see Sidgwick (1907). An entirely different kind of case for utilitarianism (or what is sometimes called neo-utilitarianism) is presented by Harsanyi (1955). The foremost modern critic of utilitarianism is Rawls; see Rawls (1971).

The concept of a social welfare function derives from Bergson (1938).

15. The Discount Rate in Cost-benefit Analysis

15.1. Introduction

Cost-benefit analysis typically is applied to problems that involve the dimension of time. Choices have to be made about whether to sacrifice consumption in one period in order to have more consumption in another. Throughout Part III of this book we have simply assumed that such choices could be made by applying an appropriate discount rate (a 'social discount rate'). We have said nothing, however, about how such a discount rate should be identified. In Chapter 4 we considered the problems involved in selecting an appropriate discount rate for a public agency, but we were able to reach no firm conclusions. We ended the chapter simply by arguing that an individual agency could regard the discount rate it was to use as being given as part of its objectives; the value of this rate was for the government to determine. It is now time to consider how a government should set about the task of choosing a social discount rate.

We shall consider two alternative approaches to this problem. One is based on the pursuit of consistency between decision-making in the public and in the private sectors, the other on the concept of 'social time preference'. We shall then try to reach some kind of synthesis.

15.2. Consistency in the appraisal of private and public projects

One approach to the problem of selecting a social discount rate to use when appraising public projects is to seek for consistency between the criteria used to appraise projects in the public sector and those used in the private sector. It has been shown already that inconsistent decision-making implies inefficiency. If the criteria used for decision-making by different agencies are not consistent with each other, it will in general be possible to reallocate resources between these agencies so as to produce what is unambiguously an increase in social welfare. (See Section 13.5.)

If public and private decisions are to be made consistent they must be assessed within a common framework. Since we are concerned here with social welfare, this framework should be that of cost-benefit analysis. That is, consistency requires that projects with the same time streams of *social* costs and benefits should be treated in the same way whether they are proposed in the public or in the private sectors.

This approach requires us to consider the *social* costs and benefits of private projects, rather than the financial outlays and receipts that would be considered by decision-makers in private firms. There are a number of reasons for expecting social costs and benefits to be different from private outlays and receipts.

First, there is the whole array of external effects. Actions by a private firm may affect people other than the firm's shareholders in a large number of different ways. Increased production by a firm, for example, might benefit consumers by lowering the price of a product, while inflicting costs—say, in the form of noise—on people living near the firm's factory. There is no firm ground for presuming that such external effects will, as a general rule, tend in one particular direction (that is, towards increasing or towards decreasing the net social benefits of a private project).

There is, however, one particular and very important type of external effect which must be singled out. This is the effect of taxes levied on the profits of private firms. If earning additional profits obliges a firm to pay additional tax, then a project that provides benefits to shareholders will simultaneously provide benefits to tax-payers. Suppose, for example, that the market rate of interest is 6% (tax-free) while profits are subject to a 50% rate of tax. To simplify the discussion and to avoid the need for a discussion of the way that depreciation is treated for tax purposes,[1] suppose that each private project consists of an outlay followed by a perpetual and constant stream of receipts and that no allowance for depreciation may be set against tax. A shareholder in a private firm will want the firm to undertake a project if, and only if, its net-of-tax outlays and receipts have a positive present value when discounted at 6% (that is, at his MTPR). We may restate this condition in terms of outlays and receipts gross of tax: a project should be undertaken if, and only if, its gross outlays and receipts—that is, its social costs and benefits—have a positive present value when discounted at 12%. A firm that appraises projects by applying a discount rate of 6% to their net-of-tax outlays and receipts, when profits are taxed at a rate of 50%, is behaving *as if* it were conducting a cost-benefit analysis using a social discount rate of 12%.

A final source of possible divergences between private receipts and social benefits arises out of uncertainty. If a particular type of investment project is risky, and if shareholders are not able to spread these risks, shareholders will regard the uncertain prospect of gain that a project confers on them as being worth less than its expected value. For convenience, we may express this risk aversion by way of a risk premium. Suppose that, as before, the market rate of interest is 6%. Shareholders may insist that their firm undertakes risky projects only if their net-of-tax outlays and receipts have a positive expected present value when discounted at 7%. (In other words, a risk premium of one percentage point should be used.) If the rate of tax on profits is 50%, this criterion is equivalent to requiring that a project's gross-of-tax outlays and receipts have a positive expected present value when discounted at 14%.

According to one school of thought,[2] this is exactly equivalent to conducting a cost-benefit analysis of projects, using a social discount rate of 14%. To reach this conclusion we must intepret the expected value of a cost or benefit as a measure of its social value. That is, we must argue that a cost-benefit analysis of a private project should use the expected value criterion. There is no difficulty in this so far as those benefits that accrue to taxpayers are concerned; the tax system is a highly effective risk-spreading institution. But the proposition that benefits accruing to shareholders should, for the purposes of cost-benefit analysis, be valued at their expected values is more debatable. The case in its favour is that, taken as a whole, the total returns of *all* private projects can probably be predicted quite accurately. Thus, the argument goes, private projects are not risky to society. This argument has been discussed in some detail in a previous chapter, where it was called an after-the-event view of uncertainty. Our conclusion was that this was not a good way for a cost-benefit analyst to view uncertainty (see Section 12.2).

An alternative approach,[3] using a before-the-event view of uncertainty, is to argue that if individuals are risk-averse there is a real cost to them in bearing risks, and that this cost should not be ignored in a cost-benefit analysis. Returning to our example, consider a risky project whose gross-of-tax outlays and returns have an expected present value of zero when discounted at 14%. This is a project that would be just on the borderline between acceptance and rejection on the criteria used by our private firm. This project provides two different streams of social costs and benefits. One stream accrues to taxpayers, and for evaluating this stream, the expected value criterion is appropriate. The other stream accrues to shareholders and is worth less than its expected value because shareholders bear risks. It is, in fact, worth exactly zero; shareholders are indifferent to whether a risky project that has an expected net-of-tax rate of return of 7% is undertaken or not. It is, therefore, worth exactly the same as a riskless project that has a net-of-tax rate of return of 6% (this too is worth zero). Thus a risky project whose gross-of-tax outlays and returns have an expected present value of zero when discounted at 14% provides a social rate of return of only 13%. The deduction of one percentage point is accounted for by the cost of risk bearing on the part of shareholders. This implies that the firm in our example behaves *as if* conducting cost-benefit analyses of its projects using a social discount rate of 13%.

The important conclusion of the foregoing analysis is that it is possible to interpret decisions made by private firms as though they were the outcomes of cost-benefit analyses. Instead of regarding the decision rules used by firms as being framed in terms of financial outlays and receipts and of a market rate of interest, we may regard them as relating to social costs and benefits and to an *implicit social discount rate*. Of course, we are not arguing that private decision-makers are motivated by the desire to maximize social welfare; as far as they are concerned they are using financial appraisal, not cost-benefit analysis. But this in no way affects the validity of our conclusion.

Public and private decision-making will be consistent if the social discount rate used in the public sector for cost-benefit analysis is equal to the implicit social discount rate used in the private sector.

It is easy to show that if these two rates are not equal, there will be inefficiency. Suppose, for example, that private firms use an implicit social discount rate of 12 per cent while public agencies use a discount rate of only 8 per cent. A private firm, faced with the opportunity to invest £1 m in year 0 and to produce returns with a social value of £0·11 m per year from year 1 onwards, would reject the opportunity. A public agency, faced with the opportunity to invest £1 m in year 0 and produce social benefits of £0·09 per year, would accept it. But by not undertaking the public project, and by instead undertaking the private one, a net increase in social benefit of £0·02 m per year could be achieved at no social cost.

One possible approach is for the government to take the value of the private sector's implicit social discount rate as given exogenously and then to achieve consistency by adopting this rate as its own social discount rate. (This approach is often called the 'social opportunity cost' approach; what we have called the private sector's implicit social discount rate is usually called the 'social opportunity cost of capital'. The idea here is that this rate measures the social opportunity cost of diverting resources from private sector investment. We have avoided this terminology because it can be misleading. The true opportunity cost of diverting capital from the private sector is the value of the private investment projects that are forgone; such an opportunity cost is better measured in units of present value than in the dimension of rates of return. See Sections 2.4, 2.5, and 6.2 for discussions of the problems that arise from measuring the values of projects, or the opportunity cost of capital, in terms of rates of return.)

15.3. Social time preference

The approach set out in the preceding section made virtually no reference to time preference. The government was merely to seek to make its decision-making consistent with that in the private sector; the question of whether or not the criteria used in the private sector were themselves 'correct' was never posed.

Let us now consider an entirely different—and more fundamental—approach. When discussing the treatment of time in financial appraisal, we began from the basic concept of time preference. (See Section 2.1) An individual, it was argued, had a marginal time preference rate between consumption in different periods, and he would make decisions about the allocation of his consumption through time by reference to this rate. An analogous starting-point for cost-benefit analysis is the concept of *social time preference*. Statements about social time preference are statements about society's preferences between consumption in one period and consumption in another; that is, they are statements about the relative effects on social welfare of changes in consumption in different years. To say, for example, that the social MTPR is 5 per cent is to say that an additional unit of consumption in any one year has the same social value as 1·05 additional units of consumption in the following year. We shall discuss later how the value of the social MTPR might be inferred or postulated.

An obvious and simple approach would be to use the social MTPR as the discount rate for discounting the costs and benefits of public projects. Clearly this approach would lead to different outcomes from those implied by the 'consistency' approach, unless the social MTPR were equal to the private sector's implicit social discount rate. There is little obvious reason to suppose that these two rates will be equal, except by chance. (One reason why they *might* be equal will be suggested later, in Section 15.6.) The social MTPR is a statement about social welfare; the implicit social discount rate is a statement of fact about the conditions under which private investment decisions are made. In principle these two concepts are entirely distinct.

15.4. Consistency and social time preference: a synthesis

Our problem now is to reconcile these two approaches.

As a starting-point we may note that, ideally, all projects, public and private, would be appraised by discounting their social costs and benefits at the social MTPR. That this would maximize social welfare follows from the definition of social time preference. In this ideal world, the private sector's implicit social discount rate would be equal to the social MTPR; both of our two suggested approaches would lead to the same 'correct' conclusions. It is only if and when the two rates are not equal that problems arise.

If these two rates are not equal then neither of our two suggested approaches is necessarily correct. (In the language of economic theory, this is one instance of the general problem of the second best.)[4] This may be illustrated by considering a simple example. Suppose that there are two (independent) public projects, A and B. Each has a time stream of net social benefits (in £m) of -1, $+0\cdot08$, $+0\cdot08,\ldots$ in years 0, 1, 2, ... In each case the benefits of the project (£0·08 per year from year 1) are in the form of increased consumption enjoyed by members of the community. But the £1m costs of the two projects will be raised in different ways. The cost of project A will fall directly on private individuals; it can be predicted that they will reduce their consumption in year 0 by £1m. The cost of project B will fall on firms; it can be predicted that they will respond by reducing investment in year 0 by £1m. Suppose that the social MTPR is 6 per cent and the private sector's implicit social discount rate is 10 per cent. Then if we use the former rate as a discount rate when appraising the two projects, both will be accepted; if we use the latter rate, both will be rejected.

A little thought shows that to undertake project A is to increase social welfare, while undertaking B will probably decrease social welfare. Project A leads to changes in *consumption* over time of -1, $+0\cdot08$, $+0\cdot08$, ... These changes have a positive net present value when discounted at the social MTPR, which means that they increase social welfare. It is true of course that a private firm would not undertake such a project, but if our aim is to maximize social welfare this is immaterial. Here the use of the social MTPR as a discount rate has led to the right answer. But now consider project B. Undertaking this project means that £1m of private investment will be forgone. If this investment is marginal, its social costs and benefits will have had a present value of zero when discounted at the private sector's implicit social discount rate (10 per cent). Suppose, for simplicity, that it would have produced benefits, in the form of additional consumption, of £0·10m per year from year 1. Then the decision to undertake project B implies a *fall* in total consumption by £0·02m per year from year 1 on, with no compensating gains at any time. The project should be rejected. In this case it is the use of the implicit social discount rate in the appraisal of the public project that has led to the correct conclusion.

What is needed is some synthesis of the two approaches. All we need to do is to interpret more carefully the ideas of the 'costs' and 'benefits' of projects. In our discussion so far in this chapter we have, implicitly, defined these costs and benefits in terms of their effects on people's *incomes*, and have sought a discount rate to apply to these. But we have defined the concept of a social MTPR in terms of society's relative valuations of changes in *consumption* in different periods. Problems arise because the effects of a project on incomes are not always the same as its effects on consumption. (In the previous example, project B produced changes in income of -1, $+0\cdot08$, $+0\cdot08$, . . . in years 0, 1, 2, . . .; it produced changes in consumption of 0, $-0\cdot02$, $-0\cdot02$, . . .). The correct procedure to follow is to express the costs and benefits of a project in terms of changes in consumption. To calculate the costs of a public project in forgone consumption we need to use the sort of analysis of the characteristics of private investment that was introduced in Section 15.2. Then, when we know what the 'consumption costs' and 'consumption benefits' of a public project are, these should be appraised by using a social MTPR.

At first sight, this approach may seem involved. In practice, however, an analyst does not need to go through the whole process of tracing the consumption costs and consumption benefits of every project he examines—or, at least, he does not need to do this explicitly. The key to simplifying the problem is the idea of a *shadow price of capital*. This is a measure of the social value of a marginal unit of private investment. To calculate the value of this shadow price, we must predict the stream of additional *consumption*, over time, that will be enjoyed by the community as a whole if an additional £1 is invested privately. Discounting this stream to its present value (that is, its value in the period the investment is made) by using the social MTPR, we arrive at the shadow price of capital. Then, for the purposes of cost-benefit analysis, changes in private investment should be valued at the shadow price rather than at their nominal value.

The shadow price of capital need not be calculated separately for every cost-benefit analysis; once calculated, it may be used again and again until circumstances change its value. To derive its value, it is necessary (as at almost all stages of a cost-benefit analysis) to make some simplifying assumptions. Different writers have used different sets of assumptions and thus produced different formulae for this shadow price. For illustrative purposes, a particular set of assumptions, and the formula for the shadow price of capital that these assumptions imply, are presented in an appendix to this chapter.

15.5. Deriving the value of the social MTPR from individuals' valuations

Having seen the role of the social MTPR in cost-benefit analysis, let us now consider the problems of attaching a value to it.

Since society is an aggregate of individuals, there seems to be a strong case that social time preference should be determined by the time preferences of the individuals who make up society. Each individual has his own 'private' MTPR—an expression of his preferences between claims on consumption in different periods. It seems plausible to argue that the social MTPR should be formed by combining in some way the private MTPRs of individuals. This certainly would be convenient for the cost-benefit analyst for, as we have seen, private MTPRs can be inferred from observations of market opportunities to borrow and lend. (See Sections 2.1 and 4.2.) But we must consider more carefully whether it is either possible in practice or correct in principle to derive a social MTPR from individuals' private MTPRs.

'Tradable' and 'untradable' goods

A social MTPR is used to express the relative values of consumption in different time periods. 'Consumption' is a broad category, as far as cost-benefit analysis is concerned. As we have seen, it includes not only goods that can easily be bought and sold at money prices (television sets, for example), but also such goods as states of health and the experience of visiting areas of natural beauty. Individuals' MTPRs are usually inferred from observations of market interest rates—that is, rates at which claims on *money* in different time periods are exchanged. People are often unhappy with the suggestion that the value of future consumption of 'untradable' goods like health and natural beauty should be discounted at the rate used for discounting the value of money.

This feeling arises out of a misunderstanding of the role of money units in cost-benefit analysis. Money is used simply as a convenient common standard in relation to which preferences may be expressed. In principle, any other goods, including health and natural beauty, could be used as a standard of measurement.

Suppose, for example, that someone is indifferent between receiving £5 now and visiting a national park now. Suppose, too, that next year he will also be indifferent between receiving £5 and visiting the park. And suppose, finally, that he has a MTPR of 10% for money income; he is indifferent between the prospect of receiving £5 next year and that of receiving £4·55 now. Given all this, it would clearly be inconsistent of our individual to maintain, in the present, that the prospect of a visit to the park next year was worth anything other than £4·55. The money value of consumption of this good, like that of any other good, must be discounted at the same MTPR.

This is not to say, of course, that individuals' valuations of goods in terms of money may not change over time. One might, for example, predict that over time the processes of economic growth will increase people's money incomes while reducing the supply of natural beauty, and that the effect of this will be to increase the demand (measured in money units) for what beauty remains. But this does not affect the argument for discounting the money value of natural beauty at a MTPR that has been inferred from people's behaviour in borrowing or lending money.

'Short-sightedness'

It is sometimes argued that, when choosing between present and future consumption, people tend to act against their own interests. They tend to be short-sighted, making choices, which they will later regret, in favour of spending rather than saving. Thus, it is alleged, the MTPR revealed in someone's private choices does not reflect the 'true' relative value to him of present and future consumption. Private MTPRs are 'too high'.

This argument is, in principle, a merit good argument, similar to one we have already looked at concerning the consumption of narcotic drugs (see Section 13.2). It can have no place in what we have called the Paretian interpretation of cost-benefit analysis. That interpretation takes as one of its foundation-stones the principle that, for the purposes of cost-benefit analysis at least, the individual should be regarded as the best judge of his own welfare. With the decision-making interpretation of cost-benefit analysis, however, a decision-maker might legitimately choose to replace individuals' valuations of future consumption (relative to present consumption) with a decision-maker's valuation selected by himself.

Transfers between generations

So far, our discussion of time preference has ignored one of the most obvious aspects of time—that, as time passes, people are born and people die. Thus choices between more consumption for society now and more later may involve choices about the distribution of resources between generations. Suppose, for example, that taxes are raised in the present so as to finance the building of a reservoir that will supply a city with water for the next 50 years. Some of the people who bear the costs of the project will die before being able to receive much, or perhaps any, benefit; some of the future beneficiaries are at present too young to be able to register their preferences, or are yet to be born. To undertake an investment of this kind is to transfer income between generations, from the living to the unborn. Only the living, of course, are in a position to decide whether such a transfer should be made.

Transfers between generations raise deep moral and philosophical problems; here we shall be able only to touch on some of these. Our task is to consider whether the social MTPR, which will be used to appraise projects that transfer income between generations, should be determined by private MTPRs—or, more accurately, by the private MTPRs of the living, since these are what we are able to infer from observations of behaviour. Essentially, there are two distinct sets of questions here. First, what social MTPR would an individual, living in the present, wish to be used to appraise public projects? Would he want his private MTPR to be used, or some other rate? Second, should the value of the social MTPR be determined solely by the preferences of the living? We shall consider these two problems in turn.

The relationship between an individual's private MTPR and his view about what the social MTPR ought to be is a complex one. A private MTPR expresses someone's preferences between claims on consumption in different time periods. The person expressing the preference hopes that he will be alive in the future to convert these claims into consumption, but there is a probability that he will die in the meantime and thus that the claims will be enjoyed only by his heirs. If he is not totally indifferent to the welfare of his heirs, his private MTPR will express the combined influences of his valuation of additional future consumption by himself and his valuation of additional future consumption by his heirs. But it is possible also that people feel a concern about the welfare of future generations in general—that is, that people are not indifferent to the welfare of other people's heirs. If this is the case, then one person's decision to save will provide an external benefit to other people currently alive; they feel themselves to benefit from the prospect that future generations will enjoy additional consumption. There is a clear analogy here with other and more familiar external effects—with, for example, the external benefits provided to tree-loving ramblers by a landowner's decision to plant hedgerow trees. Just as the landowner's valuation of the trees understates their social value, so an individual's private MTPR may understate the social value of saving.

Suppose that every member of the community were to agree that each should invest an additional £1 for the future. If an individual has the preferences we have assumed, he will regard this agreement as preferable to the prospect of himself investing £1 but of no one else doing so. Or to put this another way, consider the criteria he would wish to use to appraise the two kinds of investment. He would be willing to invest unilaterally only if the project in which he was investing had a positive present value when discounted at his private MTPR. But he might be willing to invest in a project that failed this test, provided that others did the same. That is, he would wish 'social investments'—investments undertaken jointly by everyone—to be appraised by reference to a lower discount rate than his private MTPR.

The arguments sketched out here have been worked through much more carefully and more analytically by a number of economists, each of whom has used slightly different assumptions about the nature of investment and the preferences of individuals.[5] One general conclusion emerges from most of this analysis: people will not necessarily choose that the social MTPR should equal their own private MTPRs.

Qualitatively, this conclusion is an important one. Unfortunately, however, virtually nothing is known about the numerical values of the social MTPR that people would wish to be used. That is, of course, understandable, for it is very difficult to conceive of any situation in which people would be called on to make choices that would reveal their ideas of what the social MTPR ought to be. If we take a practical viewpoint, then, the conclusion of this analysis, however inescapable, is a somewhat unhelpful one.

Ethically, it is a nice question whether the value of the social MTPR ought to be determined solely by the preferences of the living. On the one hand, there are good moral reasons for asserting that the living *ought* to take account of the interests of the unborn, irrespective of whether or not they *want* to. On the other hand, it can be argued that decisions can only be taken by the living, and that to propose the rejection of the preferences of the living as the sole determinants of social time preference is to seek to impose one's own ethics on others in an authoritarian way.

Most proponents of the Paretian interpretation of cost-benefit analysis hold the second of these two positions, and assert as a matter of principle that the social MTPR ought to reflect only the preferences of the living.[6] Given this approach, the main stumbling-block is the difficulty of discovering what these preferences are. (A further problem is that of reconciling differences between individuals about what the value of the social MTPR should be.)

With the alternative decision-making interpretation of cost-benefit analysis, it is for the decision-maker to decide whether the social MTPR should be determined solely by the preferences of the living— that is, by a particular set of individuals' valuations. In a democracy there will be some pressure on a political decision-maker to respond to the preferences of the living; they have votes while the unborn do not. But, just as in the case of merit goods, a decision-maker may choose to substitute a valuation of his own for the valuations revealed by individuals. He may choose to postulate a value of the social MTPR that takes more (or, conceivably, less) account of the welfare of future generations than is to the taste of those currently alive.

Differences in MTPRs between individuals

A further problem involved in deriving the social MTPR from individuals' private MTPRs is that private MTPRs differ between individuals (see Section 4.2). How then are these different rates to be consolidated into a single social time preference rate?

To isolate this particular problem, we shall for the present assume that investment confers no external benefits of the type considered in the previous subsection; individuals, we shall suppose, are totally indifferent to the welfare of people other than themselves. Differences in private MTPRs are potential sources of disagreement between members of the community about whether projects ought to be undertaken. Other things being equal, someone with a low MTPR is more likely to favour a public investment project than is someone with a high MTPR. In principle this is not unlike other kinds of disagreement about whether projects should be undertaken—for example, the disagreement between the residents of different areas over which area is the best site for a new airport. In cost-benefit analysis such disagreements are usually handled by applying the potential Pareto improvement criterion and discovering whether the gainers from a project gain more, in money units, than the losers lose. It might seem, therefore, that differences in MTPRs could be handled in a similar way, and that the potential Pareto improvement criterion would point the way to a single social MTPR. Unfortunately, however, this is not the case.

The potential Pareto improvement criterion, it will be remembered, is defined by reference to hypothetical transfers of money income between individuals. (A project should be undertaken if, and only if, an actual Pareto improvement could be achieved by combining the project with some set of transfers of money income.) In the present case, the outcome of applying this criterion depends upon which time period is taken to be the hypothetical date for these hypothetical transfers.

This point may be illustrated with a very simple example. Suppose that a project imposes a cost of £10 on Mr. A in period 0 and confers a benefit of £11 on Mr. B in period 1. A has a MTPR of 8% while B has a MTPR of 12%. Let us consider the possibility of linking the project with transfers of income in period 0. B, with a MTPR of 12%, will regard his benefit as equivalent to one of approximately £9·8 occurring in period 0. The project, then, provides a benefit of £9·8 at a cost of £10; it fails the test of the potential Pareto improvement criterion. In effect, we are appraising the project as a whole by using B's MTPR. But now consider the possibility of linking the project with transfers of income in period 1. A, with a MTPR of 8%, will regard the cost he bears in period 0 as equivalent to one of £10·8 in period 1, which is less than B's gain in that period. The project is a potential Pareto improvement. (B could, for example, undertake to pay £10·9 to A in period 1 if the project were undertaken; both would then be made better off.) This time we have, in effect, appraised the project as a whole using A's MTPR.

There is, then, an ambiguity in the whole notion of the potential Pareto improvement criterion which prevents it being used to reconcile different private MTPRs. If private MTPRs differ—as they do—a social MTPR can be constructed from these private rates only in a highly arbitrary way.

15.6. Postulated social MTPRs

The conclusions of the preceding section were, unfortunately, rather negative. Individuals' judgements about what the social MTPR ought to be cannot be inferred from their observable behaviour in borrowing and lending. At present we know virtually nothing about the values of the social MTPR that would be favoured by individuals. Further, it is not at all clear how differences in MTPRs between individuals can be reconciled.

But despite all this, decision-makers must made decisions. If we adopt the decision-making interpretation of cost-benefit analysis, there is a strong case that the social MTPR should be a valuation postulated by decision-makers. Such a postulated value may be justified by the necessity for someone to express a valuation on behalf of the community, given that individuals' preferences are not known. It may also be justified if decision-makers do not want public decisions about the distribution of income between generations to be determined solely by the preferences of the living. Or again, it may be justified by a belief on the part of decision-makers that individuals' current valuations of their own future consumption should be disregarded on the grounds that these valuations are too short-sighted.

As with other decision-makers' valuations, a postulated social MTPR should be consistent with the existing, or at least the intended, policies of these who postulate it. The need for such consistency sheds some light on the problem of selecting a value for the social MTPR.

The volume of public investment

Other things being equal, the lower is the social MTPR, the more likely is a given investment project to satisfy the criteria of a cost-benefit analysis. Thus, if, as consistency requires, all public projects are appraised by using the same cost-benefit criteria, the lower the social MTPR, the greater will be the volume of public investment to be undertaken. While the idea of a postulated social MTPR may seem to be an antiseptic analytical device, the volume of public investment is a magnitude of some political significance. It is helpful to think of the problem of choosing a social MTPR as an embodiment of the problem of choosing the volume of public investment.

Suppose, for example, that a government initially postulates a value of the social MTPR that, in the abstract, seems appropriate. The government might, for example, be swayed by the argument that present generations ought to put a high weight on the interests of future generations, and postulate a relatively low value. But then suppose that it emerges that this implies a very great increase in the rate of public investment and that this increase is politically unacceptable. In other words, given the time preferences of individuals in the community, the government feels unable to call for the sacrifice of present consumption that the initially postulated social MTPR implies. If it is to be consistent, the government must then admit that the social MTPR that it wishes to use as its objective is rather higher than the rate first postulated. It must select a rate whose implications it is prepared to act on.

The volume of private investment

The value of the social MTPR also has implications for what the volume of private investment ought to be. Ideally, all investment projects would be appraised by evaluating their social costs and benefits in the light of a social MTPR. Other things being equal, the lower is the social MTPR, the greater should be the volume of private investment. More particularly, if the social MTPR is less than the private sector's implicit social discount rate then—in the judgement of whoever postulated the former rate—the volume of private investment is too small. (It should be possible to find private investment projects that have failed to satisfy the criteria used in the private sector but that would satisfy the criteria of cost-benefit analysis.) Conversely, if the social MTPR is greater than the private sector's implicit rate, there is too much private investment.

Such statements as these would be of little interest to governments if governments were unable to influence the volume of private investment. But this is not the case. As we have seen, the private sector's implicit social discount rate is in part determined by the tax rates that the government imposes on company profits. (See Section 15.2 pp. 211–14.) Governments typically attempt to influence the volume of private investment—for example, by providing subsidies for investment. (Such subsidies may be regarded as negative taxes on companies.)

For the moment, let us suppose that the government has complete control of the volume of private investment, and consider what this implies for the determination of the social MTPR. Whatever value of this rate the government postulates, the volume of private investment ought to be made such that the implicit social discount rate in the private sector is equal to the postulated social MTPR. Any other policy would be inconsistent. A decision about the proper volume of private investment thus embodies a decision about the proper value of the social MTPR.

This points the way to another thought process by which a government might choose the value of the social MTPR. Again, the process is an iterative one. The government might begin by postulating a value of the social MTPR. It would then be told what volume of private investment was correct, given this rate. If this 'correct' volume of private investment were different from the actual volume, the government, if it were to be consistent, would either change its policies towards private investment so as to make the volume of private investment 'correct', or admit that the social MTPR it had postulated initially did not represent its objectives; a different rate would then need to be postulated. The final outcome would be a social MTPR that the government was willing to approve and that was consistent with policies towards private investment that the government was willing to implement. (This social MTPR should also, of course, be consistent with policies towards public investment that the government is willing to implement; nothing in the present argument reduces the force of the arguments of pp. 223–24 above.)

This approach is a convenient one, for it greatly simplifies cost-benefit analysis. *If* the volume of private investment that actually takes place can be interpreted as being the volume that the government judges to be optimal, then the social MTPR and the private sector's implicit social discount rate ought to be equal. And if these two rates are equal, there is no need to use shadow prices to value private capital (see Section 15.4 and the appendix to this chapter). Arguably, this provides a justification for the way that public investment projects are appraised in the U.K.—the costs and benefits of projects are evaluated by reference to a 'test rate of discount' which is set equal to the private sector's implicit social discount rate (the so-called 'social opportunity cost of capital').

It can, however, be argued against this approach that the government is not, in reality, able to control the volume of private investment in the way assumed. Taxes on company profits are not designed solely as a tool for controlling private investment; they are primarily a means of raising revenue. Like all practical taxes, taxes on companies impose excess burdens. In this case the excess burden takes the form of reducing the rate of private investment below its optimal level. To say that private investment is too low, then, is not to say that the government is able to increase social welfare by reducing company taxation. To reduce one tax is to increase another one (if public spending and public borrowing is to remain unchanged), and the other tax may be equally or more distorting than the first.

Sensitivity analysis

It may be that the analyst feels that he does not have enough guidance from the decision-maker to allow him to use confidently any single value for the social MTPR. If so, there is a strong pragmatic argument for using sensitivity analysis (see Section 5.1) and presenting the results of a cost-benefit analysis for each of a number of hypothetical social MTPRs. If it emerges that the outcome of the analysis is not sensitive to changes in the value of this rate within a plausible range, then there is no need to pursue the matter further. If the outcome is sensitive in this way, then the decision-maker will be obliged to commit himself to some statement about the social MTPR, even if only implicitly. One may at least hope that the process of taking decisions in this way will lead the decision-maker towards making a clear statement of the rate he wishes to use.

Appendix: The shadow price of capital

This appendix shows how a formula for the shadow price of capital can be derived from a particular set of simplifying assumptions. It is then shown that, in certain special circumstances, it is not necessary to know the value of the shadow price of capital.

Let the implicit social discount rate in the private sector be i. Assume that all private projects that are on the borderline between being accepted and being rejected have the same time stream of net social benefits; this time stream is -1, $i, i, i, \ldots$ in years 0, 1, 2, 3, ... (By 'social benefit' is meant 'increase in community income'.) Of the extra income generated by a private project in any year, the proportion c will be consumed and the proportion $(1 - c)$ will be reinvested in a project with the same characteristics as the first one. That is, the new project will also produce increases in income, some of which will be consumed and some of which will be reinvested, and so on. Given that the social MTPR is r, what is the present value of the time stream of consumption generated by an initial investment of one unit in a 'marginal' private project?

We can most conveniently begin by denoting by S the present value of this time stream; in other words S is the shadow price of capital that we are seeking. If one unit of money is invested in a marginal private project, i units of additional income are generated in each subsequent year. Of these i units, ci are consumed and $(1 - c)i$ are invested. Since we have defined the social value of the consumption generated by one unit of investment to be S, it follows that our original project produces social benefits equivalent in value to

$$ci + (1 - c)iS \qquad\qquad 15.1$$

per year. Discounting at the social MTPR, the present value of these benefits, which we have defined to be S, is given by

$$S = \frac{ci + (1 - c)iS}{r} \qquad\qquad 15.2$$

which rearranges to give an expression of the shadow price of capital in terms of c, i and r[7]

$$S = \frac{ci}{r - (1 - c)i}$$ 15.3

(Two mathematical asides may be made here. First, the derivation of the value of S assumes that S is finite; this is so if $r > (1 - c)i$. Second, Equation 15.3 implies that if $i = r$, $S = 1$. This restates a previous conclusion, that if the social MTPR and the private sector's implicit social discount rate are equal, the costs and benefits of public projects should be discounted at this common rate; there is no need for shadow prices.)

In some circumstances it is not necessary to know the value of the shadow price of capital. Paradoxically, the concept of a shadow price can be used to show that it is itself redundant.[8] Suppose that of every £1 of the costs of a public project, £a is at the expense of forgone private investment and £$(1 - a)$ is at the expense of consumption. And suppose—this is the crucial assumption—that the same ratio applies to the benefits of a project; of every £1 of benefit, £a is invested privately and £$(1 - a)$ is consumed. Thus, if the shadow price of private capital is S, the social value of a project cost or benefit with a nominal value of £1 is

$$aS + 1 - a \text{ pounds.}$$

Now consider a typical public project which produces net changes in the community's income of x_0, x_1, ..., x_n in periods 0, 1, ..., n. Using the shadow price of capital, S, and the social MTPR, r, we can calculate the present value of this project to be

$$[aS + 1 - a] \left[x_0 + \frac{x_1}{1 + r} + \ldots + \frac{x_n}{(1 + r)^n} \right].$$ 15.4

This expression will be positive if and only if

$$x_0 + \frac{x_1}{1 + r} + \ldots + \frac{x_n}{(1 + r)^n} > 0.$$ 15.5

In words, a project should be undertaken if and only if the changes in *income* that it generates have a positive present value when discounted at the social MTPR. There is no need to use shadow prices at all; that is, there is no need to consider the characteristics of private investment.

Notes

[1] For a discussion of some of these issues, see Bierman and Smidt (1975), Chapter 7 or Merrett and Sykes (1973), Chapter 3.

[2] Hirshleifer (1965 and 1966). See Note 3 below.

[3] The argument which follows is based on that in Arrow and Lind (1970). Arrow and Lind consider the case where a given risky investment would be undertaken if costs and returns could be spread amongst all taxpayers but would not be undertaken by a private firm because of risk aversion on the part of the firm's owners. If the investment can only be made in the private sector, should the government subsidize the firm to invest? This question is equivalent to, 'are the social benefits of the private investment greater than the private receipts?'. Arrow and Lind say 'no' while Hirshleifer (1965 and 1966) says 'yes'.

[4] This general theory derives from Lipsey and Lancaster (1956).

[5] See Sen (1961 and 1967), Marglin (1963a), Lind (1964), Tullock (1964) and Usher (1964).

[6] e.g. Krutilla and Eckstein (1958), pp. 91–92, and Marglin (1963a), p. 97.

[7] This result was first derived by Marglin (1963*b*). Our Equation 15.3 corresponds to his Equation 15. The recursive method by which we have derived this result, however, is not Marglin's.

[8] The conclusion which follows has been derived much more formally by Arrow (1966), Kay (1972) and Dreze (1974).

Further reading

The technical literature on social discount rates is vast.

Baumol (1968) provides a general introduction to the central issues of a difference between the social time preference rate and the private sector's implicit social discount rate (the social opportunity cost rate). Many economists have argued that public projects should be appraised by reference to a social discount rate that is a weighted average of the social time preference rate and the social opportunity cost rate. See Harberger (1969), Ramsey (1969), Usher (1969) and Sandmo and Dreze (1971). The model that underlies the analyses of these writers is a two-period one. Marglin (1963*b*) and Feldstein (1972) show that, if this artificial assumption is relaxed, the case for using a weighted average of the two rates breaks down. The correct procedure is to use a shadow price for capital (as was advocated in our Section 15.4). A (very technical) synthesis of the arguments on both sides of this debate is given by Diamond (1968).

Other writers have argued that there is no need to take any explicit account of the social opportunity cost of capital; the costs and benefits of projects should be discounted at the social time preference rate. The kernel of this argument was presented in our appendix to this chapter. The pioneer of this approach is Arrow (1966); later restatements of this position have been made by Kay (1972) and by Dreze (1974).

In Section 15.5 we considered the possibility that an individual might choose that public investments be appraised by reference to a social MTPR that was different from his own private MTPR. This issue was first analysed formally by Sen (1961). A paper on this subject by Marglin (1963*a*) prompted a lot of debate; see Lind (1964), Tullock (1964) and Usher (1964). A clear synthesis of this debate is given in Sen (1967).

For a discussion of the problems that arise for the Paretian approach to cost-benefit analysis when individuals have different private MTPRs, see Sugden (1974).

16. Epilogue: The Analyst, the Decision-maker and the Community

16.1. Introduction

In this final chapter we shall consider cost-benefit analysis in a rather deeper perspective than we have been able to do so far. We shall explore some fundamental questions which previous chapters have, at most, only touched on. We shall ask what the underling purpose of cost-benefit analysis is, and what the roles of analyst and decision-maker should be in determining the nature of a cost-benefit analysis.

It should be said at the outset that answers to such questions are 'right' or 'wrong' only in the framework of value judgements of a kind that rational and well-intentioned men may—and do—disagree about. We do not intend to try to resolve such disagreements; that would be impossible. We shall merely set out some of the questions that an economist must ask himself, and perhaps also ask others, before he can begin a cost-benefit analysis. Much unnecessary confusion can be avoided by being clear at the outset about first principles—or, in other words, about what the analyst's terms of reference are. We shall not try to suggest that only one set of first principles is valid, although some of our preferences will emerge in the course of the discussion.

The starting-point for a cost-benefit analysis is a desire to compare two or more 'social states'. Usually, but not invariably, the social states to be compared are the outcomes of alternative courses of action—that is, cost-benefit analysis is used in relation to a decision problem. (Comparing alternatives is a necessary part of any cost-benefit analysis, but the comparison need not be in preparation for a choice. One might, for example, wish to examine a choice made in the past, to see whether it had proved to be the correct one according to some particular criterion. The pathbreaking cost-benefit analysis of the M1 (London–Midlands) motorway was a study of this kind.[1] Or intellectual curiosity may prompt the question 'what would happen if . . .?', when there is no immediate prospect of change.)

The existence of a decision problem implies that there is a *decision-maker*, a person or group responsible for the decision. (As we have pointed out before, the singular noun is used for convenience only.) The idea of cost-benefit analysis implies that there is an *analyst*. Finally, public decisions affect the *community as a whole* and the public decision-maker is entrusted to act on behalf of this community. The relationships between the decision-makers, the analyst and the community are the subject-matter of this chapter.

At the very beginning of this book we made it clear that the sharp distinction between the roles of analyst and decision-maker was drawn to simplify discussion. The problems that we have discussed so far in this book would have to be faced by any person or group of people who sought to make decisions rationally and in the public interest; talking of 'the decision-maker' and 'the analyst' merely dramatized these problems. The same will be true of most of the issues raised in this chapter.

In the following discussion the decision-maker in a public agency will be taken to be a politician, or a professional administrator, or a public employee with a professional skill in the particular activity of the agency, or someone appointed to a position of responsibility in recognition of a career of public service. He will be assumed to have no special skill in economic reasoning. This assumption is true of the generality of people responsible for public choice. And there is no reason to believe that economic skills are any more necessary for a decision-maker than are many other valuable abilities. Essentially the decision-maker is, or should be, chosen for his powers of understanding and his qualities of judgement. Thus if economic reasoning is to play a part in the decision-making process—and the purpose of this book has been to argue the value of such reasoning—it must, as a general rule, be supplied by someone other than the decision-maker. We shall treat economic analysis as a form of technical advice to the decision-maker, and the source of this advice as our 'analyst'.

It should be remembered that the purpose of this book is not factual and descriptive but analytical and prescriptive. That is, we are seeking to elucidate and advocate particular ways of thinking about decision problems. Given this approach, our interest is not in the present functions of economic advisers within public agencies. Rather, it must be in the proper limits of the role of analyst, and in what the relationship between analyst and decision-maker ought to be. In a sense what we shall be sketching out will be a draft code of professional conduct for the cost-benefit analyst.

16.2.   The selection of alternatives to be compared

A problem that is to be subjected to cost-benefit analysis must generate a number of alternative social states which are to be compared. In a decision problem these states are the outcomes of alternative courses of action. Formally, the problem of cost-benefit analysis is to maximize some entity—'social welfare' or 'economic efficiency'—

subject to the constraint that one of a given set of alternatives is chosen. One of the first stages of a cost-benefit analysis, therefore, must be to choose which states—or which courses of action—to compare.

In principle, any set of (more than one) courses of action can be the subject of a cost-benefit analysis. Thus in a purely technical sense, no such set can be 'wrong'. But cost-benefit analyses typically are undertaken to assist in the formulation of policy in a particular context, and a considerable degree of skill is involved in selecting the alternatives to be compared so that the information generated by the analysis is of the greatest value to those making that policy. An unskilful selection of alternatives can lead to the production of information which, if used properly, is of very little value. The designer of a poorly thought-out cost-benefit study may believe that it will answer questions that it logically cannot. Worse, he may believe, after the study is complete, that it *has* answered them—in which case public decision-making may actually be made less rational by the use (or misuse) of his analysis.

Consider, for example, a cost-benefit analysis that compares the effects of undertaking a large programme of road-building in a city with the effects of taking no action and which finds that the former policy is to be preferred. This might then be used as an argument that the whole programme ought to be undertaken even though all that has been shown is that this is better than doing nothing at all. It might well be that undertaking only a part of the programme is preferable to either of the alternatives that has been studied.

The analyst has a dual role to play in relation to the selection of the set of alternatives to be compared. He may offer advice at this initial stage, seeking to ensure that important and practicable policy options are not ignored. Here the roles of decision-maker and analyst overlap a good deal. And at the end of the analysis, the analyst should do his best to ensure that his findings are not misinterpreted, or read as implying more than they really do. If important alternatives have not been considered in the study, intellectual honesty requires that the analyst points this out. It is possible that the decision-maker may suppress these, and perhaps other significant qualifications when presenting the analyst's work in support of his decision. This puts the analyst in a difficult position but we believe that the analyst has the professional duty to set the record straight, for otherwise analysis in general is brought into disrepute. If in the special circumstances of the case this is impossible, then it becomes a matter of conscience for the analyst whether he can continue working for that client, and whether he should dissuade other analysts from so doing.

16.3. Objectives

The criteria or objectives that the cost-benefit analyst is to use to compare alternative courses of action form an important part of his terms of reference.

If one adopts the Paretian interpretation of cost-benefit analysis, then the selection of an objective presents no problems. An advocate of this approach would maintain that the objective to be used in cost-benefit analysis is not properly within the discretion either of the decision-maker (or of whoever commissions an analysis) or of the analyst. The criterion that should be used is the potential Pareto improvement criterion. Anyone who commissions a cost-benefit analysis must accept this, rather in the way that a business that commissions a chartered accountant to audit its books must accept that certain accounting conventions will be used in valuing its assets.

But with the decision-making interpretation of cost-benefit analysis things are more difficult. The objective to be used is within the discretion of the decision-maker. But the concept of an explicit and clearly defined objective is one which has real meaning only within an analytical way of thinking; thus the decision-maker may never have thought consciously about objectives at all. Or he may regard as his objective some goal that is insufficiently precise to be used as a criterion for decision-making. For example, a public agency which sells its products to consumers (say, a public transport undertaking) may see its objective as being to break even financially; but achieving this may well be consistent with a whole range of alternative policies about the quantity and quality of the services it provides and the prices at which it sells them. Or again, a decision-maker may profess a number of different objectives without having any clear notion of how these might be made commensurable. Objectives of a kind that a cost-benefit analyst can use are likely to emerge only out of a dialogue between analyst and decision-maker.

The analyst may have to suggest to the decision-maker ways in which apparently different objectives can be collapsed into a single one. In particular, the analyst should suggest the possibility of using the potential Pareto improvement criterion, which—in principle at least—allows all the effects of a project on the welfare of members of the community to be measured in a single dimension. There is a strong case to be made that a government would want to use this criterion (see Section 7.3). In some circumstances, however, the decision-maker may wish to replace individuals' valuations with his own. The analyst should make sure that the decision-maker genuinely wants to reject individuals' valuations, and is not merely suggesting that external effects ought to be taken account of or that distributional weights should be used (see Section 13.2 and 14.3). A convenient test of this is to check that the decision-maker is prepared to assert that a policy that made some people better off and none worse off might nonetheless be one that he would choose not to undertake. If he is not prepared to make this assertion he does not reject individuals' valuations.

The analyst should make clear that the 'objectives' of an organization or government are those principles that determine its decisions. They are not pious incantations of ethical or ideological beliefs which unfortunately cannot be acted on because of 'political constraints'; they express intentions to act. The analyst must resist the temptation to mix the pragmatism of the decision-making approach to cost-benefit analysis with the ethical foundation of the Paretian approach. When, for example, trying to elicit the distributional weights that a decision-maker wishes to use, the analyst should not appear to be asking for an ethical judgement about which distribution of income would be the most just, or for judgements about how much more happiness a poor man would get from an additional £1 than a rich man would. Private individuals do not always choose to act according to the dictates of justice and neither do governments which rely on their votes. What the analyst needs is a statement of the principles that actually determine government policy—in this case, policy towards the distribution of income. Thus the analyst should, in his dialogue with the decision-maker, constantly point out the two-way relationship between objectives and policies. If the decision-maker proposes a particular objective, he should be told as much as possible about its implications for policy, so that he may be sure that this objective does express his intentions. If, for example, a government minister suggests using a set of non-unitary distributional weights, he might be told that this objective would imply the need for a particular change in income-tax rates. (See Section 14.2.) Alternatively, if the decision-maker is unsure how to express his objectives, it is helpful to tell him what implicit objectives underlie important decisions made by him or by others. For example, a government that was unsure what value to attach to the social MTPR might find it useful to know that its approval of the current volume of public investment implied the acceptance of a particular value of the social MTPR. (See Section 15.6.)

All this amounts to the point that the analyst ought to be an advocate of consistency in decision-making. If we are to argue, as we do, that the distinguishing features of cost-benefit analysis are explicitness and consistency, then to advocate consistency must be an important part of the analyst's job. If decision-makers were able to specify a different set of objectives for each decision that they had to make, cost-benefit analysis would be, as opponents of the decision-making approach have alleged,[2] little more than window-dressing. To ensure that a pet project received the sanction of cost-benefit analysis, a decision-maker would need only to revise his objectives in the appropriate way. If the analyst is to escape the charge of window-dressing he must be prepared, in the report that he makes of his analysis, to discuss the wider implications of the objectives that he has used. If, for example, he has been asked to use in a cost-benefit analysis of a particular medical treatment a valuation of the prolonging of life that is clearly inconsistent with current policy towards medical care in general, he ought to make this inconsistency clear when he reports. Otherwise the result of his work may be to mislead more than to enlighten.

16.4.   The political and ethical foundations of cost-benefit analysis

The final questions that we must consider are very fundamental ones. What is the purpose of cost-benefit analysis? What precisely is the significance of an analyst's findings for the process of decision-making? On what political or ethical principles is cost-benefit analysis grounded?

We shall continue with the framework set up in Chapter 7, distinguishing between the Paretian approach to cost-benefit analysis and the decision-making approach, for the answers to these questions are very different according to which approach is used.

The Paretian approach

The Paretian approach starts from the idea that social states, and hence alternative public decisions, may be compared in the light of fundamental ethical principles whose validity is independent of decisions taken within the political system.

In this discussion we shall draw a good deal on arguments made by Mishan, probably the most forceful advocate of this approach to cost-benefit analysis. Mishan stresses the imperfections of political systems, even in democractic states, as means of registering the preferences of the individuals who form the community:[3]

. . . economists are not alone in being unimpressed by the workaday wisdom of majority rule in modern societies . . .

The 'economist' (our 'analyst') should not accept that any decision-maker has the right to determine what constitutes social welfare. Instead, he should appeal, over the head of the decision-maker, to a body of (virtually) universally held ethical propostions whose significance 'transcends' that of 'decisions reached by political processes'.[4] Cost-benefit analysis, then, should be an ethical exercise.

Since the ethical propostions that the analyst may use are restricted to those that command wide assent in the community, there is no guarantee that it will always be possible to say which of a set of alternatives is the best. The body of 'agreed' propositions may be too weak to allow this. The exponents of the Paretian approach recognize this difficult by considering social welfare to have a number of dimensions, and claiming on behalf of the economist the ability to discriminate in only one dimension—that of economic efficiency. Changes in this dimension are identified by the potential Pareto improvement criterion, the foundation-stone of the Paretian approach. The conclusion of a cost-benefit analysis is thus an ethical prescription of a rather weak kind: 'such-and-such a course of action ought to be taken, provided that it does not adversely affect social welfare in some dimension other than that of economic efficiency'. The analyst's role stops at this point. Since he is not equipped to investigate in the other dimensions of social welfare, he cannot produce an unqualified recommendation.

The assertion that cost-benefit analysis should be an ethical exercise has important implications for the roles of decision-maker and analyst. These are not complementary roles in a decision-making process; they are completely independent of each other. The analyst is an 'independent specialist',[5] committed to applying a particular set of ethical propostions to produce ethical prescriptions. A decision-maker may choose to hire such a specialist to compare some set of alternatives, but the comparison will be made by using criteria that do not derive from the decision-maker; the decision-maker may not choose what criteria are to be used. Thus the criteria used by the analyst need not be consistent with the objectives that the decision-maker—implicitly or explicitly—pursues. If one subscribes to the ethical principles that underlie the Paretian approach, one will believe that decision-makers *ought* to act in accord with the dictates of these principles. But one cannot say that decision-makers are irrational or inconsistent if they choose to act otherwise. The practitioner of a technique that, to quote another economist,[6] 'attempts to throw light on what is right', cannot expect that his prescriptions will always be heeded by practising politicians and public officials.

The decision-making approach

According to the decision-making interpretation of cost-benefit analysis,[7] the role of the analyst is to assist the decision-maker in making choices that are consistent with his (that is, the decision-maker's) objectives. The methodology of cost-benefit analysis is not—as it is with the Paretian approach—grounded on ethical principles. It is instead very close to being value-free, presupposing no ethical principles at all.

Cost-benefit analysis is a 'scientific' technique, or a way of organizing thought, which is used to compare alternative social states or courses of action. It has two essential characteristics, consistency and explicitness. Consistency is the principle that decisions between alternatives should be consistent with objectives. Cost-benefit analysis shows how choices should be made so as to pursue some given objective as efficiently as possible. In principle, at least, any objective could be used. Cost-benefit analysis is explicit in that it seeks *to show* that particular decisions are the logical implications of particular, stated objectives.

The analyst's skill is his ability to use this technique. He is hired to use this skill on behalf of his client, the decision-maker. (Later we shall argue that people and organizations other than the decision-maker might also wish to commission cost-benefit analyses.) The decision-maker, by providing the objective that is to be used in the analysis, provides the value judgements upon which a particular cost-benefit analysis is constructed. It is no part of the analyst's job to judge whether the decision-maker's objectives are ethically right, nor whether they are acceptable to the community as a whole.

(If we are to justify our arguments, made earlier in this chapter, about the positive role that the analyst should play in eliciting objectives, advocating consistency and pointing out unconsidered alternatives, we must qualify slightly the proposition that cost-benefit analysis is value-free. The analyst must owe some allegiance to the cause of intellectual honesty. Thus, for example, he should not accept uncritically a decision-maker's stated objective if this objective is inconsistent with policies to which the decision-maker is committed. As a further aside, it should be said that the analyst, as a citizen, may properly have views about the goodness or badness of the objectives postulated by his clients. As a free man, he has the right to refuse offers of employment that would require him to use his skills in ways that he believes to be wrong. But to accept the role of analyst is to agree to work with the client's objectives.)

Because the criteria used by the analyst are—by definition—the decision-maker's objectives, cost-benefit analysis can, in principle, be comprehensive; that is, it can produce unqualified recommendations as to how the decision-maker should act. Provided that an analysis has been based on a comprehensive specification of the decision-maker's obejctives, and provided that no insurmountable technical problems have been met, the conclusion of the analysis will be a statement to the decision-maker in the form, 'Given that your objectives are . . ., this is what you should do'. For the decision-maker then to act in any other way would be for him to deny that his objectives were those he had previously postulated. It may seem that to interpret cost-benefit analysis in this way is to usurp the decision-maker's proper role. But this is to misunderstand the nature of the decision-making approach to cost-benefit analysis. The decision-maker *implicitly* decides what course of action to take when he formulates his objectives; from this point the analyst's task of working out the implications of these objectives is purely technical. The units in which costs and benefits are measured can be defined only by reference to the decision-maker's objectives. Once we admit the decision-maker's valuations into cost-benefit analysis in place of individuals' valuations, the words 'cost' and 'benefit' lose any meaning that is independent of him. Thus to say that some action produces a social benefit of £1 is to say that, in the decision-maker's judgement, this action is just as desirable as an increase of £1 in the income of one member of the community. (If distributional weights are being used, this should be rephrased as '. . . just as desirable as an increase of £1 in the income of someone in the social group whose distributional weight is unity'.) There is, then, no sense in which a decision-maker could regard the outcome of a cost-benefit analysis as an independent piece of evidence on which to base a decision; it *is* his decision.

In practice, however, cost-benefit analyses are rarely comprehensive in this sense. Some of the objectives to which decision-makers are committed are not easy to incorporate into the economic framework of cost-benefit analysis, given the present limits of knowledge and understanding. (Consider, for example, the objective of increasing harmony between different racial or religious groups—an objective that is certainly important in some areas of policy.) Sometimes it is clear in principle how some effect of a project ought to be handled but limitations on the analyst's time, resources and skill prevent the principle being turned into practice. A decision-maker, for example, might wish that the effects of a project on the natural beauty of the countryside be valued according to individuals' valuations, but the analyst may be unable to discover what these valuations are.

In such circumstances, the outcome of a cost-benefit analysis is not an unqualified recommendation but a statement of the money values of those costs and benefits that the analyst has been able to value along with a list of those that he has not been able to value.

In one sense, this outcome can be thought of as information for the decision-maker, who retains the final responsibility for making a decision. But choice implies valuation. Since the decision-maker must choose between alternatives, he must make some implicit judgement about the money values of the costs and benefits that the analyst has has merely listed (see Section 13.3). The act of decision completes the cost-benefit analysis. The analyst can make this clear by presenting his findings in a way that shows what judgements remain to be made and what relationships exist between particular valuations of the 'unvalued' costs and benefits and particular final decisions.

If cost-benefit analysis, as a technique, is value-free, the ultimate justification for its use can only be that people wish to use it—that is, that there is a demand for techniques that compare alternative courses of action in a way that is consistent and explicit.

The most obvious source of such a demand is the decision-maker himself. It is not, however, self-evident that decision-makers value consistency and explicitness, and a number of writers have argued cogently that decision-makers will often prefer that their problems remain unanalysed.[8]

Consider first the merits of consistency. We are obliged to assume that a decision-maker will prefer that the decisions he makes are consistent with *his own* objectives. Given our interpretation of objectives (see Section 16.3), any other preference would be irrational. So to the extent that using cost-benefit analysis increases consistency in this sense, it is of value to the decision-maker. This, of course, is not to say that he will want to use it to appraise every decision problem, for analysis has costs as well as benefits; but consistency is a clear benefit. However, the value of consistency is less obvious when one allows for the fact that decision-making is often a group activity. Consistency then requires that individuals agree about the proper goals of the organization in which they work, when each may have a different opinion about what these goals should be. The case for consistency is that it is 'more efficient' for a group of decision-makers to pursue a common, agreed objective than for each to pursue his own. That is, by achieving consistency rather than inconsistency it is possible to produce what every member of the group would agree to be an improvement (see Section 13.5). This is a strong argument, but it has one weakness; it ignores the costs of reaching agreement about objectives. In the short term, at least, and so far as the decision-makers themselves are concerned, these costs may be high. Critics of cost-benefit analysis stress the importance of these costs and argue that, because of them, decision-makers will often prefer that fundamental questions about objectives remain unasked.

That explicitness has a positive value to decision-makers is far from self-evident. It is quite conceivable that the objectives that are implicit in decisions are ones that decision-makers would prefer to remain implicit rather than explicit. The members of a political or bureaucratic organization may pursue goals that they do not wish outsiders to know about. In particular, it is arguable that decision-makers typically are concerned as much about securing the survival and growth of their organizations as about achieving particular ends in the world outside. A government, for example, may have as a principal objective that of remaining in office as long as possible.

In principle, there is no reason why an objective such as this should not be used in a cost-benefit analysis. In a technical sense, such an analysis might also be quite practical, for it may be possible to express a 'political' objective in a way that fits neatly into the framework of conventional cost-benefit analysis. (For example, a government's goal of remaining in office might be translated quite accurately into particular judgements about the distribution of income and about social time preference. Increments of income would presumably be more highly valued, the greater the political significance of the members of the group receiving them; this would provide the basis for a system of distributional weights. Arguably, an elected government concerned with remaining in office would wish to use a very high social time preference rate for discounting increments of consumption that were to be received after the date of the next election.)

The obstacle in the way of a cost-benefit analysis of this kind is not technical. It is that the explicitness of cost-benefit analysis would deter decision-makers from postulating their real objectives. Objectives such as survival in office can be pursued most effectively if left unstated, for publicity invites censure. Some economists have been prepared to accept that the analyst might have to observe secrecy about the objectives he is using. (Little and Mirrlees have argued that it may be best to conceal distributional weights from the public: 'It may sometimes be politically expedient to do good by stealth'.[9] They do not consider the possible expediency of doing bad by stealth.) But secrecy can never be guaranteed, and if an organization does not want outsiders to know its objectives the safest course is never to state them.

As far as the interests of decision-makers are concerned, this criticism of the value of cost-benefit analysis has considerable weight. Analysis produces the benefit of consistency at the cost of explicitness—that is, at the cost of exposing the decision-maker's objectives to the scrutiny of others. But to the people or organizations to whom the decision-maker is accountable, the explicitness of cost-benefit analysis has a corresponding value. The managers and officials of public agencies are accountable to ministers in the government. Individual ministers are accountable for the way they run their departments to the government as a whole. An elected government is accountable to voters. The more explicit a decision-maker is called upon to be in justifying his decisions, the more difficult it is for him to act against the interests of the people to whom he is accountable. If decisions are taken in an *ad hoc* way, justified by unspecific references to acceptable platitudes, it is relatively easy for a decision-maker covertly and implicitly to pursue objectives that, if stated openly, would not command support. A government might, for example, use as a criterion for deciding which investment projects to undertake, the principle that projects located in marginal constituencies ought to be favoured. Publicly, of course, some suitable formula—say, 'every case is considered on its merits'—would be used. But if projects are appraised by cost-benefit analysis, the government must choose either to state openly that it uses distributional weights that are determined by the constituency in which a person lives, or to drop this objective altogether.

Thus cost-benefit analysis should not be seen solely as a service to the decision-maker. If the analysis is not secret it exposes the logic of the decision-maker's actions to the scrutiny of those to whom he is accountable. Cost-benefit analysis may be demanded by this latter group even when the decision-maker himself would prefer to avoid using it. In a sense, cost-benefit analysis carries a stage further the function of traditional financial accounting. The obligation on the part of privately owned firms and public agencies to keep financial accounts is a very effective deterrent against embezzlement and fraud by managers, public officials and politicians. The obligation to justify public decisions within the framework of cost-benefit analysis discourages a much subtler form of abuse of responsibility—that of taking decisions on behalf of others by using criteria that these others would not approve.

There are, then, reasons for expecting the services of cost-benefit analysts to be in demand. We could leave matters here, claiming on behalf of the analyst nothing more than that he possesses skills which (fortunately for him) other people and organizations are willing to pay to hire.

Many practitioners of the decision-making variant of cost-benefit analysis wish, however, to claim more—that the use of cost-benefit analysis in public decision-making tends to increase the welfare of society in a real sense. (Of course, any decision-maker may *assert* that the objectives he chooses to pursue are the objectives of 'society' and thus that a cost-benefit analysis made on his behalf is concerned with increasing 'social welfare'. But neither the analyst nor anyone else need agree with this assertion.)

An ethical justification for the decision-making approach to cost-benefit analysis must start from beliefs about how a political system ought to operate. Given particular beliefs of this kind, one can argue that in a democractic community the use of cost-benefit analysis contributes to the good of society; cost-benefit analysis *ought* to be used. The argument begins from the assertion that the role of the analyst is to assist, not simply a decision-maker, but a decision-making process that has the assent of the community as a whole. In this process the community, as well as the decision-maker and the analyst, is involved. The decision-maker is responsible for making a decision, according to his own lights, but he is responsible to the community. His right to decide stems from the consent of the community, expressed through the political system. The community, then, ought to have the right to call upon the decision-maker to account for his decisions.

In this framework, cost-benefit analysis has a dual function. It assists the decision-maker to pursue objectives that are, by virtue of the community's assent to the decision-making process, social objectives. And by making explicit what these objectives are, it makes the decision-maker more accountable to the community.

This view of cost-benefit analysis, unlike the narrower value-free interpretation of the decision-making approach, provides a justification for cost-benefit analysis that is independent of the preferences of the analyst's immediate client. An important consequence of this is that the role of the analyst is not completely subservient to that of the decision-maker. Because the analyst has some responsibility to principles over and above those held by the decision-maker, he may have to ask questions that the decision-maker would prefer not to answer, and which expose to debate conflicts of judgement and of interest that might otherwise comfortably have been concealed. As the authors of a U.N. publication have argued, analysts (or 'technicians') should:[10]

... put political choice in the hands of those who bear the responsibility for these choices—the political leaders who are accountable to the people for the manner in which conflict is resolved. By confronting the political leadership with alternatives which emphasize the various dimensions of social welfare in different degrees, technicians will make it impossible to maintain the pretence that project analysis is technical and apolitical . . ... Muting conflict is by no means an absolute good.

It is in the nature of cost-benefit analysis that it will sometimes stimulate conflict and arouse opposition. But we, the authors, believe that to use cost-benefit analysis is to provide a framework for public decision-making and for public debate that leads to more responsible decisions.

Notes

[1] See Coburn, Beesley and Reynolds (1960).
[2] Mishan (1974).
[3] Mishan (1971a), p. 309.
[4] Mishan (1971a), p. 310.
[5] Mishan (1974), p. 94.
[6] Layard (1972), p. 37.

[7] A case for this approach is made in Williams (1972).

[8] e.g. Wildavsky (1966 and 1969), Lindblom (1959) and Braybrooke and Lindblom (1963).

[9] Little and Mirrlees (1974), pp. 54—5 and 238—42. The quotation is from p. 55.

[10] Dasgupta, Marglin and Sen (1972), pp. 258—9.

Further reading

For a statement of the underlying rationale of the Paretian brand of cost-benefit analysis, and of its relationship to the political process, see Mishan (1971a), Chapters 45—47, and Mishan (1974). For an equivalent statement for the decision-making brand of cost-benefit analysis, see Williams (1972).

For criticisms of cost-benefit analysis and of related approaches to analysing public decision problems, see Wildavsky (1966 and 1969), Lindblom (1959), Braybrooke and Lindblom (1963) and Self (1975).

Any attempt to explain why political decision-makers choose to use, or not to use, particular methods of appraising policy options must rest on some theory of how the political process works. A number of economists have attempted to construct theories about the workings of the political process that are derived from applications of economic theories of rational choice. See Downs (1957), Buchanan and Tullock (1962), Olson (1965), Niskanen (1971), Breton (1974) and Tullock (1976).

Appendix 1: Tables of Discount and Annuity Factors

TABLE A
Discount Factors
$$v_{n,r} = 1/(1+r)^n$$

$r \times 100$: discount rate period (per cent)

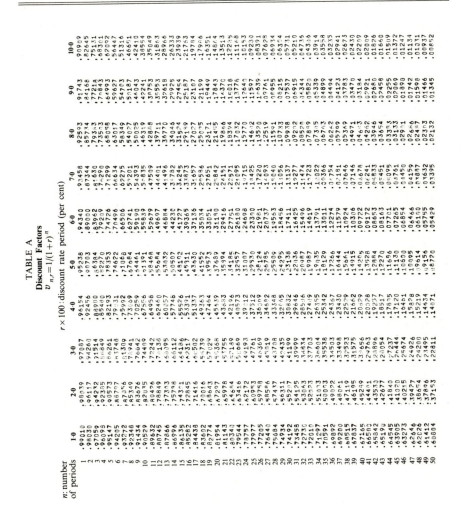

n: number of periods	1.0	2.0	3.0	4.0	5.0	6.0	7.0	8.0	9.0	10.0
1	.99010	.98039	.97087	.96154	.95238	.94340	.93458	.92593	.91743	.90909
2	.98030	.96117	.94260	.92456	.90703	.89000	.87344	.85734	.84168	.82645
3	.97059	.94232	.91514	.88900	.86384	.83962	.81630	.79383	.77218	.75131
4	.96098	.92385	.88849	.85480	.82270	.79209	.76290	.73503	.70843	.68301
5	.95147	.90573	.86261	.82193	.78353	.74726	.71299	.68058	.64993	.62092
6	.94205	.88797	.83748	.79031	.74622	.70496	.66634	.63017	.59627	.56447
7	.93272	.87056	.81309	.75992	.71068	.66506	.62275	.58349	.54703	.51316
8	.92348	.85349	.78941	.73069	.67684	.62741	.58201	.54027	.50187	.46651
9	.91434	.83676	.76642	.70259	.64461	.59190	.54393	.50025	.46043	.42410
10	.90529	.82035	.74409	.67556	.61391	.55839	.50835	.46319	.42241	.38554
11	.89632	.80426	.72242	.64958	.58468	.52679	.47509	.42888	.38753	.35049
12	.88745	.78849	.70138	.62460	.55684	.49697	.44401	.39711	.35553	.31863
13	.87866	.77303	.68095	.60057	.53032	.46884	.41496	.36770	.32618	.28966
14	.86996	.75788	.66112	.57748	.50507	.44230	.38782	.34046	.29925	.26333
15	.86135	.74301	.64186	.55526	.48102	.41727	.36245	.31524	.27454	.23939
16	.85282	.72845	.62317	.53391	.45811	.39365	.33873	.29189	.25187	.21763
17	.84438	.71416	.60502	.51337	.43630	.37136	.31657	.27027	.23107	.19784
18	.83602	.70016	.58739	.49363	.41552	.35034	.29586	.25025	.21199	.17986
19	.82774	.68643	.57029	.47464	.39573	.33051	.27651	.23171	.19449	.16351
20	.81954	.67297	.55368	.45639	.37689	.31180	.25842	.21455	.17843	.14864
21	.81143	.65978	.53755	.43883	.35894	.29416	.24151	.19866	.16370	.13513
22	.80340	.64684	.52189	.42196	.34185	.27751	.22571	.18394	.15018	.12285
23	.79544	.63416	.50669	.40573	.32557	.26180	.21095	.17032	.13778	.11168
24	.78757	.62172	.49193	.39012	.31007	.24698	.19715	.15770	.12640	.10153
25	.77977	.60953	.47761	.37512	.29530	.23300	.18425	.14602	.11597	.09230
26	.77205	.59758	.46369	.36069	.28124	.21981	.17220	.13520	.10639	.08391
27	.76440	.58586	.45019	.34682	.26785	.20737	.16093	.12519	.09761	.07628
28	.75684	.57437	.43708	.33348	.25509	.19563	.15040	.11591	.08955	.06934
29	.74934	.56311	.42435	.32065	.24295	.18456	.14056	.10733	.08215	.06304
30	.74192	.55207	.41199	.30832	.23138	.17411	.13137	.09938	.07537	.05731
31	.73458	.54125	.39999	.29646	.22036	.16425	.12277	.09202	.06915	.05210
32	.72730	.53063	.38834	.28506	.20987	.15496	.11474	.08520	.06344	.04736
33	.72010	.52023	.37703	.27409	.19987	.14619	.10723	.07889	.05820	.04306
34	.71297	.51003	.36604	.26355	.19035	.13791	.10022	.07305	.05339	.03914
35	.70591	.50003	.35538	.25342	.18129	.13011	.09366	.06763	.04899	.03558
36	.69892	.49022	.34503	.24367	.17266	.12274	.08754	.06262	.04494	.03235
37	.69200	.48061	.33498	.23430	.16444	.11579	.08181	.05799	.04123	.02941
38	.68515	.47119	.32523	.22529	.15661	.10924	.07646	.05369	.03783	.02673
39	.67837	.46195	.31575	.21662	.14915	.10306	.07146	.04971	.03470	.02430
40	.67165	.45289	.30656	.20829	.14205	.09722	.06678	.04603	.03184	.02209
41	.66500	.44401	.29763	.20028	.13528	.09172	.06241	.04262	.02921	.02009
42	.65842	.43530	.28896	.19257	.12884	.08653	.05833	.03946	.02680	.01826
43	.65190	.42677	.28054	.18517	.12270	.08163	.05451	.03654	.02458	.01660
44	.64545	.41840	.27237	.17805	.11686	.07701	.05095	.03383	.02255	.01509
45	.63905	.41020	.26444	.17120	.11130	.07265	.04761	.03133	.02069	.01372
46	.63273	.40215	.25674	.16461	.10600	.06854	.04450	.02901	.01898	.01247
47	.62646	.39427	.24926	.15828	.10095	.06466	.04159	.02686	.01742	.01134
48	.62026	.38654	.24200	.15219	.09614	.06100	.03887	.02487	.01598	.01031
49	.61412	.37896	.23495	.14634	.09156	.05755	.03632	.02303	.01466	.00937
50	.60804	.37153	.22811	.14071	.08720	.05429	.03395	.02132	.01345	.00852

TABLE A (continued)

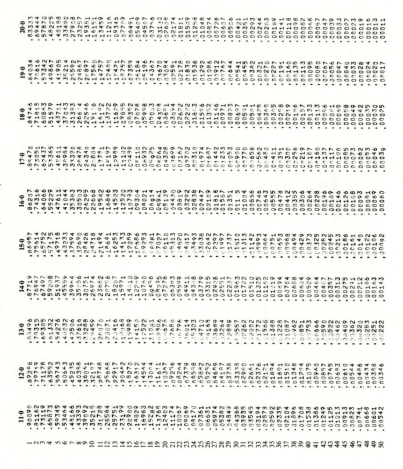

	11·0	12·0	13·0	14·0	15·0	16·0	17·0	18·0	19·0	20·0
1	.90090	.89286	.88496	.87719	.86957	.86207	.85470	.84746	.84034	.83333
2	.81162	.79719	.78315	.76947	.75614	.74316	.73051	.71818	.70617	.69444
3	.73119	.71178	.69305	.67497	.65752	.64066	.62437	.60863	.59342	.57870
4	.65873	.63552	.61332	.59208	.57175	.55229	.53365	.51579	.49867	.48225
5	.59345	.56743	.54276	.51937	.49718	.47611	.45611	.43711	.41905	.40188
6	.53464	.50663	.48032	.45559	.43233	.41044	.38984	.37043	.35214	.33490
7	.48166	.45235	.42506	.39964	.37594	.35383	.33320	.31393	.29592	.27908
8	.43393	.40388	.37616	.35056	.32690	.30503	.28478	.26604	.24867	.23257
9	.39092	.36061	.33288	.30751	.28426	.26295	.24340	.22546	.20897	.19381
10	.35218	.32197	.29459	.26974	.24718	.22668	.20804	.19106	.17560	.16151
11	.31728	.28748	.26070	.23662	.21494	.19542	.17781	.16192	.14757	.13459
12	.28584	.25668	.23071	.20756	.18691	.16846	.15197	.13722	.12400	.11216
13	.25751	.22917	.20416	.18207	.16253	.14523	.12989	.11629	.10421	.09346
14	.23199	.20462	.18068	.15971	.14133	.12520	.11102	.09855	.08757	.07789
15	.20900	.18270	.15989	.14010	.12289	.10793	.09489	.08352	.07359	.06491
16	.18829	.16312	.14150	.12289	.10686	.09304	.08110	.07078	.06184	.05409
17	.16963	.14564	.12522	.10780	.09293	.08021	.06932	.05998	.05196	.04507
18	.15282	.13004	.11081	.09456	.08081	.06914	.05925	.05083	.04367	.03756
19	.13768	.11611	.09807	.08295	.07027	.05961	.05064	.04308	.03670	.03130
20	.12403	.10367	.08678	.07276	.06110	.05139	.04328	.03651	.03084	.02608
21	.11174	.09256	.07680	.06383	.05313	.04430	.03699	.03094	.02591	.02174
22	.10067	.08264	.06797	.05599	.04620	.03819	.03162	.02622	.02178	.01811
23	.09069	.07379	.06015	.04911	.04017	.03292	.02702	.02222	.01830	.01509
24	.08170	.06588	.05323	.04308	.03493	.02838	.02310	.01883	.01538	.01258
25	.07361	.05882	.04710	.03779	.03038	.02447	.01974	.01596	.01292	.01048
26	.06631	.05252	.04169	.03315	.02642	.02109	.01687	.01352	.01086	.00874
27	.05974	.04689	.03689	.02908	.02297	.01818	.01442	.01146	.00912	.00728
28	.05382	.04187	.03264	.02551	.01997	.01567	.01233	.00971	.00767	.00607
29	.04849	.03738	.02889	.02237	.01737	.01351	.01053	.00823	.00644	.00506
30	.04368	.03338	.02557	.01963	.01510	.01165	.00900	.00698	.00542	.00421
31	.03935	.02980	.02262	.01722	.01313	.01004	.00770	.00591	.00455	.00351
32	.03545	.02661	.02002	.01510	.01142	.00866	.00658	.00501	.00382	.00293
33	.03194	.02376	.01772	.01325	.00993	.00746	.00562	.00425	.00321	.00244
34	.02878	.02121	.01568	.01162	.00864	.00643	.00480	.00360	.00270	.00203
35	.02592	.01894	.01388	.01019	.00751	.00555	.00411	.00305	.00227	.00169
36	.02335	.01691	.01228	.00894	.00653	.00478	.00351	.00258	.00191	.00141
37	.02104	.01510	.01087	.00784	.00568	.00412	.00300	.00219	.00160	.00118
38	.01896	.01348	.00962	.00688	.00494	.00355	.00256	.00186	.00135	.00098
39	.01708	.01204	.00851	.00604	.00429	.00306	.00219	.00157	.00113	.00082
40	.01538	.01075	.00753	.00529	.00373	.00264	.00187	.00133	.00095	.00068
41	.01386	.00960	.00666	.00464	.00325	.00228	.00160	.00113	.00080	.00057
42	.01249	.00857	.00590	.00407	.00282	.00196	.00137	.00096	.00067	.00047
43	.01125	.00765	.00522	.00357	.00245	.00169	.00117	.00081	.00056	.00039
44	.01013	.00683	.00462	.00314	.00213	.00146	.00100	.00069	.00047	.00033
45	.00913	.00610	.00409	.00275	.00186	.00126	.00085	.00058	.00040	.00027
46	.00823	.00544	.00362	.00241	.00161	.00108	.00073	.00049	.00033	.00023
47	.00741	.00486	.00320	.00212	.00140	.00093	.00062	.00042	.00028	.00019
48	.00668	.00434	.00283	.00186	.00122	.00081	.00053	.00035	.00024	.00016
49	.00601	.00388	.00251	.00163	.00106	.00069	.00046	.00030	.00020	.00013
50	.00542	.00346	.00222	.00143	.00092	.00060	.00039	.00025	.00017	.00011

TABLE B
Annuity Factors

$$a_{n,r} = 1/(1+r) + 1/(1+r)^2 + \cdots + 1/(1+r)^n$$

$r \times 100$: discount rate period (per cent)

n: number of periods	1.0	2.0	3.0	4.0	5.0	6.0	7.0	8.0	9.0	10.0
1	.990099	.980392	.970874	.961538	.952381	.943396	.934579	.925926	.917431	.909091
2	1.970400	1.941561	1.913470	1.886095	1.859410	1.833393	1.808018	1.783265	1.759111	1.735537
3	2.940990	2.883883	2.828611	2.775091	2.723248	2.673012	2.624316	2.577097	2.531295	2.486852
4	3.901970	3.807729	3.717098	3.629895	3.545951	3.465106	3.387211	3.312127	3.239720	3.169865
5	4.853430	4.713460	4.579707	4.451822	4.329477	4.212364	4.100197	3.992710	3.889651	3.790787
6	5.795480	5.601431	5.417191	5.242137	5.075692	4.917324	4.766540	4.622880	4.485919	4.355261
7	6.728190	6.471991	6.230283	6.002055	5.786373	5.582381	5.389289	5.206370	5.032953	4.868419
8	7.651680	7.325481	7.019692	6.732745	6.463213	6.209794	5.971299	5.746639	5.534819	5.334926
9	8.566020	8.162237	7.786109	7.435332	7.107822	6.801692	6.515232	6.246888	5.995247	5.759024
10	9.471300	8.982585	8.530203	8.110896	7.721735	7.360087	7.023582	6.710081	6.417658	6.144567
11	10.3676	9.78685	9.25262	8.76048	8.30641	7.88687	7.49867	7.13896	6.80519	6.49506
12	11.2551	10.57534	9.95400	9.38507	8.86325	8.38384	7.94269	7.53608	7.16073	6.81369
13	12.1337	11.34837	10.63496	9.98565	9.39357	8.85268	8.35765	7.90378	7.48690	7.10336
14	13.0037	12.10625	11.29607	10.56312	9.89864	9.29498	8.74547	8.24424	7.78615	7.36669
15	13.8651	12.84926	11.93794	11.11839	10.37966	9.71225	9.10791	8.55948	8.06069	7.60608
16	14.7179	13.57771	12.56110	11.65230	10.83777	10.10590	9.44665	8.85137	8.31256	7.82371
17	15.5623	14.29187	13.16612	12.16567	11.27407	10.47726	9.76322	9.12164	8.54363	8.02155
18	16.3983	14.99203	13.75351	12.65930	11.68959	10.82760	10.05909	9.37189	8.75563	8.20141
19	17.2260	15.67846	14.32380	13.13394	12.08532	11.15812	10.33560	9.60360	8.95011	8.36492
20	18.0456	16.35143	14.87748	13.59033	12.46221	11.46992	10.59401	9.81815	9.12855	8.51356
21	18.8570	17.01121	15.41502	14.02916	12.82115	11.76408	10.83553	10.01680	9.29224	8.64869
22	19.6604	17.65805	15.93692	14.45112	13.16300	12.04158	11.06124	10.20074	9.44243	8.77154
23	20.4558	18.29220	16.44361	14.85684	13.48857	12.30338	11.27219	10.37106	9.58021	8.88322
24	21.2434	18.91393	16.93554	15.24696	13.79864	12.55036	11.46933	10.52876	9.70661	8.98474
25	22.0232	19.52346	17.41315	15.62208	14.09394	12.78336	11.65358	10.67478	9.82258	9.07704
26	22.7952	20.12104	17.87684	15.98277	14.37519	13.00317	11.82578	10.80998	9.92897	9.16095
27	23.5596	20.70690	18.32703	16.32959	14.64303	13.21053	11.98671	10.93516	10.02658	9.23722
28	24.3164	21.28127	18.76411	16.66306	14.89813	13.40616	12.13711	11.05108	10.11613	9.30657
29	25.0658	21.84438	19.18845	16.98371	15.14107	13.59072	12.27767	11.15841	10.19828	9.36961
30	25.8077	22.39646	19.60044	17.29203	15.37245	13.76483	12.40904	11.25778	10.27365	9.42691
31	26.5423	22.93770	20.00043	17.58849	15.59281	13.92909	12.53181	11.34980	10.34280	9.47901
32	27.2696	23.46834	20.38877	17.87355	15.80268	14.08404	12.64656	11.43500	10.40624	9.52638
33	27.9897	23.98856	20.76579	18.14765	16.00255	14.23023	12.75379	11.51389	10.46444	9.56943
34	28.7027	24.49859	21.13184	18.41120	16.19290	14.36814	12.85401	11.58693	10.51784	9.60858
35	29.4086	24.99862	21.48722	18.66461	16.37419	14.49825	12.94767	11.65457	10.56682	9.64416
36	30.1075	25.48884	21.83225	18.90828	16.54685	14.62099	13.03521	11.71719	10.61176	9.67651
37	30.7995	25.96945	22.16723	19.14258	16.71129	14.73678	13.11702	11.77518	10.65299	9.70592
38	31.4847	26.44064	22.49246	19.36786	16.86789	14.84602	13.19347	11.82887	10.69082	9.73265
39	32.1630	26.90259	22.80822	19.58448	17.01704	14.94908	13.26493	11.87858	10.72552	9.75696
40	32.8347	27.35548	23.11477	19.79277	17.15909	15.04630	13.33171	11.92461	10.75736	9.77905
41	33.4997	27.79949	23.41240	19.99305	17.29437	15.13802	13.39412	11.96723	10.78657	9.79914
42	34.1581	28.23479	23.70136	20.18563	17.42321	15.22454	13.45245	12.00670	10.81337	9.81740
43	34.8100	28.66156	23.98190	20.37079	17.54591	15.30617	13.50696	12.04324	10.83795	9.83400
44	35.4555	29.07996	24.25427	20.54884	17.66277	15.38318	13.55791	12.07707	10.86051	9.84909
45	36.0945	29.49016	24.51871	20.72004	17.77407	15.45583	13.60552	12.10840	10.88120	9.86281
46	36.7272	29.89231	24.77545	20.88465	17.88007	15.52437	13.65002	12.13741	10.90018	9.87528
47	37.3537	30.28658	25.02471	21.04294	17.98101	15.58903	13.69161	12.16427	10.91760	9.88662
48	37.9740	30.67312	25.26671	21.19513	18.07716	15.65003	13.73047	12.18914	10.93358	9.89693
49	38.5881	31.05208	25.50166	21.34147	18.16872	15.70757	13.76680	12.21216	10.94823	9.90630
50	39.1961	31.42361	25.72976	21.48218	18.25593	15.76186	13.80075	12.23348	10.96168	9.91481

TABLE B (continued)

	110	120	130	140	150	160	170	180	190	200
1	.900901	.892857	.884956	.877193	.869565	.862069	.854701	.847458	.840336	.833333
2	1.71252	1.69005	1.66810	1.64666	1.62571	1.60523	1.58521	1.56564	1.54650	1.52778
3	2.44371	2.40183	2.36115	2.32163	2.28323	2.24589	2.20958	2.17427	2.13992	2.10648
4	3.10245	3.03735	2.97447	2.91371	2.85498	2.79818	2.74324	2.69006	2.63859	2.58873
5	3.69590	3.60478	3.51723	3.43308	3.35216	3.27429	3.19935	3.12717	3.05763	2.99061
6	4.23054	4.11141	3.99755	3.88867	3.78448	3.68474	3.58918	3.49760	3.40978	3.32551
7	4.71220	4.56376	4.42261	4.28830	4.16042	4.03857	3.92238	3.81153	3.70570	3.60459
8	5.14612	4.96764	4.79877	4.63886	4.48732	4.34359	4.20716	4.07757	3.95437	3.83716
9	5.53705	5.32825	5.13166	4.94637	4.77158	4.60654	4.45057	4.30302	4.16333	4.03097
10	5.88923	5.65022	5.42624	5.21612	5.01877	4.83323	4.65860	4.49409	4.33893	4.19247
11	6.20652	5.93770	5.68694	5.45273	5.23371	5.02864	4.83641	4.65601	4.48650	4.32706
12	6.49236	6.19437	5.91765	5.66029	5.42062	5.19711	4.98839	4.79322	4.61050	4.43922
13	6.74987	6.42355	6.12181	5.84236	5.58315	5.34233	5.11828	4.90951	4.71471	4.53268
14	6.98187	6.62817	6.30249	6.00207	5.72448	5.46753	5.22930	5.00806	4.80228	4.61057
15	7.19087	6.81086	6.46238	6.14217	5.84737	5.57546	5.32419	5.09158	4.87586	4.67547
16	7.37916	6.97399	6.60388	6.26506	5.95424	5.66850	5.40529	5.16235	4.93770	4.72956
17	7.54880	7.11963	6.72909	6.37286	6.04716	5.74870	5.47461	5.22233	4.98966	4.77463
18	7.70162	7.24967	6.83991	6.46742	6.12797	5.81785	5.53385	5.27316	5.03333	4.81219
19	7.83930	7.36578	6.93797	6.55037	6.19823	5.87746	5.58449	5.31624	5.07003	4.84349
20	7.96333	7.46944	7.02475	6.62313	6.25933	5.92884	5.62777	5.35275	5.10086	4.86958
21	8.07507	7.56200	7.10155	6.68696	6.31246	5.97314	5.66476	5.38368	5.12677	4.89132
22	8.17574	7.64465	7.16951	6.74294	6.35866	6.01133	5.69637	5.40990	5.14855	4.90943
23	8.26644	7.71843	7.22966	6.79206	6.39884	6.04425	5.72340	5.43212	5.16685	4.92453
24	8.34814	7.78432	7.28288	6.83514	6.43377	6.07263	5.74649	5.45095	5.18223	4.93710
25	8.42175	7.84314	7.32998	6.87293	6.46415	6.09709	5.76623	5.46691	5.19515	4.94759
26	8.48806	7.89566	7.37167	6.90608	6.49056	6.11818	5.78311	5.48043	5.20601	4.95632
27	8.54780	7.94256	7.40856	6.93515	6.51353	6.13637	5.79753	5.49189	5.21513	4.96360
28	8.60163	7.98442	7.44120	6.96066	6.53351	6.15204	5.80985	5.50160	5.22280	4.96967
29	8.65011	8.02181	7.47009	6.98304	6.55088	6.16555	5.82039	5.50984	5.22924	4.97472
30	8.69380	8.05518	7.49565	7.00266	6.56598	6.17720	5.82939	5.51681	5.23466	4.97894
31	8.73315	8.08499	7.51828	7.01988	6.57911	6.18724	5.83709	5.52272	5.23921	4.98245
32	8.76860	8.11159	7.53830	7.03498	6.59053	6.19590	5.84366	5.52773	5.24303	4.98537
33	8.80054	8.13535	7.55602	7.04823	6.60046	6.20336	5.84928	5.53197	5.24625	4.98781
34	8.82932	8.15656	7.57170	7.05985	6.60910	6.20979	5.85409	5.53558	5.24895	4.98984
35	8.85524	8.17550	7.58557	7.07005	6.61661	6.21534	5.85820	5.53862	5.25122	4.99154
36	8.87860	8.19241	7.59785	7.07898	6.62314	6.22012	5.86171	5.54120	5.25312	4.99295
37	8.89964	8.20751	7.60872	7.08683	6.62882	6.22424	5.86471	5.54339	5.25472	4.99412
38	8.91859	8.22099	7.61833	7.09371	6.63375	6.22780	5.86727	5.54525	5.25607	4.99510
39	8.93567	8.23303	7.62684	7.09975	6.63805	6.23086	5.86946	5.54682	5.25720	4.99592
40	8.95106	8.24378	7.63438	7.10504	6.64178	6.23350	5.87133	5.54815	5.25815	4.99660
41	8.96492	8.25337	7.64104	7.10969	6.64502	6.23577	5.87294	5.54928	5.25895	4.99717
42	8.97740	8.26194	7.64694	7.11376	6.64785	6.23774	5.87430	5.55024	5.25962	4.99764
43	8.98865	8.26959	7.65216	7.11733	6.65031	6.23943	5.87547	5.55105	5.26019	4.99803
44	8.99878	8.27642	7.65678	7.12047	6.65244	6.24089	5.87647	5.55174	5.26066	4.99836
45	9.00791	8.28252	7.66086	7.12322	6.65429	6.24214	5.87733	5.55232	5.26106	4.99863
46	9.01614	8.28796	7.66448	7.12563	6.65591	6.24324	5.87806	5.55281	5.26140	4.99886
47	9.02355	8.29282	7.66768	7.12774	6.65731	6.24416	5.87868	5.55323	5.26168	4.99905
48	9.03022	8.29716	7.67052	7.12960	6.65853	6.24498	5.87922	5.55359	5.26191	4.99921
49	9.03624	8.30104	7.67302	7.13123	6.65959	6.24566	5.87967	5.55389	5.26211	4.99934
50	9.04165	8.30450	7.67524	7.13266	6.66051	6.24626	5.88006	5.55414	5.26226	4.99945

Appendix 2: Notes on and Suggested Solutions to Problems

Notes on the 'Problems'

The 'problems' which follow most of the chapters of this book are designed to illustrate and to apply the principles expounded in the preceding chapters. Some problems require only a fairly straightforward application of clearly defined principles, but most require a degree of ingenuity on the part of the reader. This is deliberate; project appraisal is not a mechanical process but a craft whose practitioners must be able to think their way through the new problems raised by each study they tackle.

The 'suggested solutions' given below are not necessarily the *only* possible ones. In some cases there may be one, or even more than one, alternative and equally valid approach which leads to different conclusions. However, the reader who tries one of these alternative approaches will probably find that insufficient information is given for him or her to proceed. In this case it is a useful exercise to ask oneself, 'precisely what information do I need and how would I use it if I had it?'. Sufficient information is always given to allow each problem to be solved in some way. (Frequently some irrelevant information is given in addition; it is for the reader to decide what is relevant and what is not.)

A number of working assumptions are built into the derivations of the suggested solutions. *These should be taken as read whenever they are not explicitly contradicted by the information given with a problem.* These working assumptions are made primarily to avoid confusing the reader; each chapter concentrates on a particular set of issues and it is these issues that are highlighted in the associated problems. Difficulties arising out of issues dealt with in other chapters are assumed away as far as possible. This way of proceeding is not as artificial as it may seem; every practical cost-benefit analyst, working with limited skills, time and money, has to make simplifying assumptions when dealing with matters which seem peripheral to the main problem under study.

These working assumptions are as follows:

1. Time periods (invariably years) are taken to be discrete for the purposes of discounting.

2. All prices, interest rates and discount rates are expressed in real (constant price) terms.

3. All individuals in the relevant community are able to borrow and lend freely at a single market interest rate. All public agencies are required to use this rate as their discount rate.

4. The price of each good is equal to the marginal social cost of its production and also to the marginal social value of consumption of the good.

5. There is no involuntary unemployment of labour.

6. All income effects are zero.

7. Problems typically concern choices between alternative courses of action. The prices of all goods not mentioned explicitly in the problem will not be affected by the taking of any one of these courses of action rather than any other.

Where numerical solutions are given, only 3 or 4 significant figures are usually shown. (The measurements used in cost-benefit analyses almost invariably have quite wide margins of error; to present findings accurate to many significant figures would be to give a false impression of precision.) Occasionally very slight numerical inaccuracies may occur in the suggested solutions as the result of the accumulation of rounding errors. Tables associated with problems are numbered consecutively for each chapter. In the suggested solutions table numbers continue the sequence of the corresponding chapter.

Suggested solutions

CHAPTER 2

1. The present value in year 0 of a stream of income of £1900 per year from year 1 to year 20 inclusive is £18 654 if the discount rate is 8 per cent. (1900 $a_{20,0\cdot08}$ = 1900 × 9·818 = 18 654). Subtracting the present value of the costs of modernizing a crossing, £20 200, the project of modernizing a crossing has a negative present value (*minus* £1550) and is not worth undertaking. But repeating the calculation for a discount rate of 6 per cent shows that the project then has a positive present value (£1590); it would thus be financially worthwhile to modernize the crossing if the interest rate were as low as 6 per cent.

2. The proposal to build a wide bridge rather than a narrow one in year 0 is an investment project, involving a cost of £120 000 in year 0 (the extra cost of the wide bridge) and a return of £240 000 in year 8 (the saving from not having to rebuild the bridge). Discounting at 10 per cent the present value of this project is *minus* £8040 in year 0. It is thus in the taxpayers' interests to build the bridge in year 0 only wide enough to carry the existing road.

3. This problem can be treated as involving a set of mutually exclusive projects, each project being the possibility of carrying out the improvement in a particular year. The net financial returns resulting from each of five possible starting dates are summarized in Table (i). (The initial cost of the improvements

Table (i)

Starting date for project: year	Net financial returns (in £'000) of project in year(s)						Present value in year 0 of net financial returns (£'000)
	0	1	2	3	4	5—19	
0	−110	8	10	12	14	16 *per year*	7·23
1		−110	10	12	14	16 *per year*	9·96
2			−110	12	14	16 *per year*	10·78
3				−110	14	16 *per year*	10·04
4					−110	16 *per year*	7·99

is followed by a stream of returns in the form of cost savings.) The present value in year 0 of each of these streams of outlays and returns is also shown in the table. The objective is to maximize the present value in year 0 of net financial returns (this is equivalent to minimizing the present value of the hospital's net subsidy requirement.) Consequently the best course of action is to carry out the improvements in year 2.

4. The government is proposing to take from shareholders a stream of income of £1·475 m per year in years 1 to 30. Since the market interest rate (and hence

each shareholder's marginal time preference rate) is 8 per cent, the present value in year 0 of this income stream is £16·61 m. This is the sum that, if received in year 0, would just compensate shareholders for their loss of income in the future. By proposing to pay only £9·10 m as compensation, the government is, in effect, proposing to expropriate £7·51 m of the shareholders' current wealth.

The logic of the government's argument is that, *if shareholders' MTPRs were 16 per cent*, the present value in year 0 of the stream of income taken by the government would be approximately £9·1 m. Only in this event would the government's proposed 'compensation' in fact just compensate shareholders.

CHAPTER 3

1. The engineer's argument is incorrect.

In any year (say, year 0) a certain amount of road must be reconstructed. We may compare the costs over years 0—39 of two alternative policies. Policy A is to reconstruct in asphalt in year 0 and again in year 20. Policy B is to reconstruct in concrete in year 0. By year 40, whichever policy has been chosen, the roads reconstructed in year 0 will require reconstructing again. There is, therefore, no need to look beyond year 39 when comparing the two alternatives.

For each lane kilometre of road reconstructed in year 0, the present value in year 0 of the cost implied by policy A is

$$30\,000 + 30\,000\,v_{20,0·10} = 34\,460 \text{ pounds}$$

if the market interest rate is 10 per cent. The equivalent present value for policy B is £38 000, the cost per lane kilometre of reconstructing in concrete. Policy A thus is the less costly of the two alternatives.

The error in the engineer's argument lies in his use of depreciation allowances. His calculations imply, for example, that a payment of £30 000 in year 0 (to reconstruct one lane kilometre in asphalt) is equivalent to payments of £1500 per year in each of years 1 to 20. This would be correct only if the market rate of interest were zero. If this *were* the case, it would be less costly to build roads of concrete.

2. The real rate of interest is 8 per cent (the nominal rate of interest *minus* the expected rate of increase in the prices of consumption goods). Relative to the price level for consumption goods, wages are expected to increase by 2 per cent per year. Thus in real terms, relative to the prices current in year 0, the cost savings from modernizing a crossing are £1900 $(1 + 0·02)$ in year 1, £1900 $(1 + 0·02)^2$ in year 2, and so on. Discounting at the real interest rate of 8 per cent, the present value of these cost savings is (in year 0 pounds)

$$1900 \left[\frac{1 + 0·02}{1 + 0·08} + \frac{(1 + 0·02)^2}{(1 + 0·08)^2} + \ldots + \frac{(1 + 0·02)^{20}}{(1 + 0·08)^{20}} \right]$$
$$\simeq 1900\,a_{20,0·06}$$
$$\simeq 21\,790.$$

This is greater than the cost of modernizing a crossing; modernizing is thus financially worthwhile.

3. The opportunity cost of using the land at A on which to build the hospital is that by using it in this way the health authority forgoes the opportunity to sell it. If a decision were made in year 0 to build the hospital at B, the site at A could be sold for its current market value of £415 000. The sum of money that the health authority paid in year −8 is irrelevant to the present problem: bygones are bygones.

An 18-hectare site at B would cost £1 260 000. However, it would be misleading to compare this cost with the opportunity cost of using a 12-hectare site at A. It is more useful to compare the costs of building at A with the costs that would be implied by building on a 12-hectare site at B. If the latter are less than the former, it is clear that site B is to be preferred, for B has an additional advantage—there is the opportunity to buy an extra 6 hectares. The health authority would only take up this opportunity (as it has, in fact, said it would) if it judged the benefits of having the additional land to be at least as great as the extra costs. Thus this opportunity cannot have a negative value and may have a positive value. A 12-hectare site at B would cost £840 000, £425 000 more than the opportunity cost of the site at A.

The net financial advantages from building at B rather than at A are summarized in Table (i).

Table (i)

Item	Net financial advantage in favour of site B (£m present value in year 0)
Cost of 12-hectare site	—0·425
Opportunity to buy additional 6 hectares	0·000 or greater
Operation of ambulances	—0·105
Building and maintenance	0·920
Total	0·390 or greater

The present value of these net financial advantages is *at least* £390 000; site B is to be preferred.

(In Chapter 5 we take up the problem of attaching a more precise value to the opportunity to buy the additional 6 hectares at site B (see Problem 1 p. 70).)

CHAPTER 5

1. The expected value criterion seems appropriate for appraising the choice between buying the smaller and buying the larger site. (Since costs are to be divided amongst many taxpayers, no individual will risk significant changes in his wealth. There is no obvious reason why taxpayers in general should be more or less wealthy if the state of the world 'hospital extension built' occurs than if the state 'hospital extension not built' occurs; the risks involved in this choice thus are independent.)

Consider the net financial returns that result from buying the larger site rather than the smaller one. This is a project whose returns are different according to which of the two states of the world ('extension built' and 'extension not built') occurs.

If the extension is built, the project involves a cost of £420 000 in year 0 (the cost of the additional 6 hectares of land) and produces returns of £400 000 in each of years 6—8 (the savings in the costs of building the extension). Using a discount rate of 10 per cent, the present value of the project is £197 600 in year 0.

If the extension is not built, the project involves, as before, a cost of £420 000 in year 0. Its only return is of £420 000 in year 8 (the proceeds from reselling the surplus land). The present value of the project is *minus* £182 900 in year 0.

If the probability that the extension will be built is p, the expected present value of the project is

$$197\ 600\ p - 182\ 900(1 - p).$$

The larger site would be preferable to the smaller one if this expected present value were positive. This is the case if p is greater than 0·48. Very roughly, the larger site should be bought if and only if it is judged that the extension is more likely to be built than not.

2. Let the years in which the railway is electrified be n and $n + 1$. Then the project of immunizing the signalling system now rather than later involves costs of £150 000 in each of years 0 and 1 (the additional capital costs of immunizing the system) followed by costs of £3000 in each of years 2 to $n + 1$ (the additional maintenance costs). It produces a return of £300 000 in each of years n and $n + 1$ (the savings from not having to convert the system).

The present value in year 0 of immunizing now rather than later is thus (in £)

$$-150\ 000 - 150\ 000\ v_{1,0\cdot08} - 3000\ a_{n,0\cdot08}\ v_{1,0\cdot08} + 300\ 000\ a_{2,0\cdot08}\ v_{n-1,0\cdot08}.$$

Substituting the appropriate values of n into this equation, this present value can be calculated for each possible electrification date. A further calculation gives the present value of the extra costs of immunizing now if the railway is never electrified (during the whole 40-year life of the equipment). These results are summarized in Table (iii). Such a table of outcomes would provide the decision-maker with valuable information on which to base a decision. It does not

Table (iii)

Electrification begins in year	*Present value in year 0 of immunizing now rather than later (£)*
5	93 200
6	62 400
7	33 800
8	7300
9	−17 200
10	−39 900
11	−60 900
12	−80 400
13	−98 400
14	−115 100
15	−130 500
not during life of equipment	−322 000

however, show one course of action to be clearly preferable to the other (unless the decision-maker feels certain *either* that electrification will begin not later than year 8, in which case the system should be immunized immediately, *or* that electrification will not begin before year 9, in which case the system should not be immunized now).

The expected value criterion seems appropriate to this decision problem. Given the probability judgements that were shown in Table (i), the 'expected present value of immunizing now rather than later' can be calculated.

There is one difficulty here—how to take account of the possibility of electrification beginning after year 14. One way to proceed is to calculate an upper and a lower estimate of the 'expected present value of immunizing now', the upper estimate being based on the assumption that there is a probability of 0·05 that electrification will begin in year 15, and the lower estimate being based on the assumption that there is a probability of 0·05 that electification will not take place during the life of the equipment. The upper estimate of the 'expected present value of immunizing now' can be calculated to be *minus* £13 000; the lower estimate is *minus* £22 600. Thus the judgements of the probabilities of different electrification dates that were given in Table (i) imply that the railway undertaking's request for the approval of its plan to immunize the signalling system should be turned down.

3. The finance officer's report implies that the authority is risk-averse (it wishes to 'avoid taking risks with the electors' money'). This risk aversion is incorporated into the appraisal of the three schemes by using a risk premium when discounting the 'most likely' net returns of the schemes. This approach is potentially misleading (see Section 5.4).

A sounder approach is to keep judgements about uncertainty separate from statements about time preference. Using as the discount rate the interest rate at which the authority can borrow—that is, 6 per cent—the outcomes of each investment project can be calculated for each possible date of completion of building work. These outcomes are shown in Table (iv).

Table (iv)

Building work completed in year:	Present value of net financial returns from adopting:	
	B rather than A	C rather than A
2	233·5	241·5
3	137·2	171·2
4	44·6	105·0
5	-- 42·8	42·5
6	−125·3	− 16·6

Notes

1. Present value in £'000 in year 0.
2. Discount rate: 6 per cent.

It emerges that scheme C produces a more favourable outcome than scheme B whichever year building work is completed (given that it will not be completed before year 2). Figures are not presented for completion dates beyond year 6, but it is not difficult to prove that, the later the completion date, the greater is the financial advantage from adopting scheme C rather than scheme B. Thus, whatever degree of risk aversion the authority thinks it proper to show, scheme C is clearly preferable to scheme B. There can be no case for adopting scheme B (the course of action recommended by the finance officer). If the local authority were confident that building work would be completed before year 6, scheme C clearly would be the best to adopt. It is *conceivable*, however, that the authority's decision-makers might feel so pessimistic about the date when building work will be completed, and be so risk-averse, as to prefer scheme A.

CHAPTER 6

1. The authority's objective, so far as the current problem is concerned, is to minimize the total cost of undertaking the 6 projects. This objective may be stated in another, and equivalent, form. If all probjects were undertaken by contractors, the total cost would be £243 700. By using its own labour force for some projects, total costs can be reduced. The authority's objective is to

maximize the total cost saving that is achieved by using its own labour force rather than contractors. This implies that its own labour force should be used on those projects where the cost saving per man year of labour is greatest. The project with the highest cost saving per man year of labour is B, followed, in descending order, by D, F, C, A and E. (See Table (iii).) Consequently the 30

Table (iii)

Project	Man years of labour required	Cost using own labour (£'000)	Cost using contractors (£'000)	Cost saving from using own labour (£'000)	Cost saving per man year of labour (£'000)
A	20	60·0	61·3	1·3	0·065
B	15	51·1	54·8	3·7	0·247
C	12	40·6	41·9	1·3	0·108
D	10	58·0	59·8	1·8	0·180
E	5	18·3	18·6	0·3	0·060
F	2	7·0	7·3	0·3	0·150

man years of labour should be used to undertake the whole of projects B, D and F, and part of project C. Were additional labour to be available, the best use for it would be on project C, where the cost saving per man year of labour is £108. This is the maximum sum that it would be worth paying, in addition to the current wage, to secure an additional man year of labour. (That is, the shadow price of labour is equal to the wage plus £108 per man year.)

2. Consider the investment of £2500 in project A in year 0. The present value of the net financial returns from this investment (including the initial capital outlay) is £533. Compare this with the present value, in year 0, of investing £2500 in project A in year 1. This is £33. The present value of the net gain from not postponing investment in project A is thus £500 per £2500 of capital spending, or £0·20 per £1 of capital.

Now consider project B. If one piece of equipment is bought in year 0, the present value of the net financial returns from this piece of equipment (that is, not counting the net returns to be expected from later replacements) is £4921. This is equivalent, in present value terms, to a financial return of £1799 per year in each of years 0 to 2. Similarly, the net financial returns from the first piece of equipment bought in replacement are equivalent in present value to a financial return of £1799 per year in each of years 3 to 5. Thus the project as a whole, of buying one peice of equipment in year 0 and buying replacements every three years, is equivalent in present value to a perpetual stream of revenue of £1799 per year. Postponing this project for one year is thus equivalent to incurring a cost of £1799 in year 1. The net gain from not postponing investment in project B is £1799 per £10 000 of capital spending, or £0·18 per £1 of capital.

The agency's objective is to maximize the 'net gain from not postponing', subject to the constraint that capital spending must not exceed £120 000 in year 0. This would be achieved by reducing its investment in project B (the project with the lower 'net gain from not postponing' per £1 per capital) to £40 000 (that is, 4 pieces of equipment) while keeping to its original plan of investing £80 000 in project A. The marginal value of capital to the agency is its value in project B, £0·18 per £1 of capital in excess of its nominal value. That is, the spending of £1 in year 0 should be shadow priced at a notional cost of £1·18.

3. If the agency followed its normal policy of buying replacements in year 0 and then buying further replacements in years 3, 6, 9, . . ., it would incur costs (per item of equipment) of £11 000 in year 0, £2000 in year 1, £5000 in year 2, and then £11 000, £2000, £5000 in years 3, 4 and 5, and so on. This stream of costs has the same present value as a perpetual stream of costs of £6180 per year from year 0 onwards. By not replacing one item of equipment in year 0 the agency postpones by one year the incidence of this stream of costs; the present value of the gain from doing this is thus £6180. This gain must be set against the costs incurred in year 0 to maintain the old equipment. These amount to £8000 per item of equipment. The net loss from postponing replacement thus has a present value of £1820 per item. By postponing replacement, the agency reduces its spending in year 0 by £3000 per item (£11 000 *minus* £8000). Thus each £1 reduction in spending in year 0 is being achieved at a cost of £0·61 in present value terms (1820/3000 = 0·61). The government's decision that the equipment should not be replaced is consistent with a declaration that public agencies should treat each £1 of spending in year 0 as if it had some shadow price no less than £1·61.

Now consider the investment by the 'other agency'. It is not known whether or not this project could have been postponed. Let us therefore make the assumption most favourable to the government's decision that the project be undertaken; we shall assume that there was no possibility of postponing it. The present value in year 0 of this project is £214 500. This is to be achieved by spending £400 000 in year 0. The net return per £1 of spending in year 0 is £0·54. The government's decision in favour of the project is consistent with a declaration that each £1 of public spending in year 0 should have a shadow price no greater than £1·54.

If the government's policies were consistent, both agencies would be required to act as if facing the same shadow price of public spending. In fact, the shadow price for one agency is higher than that for the other. The government, it seems, is inconsistent.

CHAPTER 8

1. (*i*) Consumption of oil should be shadow priced at the net-of-tax price. (The price elasticity of supply is infinite; in the notation used in Section 8.3, $a = 0$.)

(*ii*) Consumption of oil should be shadow priced at the gross-of-tax price. The relevant good is 'foreign currency'. Since the supply of foreign currency is constrained, each additional unit used by one individual or firm corresponds to one less unit used by others; the social value of what is forgone by the latter is measured by the gross-of-tax price. (The government's taxation of imports can be regarded as a means of rationing the available foreign currency between competing users; the gross-of-tax price of an imported good thus is a government-determined shadow price.)

2. The shadow price of labour should be a weighted average of the gross-of-tax and net-of-tax wage rates, with the weights being in the ratio 2:1. (In the notation used in Section 8.3, $a = \frac{2}{3}$).

In case (*i*) changes in the quantity of labour employed represent changes in the number of workers who are working 40 hours per week. The relevant wage rate is thus the wage received for 40 hours of work. This is £60 per week gross and £51 per week net. The shadow price of labour is thus £57 per week (or £1·43 per hour).

In case (*ii*) changes in the quantity of labour employed represent changes in the number of hours worked per worker. The relevant wage rate is thus the hourly rate of £1·50 per hour. Since all workers pay tax, the relevant net-of-tax wage rate is £1·00 per hour. (Each additional hour of labour earns £1·00 net of tax.) The shadow price of labour is £1·33 per hour.

3. The effect of building the new hotel is to increase the supply of hotel rooms and thus (marginally) to reduce the price at which rooms are let. Of the *increase* in the number of visitors that is induced by this price change, two-thirds is accounted for by an increase in the number of foreign visitors. Thus although the new hotel itself earns only $180 000 per year from foreigners, all hotels taken together will earn an additional $240 000 per year from abroad. Producers of other goods and services will earn an additional $192 000 per year from abroad. The social value of the additional foreign currency earned exceeds its nominal value by $86 400 per year.

CHAPTER 9

1. (*i*) Suppliers of labour are interested in the wage rate net of tax. The net wage increases from £21 to £22·30 per week and the number of workers increases from 3200 to 4000. This implies an increase in producers' surplus to suppliers of labour of approximately £4680 per week.

(*ii*) Employers of labour are interested in the gross wage rate they have to pay. When the gross wage increases from £25 to £27 per week the number of workers employed outside the new factory falls from 3200 to 3000. This implies a decrease in producers' surplus to employers (that is, to owners of capital) of appoximately £6200 per week.

(*iii*) The government's income-tax revenue increases by £6000 per week.

2. The price of bus trips falls from 4p per passenger kilometre to 3p; the quantity demanded increases from 120 m passenger kilometres per year to 135 m per year. The increase in consumers' surplus is approximately £1·275 m per year. This benefit to bus users exceeds the financial cost to the bus company (£0·985 m per year) by £0·29 m per year. This latter figure is the net social benefit of reducing bus fares.

3. The information given in Table (i) can be interpreted as information about points on the demand curve for 'improvements'.

If no grants were given, the cost to a house owner of improving his house would be £2000 and, in equilibrium, the market value (or 'price') of an improvement would also be £2000. (That is, improved houses would have a price £2000 greater than unimproved houses would have.) There would be 2000 improved houses in the city and no tendency for this number to increase. Thus the number of improvements demanded at the price of £2000 is 2000. Similarly, if grants of 10 per cent were given, the cost to a house owner of improving his house would be £1800. The number of improved houses would tend to that at which the market value of an improvement was £1800 (that is, unimproved houses would sell for £8000 and improved ones for £9800). This number, it has been predicted, would be 2200. This is the number of improvements demanded at the price of £1800. The demand curve that can be plotted from the information given in Table (i) is shown in Figure (i) as the curve *D*.

The effect of the government's policy of introducing 50 per cent grants is to reduce the 'price' or 'market value' of improvements from £2000 to £1000 'Consumers' of houses thus gain in consumers' surplus a sum equal to the shaded strip in the diagram (approximately £2·8 m). Of this £2·8 m, £2·0 m is accounted for by the fall in the market value of the 2000 houses that were improved before the introduction of grants. This gain to 'consumers' is exactly counterbalanced

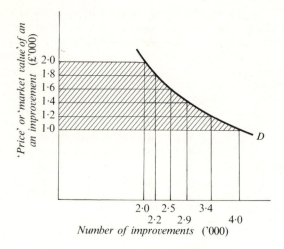

Number of improvements ('000)

Fig. (i)

by an equal and opposite loss to the owners of these houses. ('Consumers' and 'owners' cannot be distinguished as two distinct groups of individuals, for an owner-occupier simultaneously plays both roles.) We are left with a gain of £0·8 m to 'consumers' and 'owners' taken together. This gain has to be set against those costs of improving houses that are borne by the government—that is, the sum paid in grants, £2·0 m. Thus the net effect of the policy of giving 50 per cent grants is a social loss of £1·2 m (£2·0 m *minus* £0·8 m). The policy cannot be justified by reference to the potential Pareto improvement criterion.

CHAPTER 10

1. The two theatres are closed simultaneously. For the purposes of analysis, however, it is convenient to consider the two closures in sequence; one theatre is closed and then, an instant later, the other is closed. To consumers it is a matter of indifference which theatre is closed an instant before the other, and so the loss of consumers' surplus can be evaluated by considering the closures in either order.

Suppose that theatre X closes first, while theatre Y continues to sell tickets at the price p_Y. As a result, theatre-goers lose in consumers' surplus a sum equal to the area *CBE*. The demand curve for tickets for theatre *Y* shifts to D_Y'. Theatre Y is then closed. Consumers lose a sum equal to the area *IGK* (an area to the left of the 'new' demand curve, D_Y'). In total, then, theatre-goers lose the sum of area *CBE* and area *IGK*.

Alternatively, if theatre Y closes first, followed immediately by theatre X, theatre-goers lose the sum of area *IHJ* and area *CAF*.

Since the two alternative measurements are of the same loss to consumers, they are equal. That is, area *CBE plus* area *IGK* is equal to area *IHJ plus* area *CAF*. In other words, the areas *BAFE* and *HGKJ* are equal. (In formal economic theory, this equality is an implication of the theorem of the 'symmetry of (cross-) substitution effects'.)

2. This problem involves two goods, 'unimproved houses' and 'improvements', which are complementary in demand. The government's policy of introducing 50 per cent improvement grants implies a fall in the 'price' of improvements

from £2000 to £1000. This, in turn, induces an increase in the demand for unimproved houses and an increase in their price.

To evaluate the net gain to all owners of, and consumers of, houses taken together, it is necessary to know only the observed demand curve for improvements (the good whose price is affected *directly* by the government's policy). This observed demand curve is precisely the same as the curve shown in Figure (i) in the solution to the original version of this problem (Problem 3, Chapter 9; solution on p. 255). Thus the conclusions reached in relation to the original problem still stand. (The only difference between the two problems is that a pecuniary external effect has been introduced into the present one.) The net effect of the policy of giving 50 per cent improvement grants is a social loss of £1·2 m.

3. In this problem there are two relevant goods, 'output' and 'skilled labour'. The changes in the prices of these goods are represented in Figures (iv) and (v).

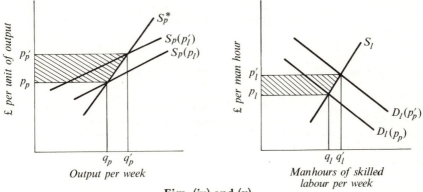

Figs. (iv) and (v)

The initial price of the product is p_p (£20). Given this price, the demand for labour is $D_l(p_p)$. The supply of labour is S_l. The market-determined wage rate is p_l (£1·50) and the quantity of labour employed is q_l (200 000 man hours per week). Given this wage rate, the supply curve for output is $S_p(p_l)$ and the quantity of output produced is q_p (20 000 units per week).

The price of the product then increases to p'_p (£25). This induces a shift in the demand for labour to $D_l(p_p')$, an increase in the wage rate to p'_l ((£1·70) and an increase in the quantity of labour employed to q'_l (225 000 man hours per week). The increase in the wage rate induces a shift in the supply curve for the product to $S_p(p'_l)$. (The marginal cost of any rate of output is higher, the higher the wage rate.) The quantity of output produced is q'_p (24 000 units per week).

Owners of capital gain the shaded area in Figure (iv) (which is associated with a price increase in their favour) *minus* the shaded area in Figure (v) (which is associated with a price increase which is not in their favour). Suppliers of labour gain the shaded area in Figure (v). The shaded area in Figure (iv) thus measures the net gain to owners of capital and suppliers of labour taken together. This area corresponds to the shaded area in Figure (iii) on page 146.

In money units, owners of capital gain approximately £67 500 per week and suppliers of labour gain approximately £42 500 per week. ('Owners of capital' includes those concerned with the production of goods other than the 'output' whose price increased.)

CHAPTER 11

1. Take as the main good in the problem 'trips by public transport'. The effect of closing the rail service would be to increase the opportunity cost price of this good from 29p per trip (20p fare *plus* 15 minutes of travelling time) to 38p (20p fare *plus* 30 minutes). This increase in the 'price' would reduce the quantity demanded from 250 000 trips per year to 150 000. This implies a loss of approximately £18 000 per year in consumers' surplus. (£13 500 per year would be lost by those who continued to use public transport after the railway closed. £4500 per year would be lost by those who no longer used public transport, either because of transferring to travelling by car or because of giving up travelling altogether.) Because the analysis has focussed on the good 'trips by public transport' (rather than 'trips'), there is no need to take any explicit account of the costs of travelling by car. The closure of the rail service—that is, the increase in the 'price' of public transport trips—would have no effect on the cost (per trip) of travelling by car; the area of a strip to the left of the demand curve for public transport trips correctly measures the change in the welfare of consumers that results from a change in the price of these trips. (See Section 10.2.)

The government would gain £17 000 per year from its being relieved of the obligation to subsidize the rail service but would lose £2000 per year because of its corresponding obligation to subsidize the replacement bus service. The net gain to the government (or to taxpayers) would be £15 000 per year.

No other parties would be affected by the closing of the rail service. To close it would lead to a net social loss of £3000 per year.

2. The line *DD* in Figure (i) is the estimate of the demand for visits that can be derived from the information available. (The cost, or opportunity cost price, of a visit includes the entrance charge as well as the cost of travel.)

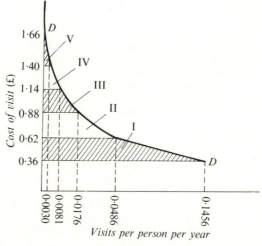

Fig. (i)

By being able to make visits at the opportunity cost price of 36p, the inhabitants of zone A receive in consumers' surplus (per person) the sum of the areas of strips I, II, III, IV and V. The inhabitants of zone B receive (per person) the sum of areas II, III, IV and V; and so on. Thus the total consumers' surplus received by the inhabitants of zones A to E is given by consumers' surplus = (area I × population of zone A) + (area II × population of zones A and B) + (area III × population of zones A, B and C) + (area IV × population of zones A, B, C and D) + (area V × population of zones A, B, C, D and E) = £26 000 per year.

Thus the policy of allowing access with a charge of 10p per person (rather than not allowing access at all) confers benefits of £26 000 per year on consumers. The public agency loses £3260 per year as a result of the policy. The net social benefit is £22 740 per year.

If the entry charge were increased to 36p, the inhabitants of zone A would face an opportunity cost price of 62p per visit—the same as that currently faced by the inhabitants of zone B. According to the estimated demand curve shown in Figure (i), the 90 000 inhabitants of zone A would make 0·0486 visits per person per year—a total of approximately 4400 visits per year. Similar calculations show that from zones B, C, and D and E the numbers of visits per year would be respectively 16 400, 8400, 6000 and 'negligible'. The total number of visits would be 35 200 per year. The agency would earn approximately £12 700 in revenue and incur costs of only £11 000 per year.

3. The original estimate overstates the true benefit. (See Section 11.4, p. 158, for a discussion of a similar problem.)

4. The effect of building the new runway is to decrease the supply of the good 'freedom from noise' from 30 000 units (that is, quiet houses) to 18 000. This causes the price of freedom from noise to rise from £750 to £1200, and causes the price of 'houses' (that is, houses without freedom from noise, or noisy houses) to fall from £11 250 to £11 050. The direction of this latter effect implies that houses and freedom from noise are complementary goods: an increase in the price of freedom from noise is associated with a decrease in the demand for houses.

The crucial construction for tackling this problem is the observed demand curve for freedom from noise. (There is no need to take any explicit account of changes in prices in the market for houses; these are pecuniary external effects of changes in the supply of freedom from noise). The observed demand curve for freedom from noise is shown in D* in Figure (ii). The area *PQTR* measures the net loss borne by people affected by the increase in the price of freedom from noise, whether as 'consumers' of freedom from noise and of the complementary good houses, or as 'suppliers' of the complementary good. All that remains to be

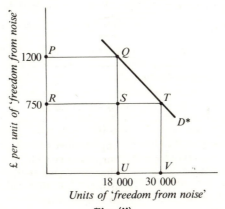

Fig. (ii)

considered is the effect of the price change on suppliers of freedom from noise. Those suppliers who own the 18 000 houses that remain unaffected by noise after the building of the new runway gain the area *PQSR* (the increase in the value of the units of freedom from noise that they own). The less fortunate suppliers who owned the 12 000 units of freedom from noise that were destroyed by the building of the new runway lose the area *STVU*. The net social loss is equal to area *PQTR plus* area *STVU minus* area *PQSR*, which is equal to area *QTVU*. In money units, this net social loss is approximately £11·7 m.

CHAPTER 12

1. (*i*) Two main groups of people would benefit from the flood relief scheme—the shareholders of insurance companies, and the owners of the 150 affected houses.

Insurance companies would benefit because they would be called on to pay less in response to claims. This benefit is approximately measured by the expected value of the payments that would be made for flood damage if the flood relief scheme were not built. Expressed as a present value in the year the scheme would be built, this benefit is £18 900 (8 × 150 × 15·7619) ≃ £18 900.

To the occupiers of flood-affected houses, flooding is a public bad. Or to put this another way, freedom from the risk of flooding is a public good to the occupiers of unaffected houses. However, access to the enjoyment of this public good is priced through the medium of property prices. The market value, and hence individuals' marginal valuations, of 'freedom from flooding' is £250 per house. By providing this good to the occupiers of 150 houses, the flood relief scheme provides a benefit of £37 500. It would be double counting to add to this any 'other' element of benefit accruing to the occupiers of houses as a result of the flood relief scheme.

The total social benefit provided by the flood relief scheme is thus (in present value terms) £56 400.

(*ii*) If there is a probability (greater than zero) that a flood relief scheme will be built, the (uncertain) prospect of the scheme being built is, in a sense, a public good. The value to house occupiers of this uncertain prospect will reveal itself in property values; houses that would benefit if the scheme were built will, by virtue of this fact, possess additional value. Thus some part of the benefits that the flood relief scheme would give are already capitalized in the prices of flood-affected houses. The true value to house occupiers of freedom from flooding is greater than £250 per house; consequently the social benefit of the flood relief scheme is greater than the original estimate of £56 400.

2. The total benefits of the road improvement are greater than £385 000 per year.

Car users and pedestrians must be considered separately. To car users, the risk of being killed or injured is one of the costs of making a trip. The road improvement reduces both the risk of being killed (per trip) and the risk of being injured (per trip). Thus the total opportunity cost of a trip is reduced not only by the money value of 10 minutes of travelling time (5p) but also by the money value of the reduction in these risks (which may be denoted by x). The annual gain in consumers' surplus to car users is approximately $(5p + x)(6·9 \text{ m} + 8·5 \text{ m})/2$, which is greater than £385 000 per year if x is positive.

In contrast, the killing and injuring of pedestrians is an external effect of the making of car trips. Here what is relevant is not the number of casualties per car trip but the number of casualties per year (which is an index of the risks imposed on individual pedestrians). Both the number of pedestrian deaths per year and the number of pedestrian injuries per year are reduced by the road improvement. The project thus provides a positive benefit to pedestrians in addition to the benefits enjoyed by car users.

3. The effect on social welfare of a reduction in the volume of betting is different according to whether one regards the uncertainty of horse races from a viewpoint before the event or after the event (see Section 12.2).

Consider first the after-the-event approach. As a result of the closure of the racecourse, bookmakers (that is, the owners of bookmaking firms) are made worse off by £8000 per year. (Their revenue decreases by £20 000 per year and their costs by £12 000 per year.) Punters are made better off by £20 000 per year. There is a net social benefit of £12 000 per year.

Now consider the before-the-event approach. Because of the 'law of large numbers' it may be assumed that individual bookmakers, at the beginning of each year, know with virtual certainty how much revenue they will earn that year from punters. Thus bookmakers as a whole feel sure, beforethe event, that closing the racecourse will impose on them losses of £8000 per year. Individual punters, however, do not know whether they will gain or lose as a result of their own bets. From the fact that someone chooses to bet it must be inferred that, before the event, he considers himself better off—or, at least, no worse off—with the uncertain claims on wealth that he acquires by betting than with the possession, with certainty, of the sum of money he stakes. Thus each punter is made worse off—or, at least, no better off—by the reduction in his opportunities for betting. Closing the racecourse implies a net social loss of *at least* £8000 per year.

(The fact that people choose to bet at odds which allow bookmakers to earn a steady income can be explained in a number of ways. It may be that those people who gamble are not risk-averse—as we have assumed people in general to be; they are the opposite of risk-averse, preferring uncertainty to certainty. An alternative explanation, which is not inconsistent with the assumption that people are risk-averse, is that punters do not always share bookmakers' subjective judgements about the probabilities of particular outcomes of horse races. Thus punter and bookmaker may each believe that the expected value to himself of a given bet is positive.)

CHAPTER 13

1. Installing grit-arresting equipment produces the good 'freedom from air pollution'; this good can be measured in units of 'grit and dust arrested' (since the total quantity of grit and dust produced at the power stations—12 000 metric tons per year—is not a variable in this problem).

Table (ii) shows the marginal cost, per metric ton, of arresting grit and dust at each power station for each of a range of levels of efficiency of the equipment installed. With the 98·8 per cent efficient equipment actually installed at the two stations, the marginal cost is £113 per metric ton at A and £225 per metric ton at B.

A rational government would seek to achieve that level of pollution control at which the marginal cost of preventing a unit of pollution from occurring is just equal to the marginal social value of freedom from pollution. Thus the decision that station A should have 98·8 per cent efficient equipment implies a judgement that the marginal social value of freedom from pollution is £113 per metric ton of grit and dust arrested. The decision that station B should have 98·8 per cent efficient equipment implies a judgement that the marginal social value of freedom from pollution is £225 per metric ton arrested. The two decisions are inconsistent.

The combined effect of these two decisions is that 11 856 metric tons of grit

Table (ii)

Efficiency (% of grit and dust arrested)	Cost (£'000 per year)	Mass of grit and dust arrested (metric tons per year)		Approximate marginal cost per percentage point of efficiency (£'000 per year)	Approximate marginal cost per metric ton arrested (£)	
		station A	station B		station A	station B
98·0	40·9	7840	3920			
98·2	42·0	7856	3928	5·5	69	138
98·4	43·2	7872	3936	6·0	75	150
98·6	44·7	7888	3944	7·5	94	188
98·8	46·5	7904	3952	9·0	113	225
98·9	47·5	7912	3956	10·0	125	250
99·0	48·6	7920	3960	11·0	138	275
99·1	49·8	7928	3964	12·0	150	300
99·2	51·4	7936	3968	16·0	200	400

and dust are arrested each year at a cost of £93 000 per year. By making different decisions it would be possible to arrest more grit and dust at the same cost (or to arrest the same quantity at less cost). For example, by installing 99·1 per cent efficient equipment at A and 98·4 per cent efficient equipment at B, 11 864 metric tons per year are arrested at the same total cost of £93 000 per year. (Both of these decisions imply the same marginal social value of freedom from pollution—£150 per metric ton of grit and dust arrested.)

2. Let the value of a prevented death be x (measured in thousands of pounds). The present value of the net social benefit of each project is shown in Table (iii), together with the lowest value of x that would imply non-negative net social benefits.

Table (iii)

Project	Net benefit (£'000)		Present value of net benefit (£'000 in year 0)	Present value of net benefit > 0 if $x >$
	year 0	years 1–50		
A	−100	$0·6x$	$-100 + 5·949x$	16·81
B	− 5	$-3·5 + 0·4x$	$- 39·7 + 3·966x$	10·01
A *minus* B	− 95	$3·5 + 0·2x$	$- 60·3 + 1·983x$	30·41
C	−150	$0·8x$	$-150 + 7·932x$	18·91

Which project or projects should be undertaken depends on the value of x:

if $x < 10·01$	none of projects should be undertaken
if $10·01 < x < 18·91$	project B should be undertaken
if $18·91 < x < 30·41$	projects B and C should be undertaken
if $30·41 < x$	projects A and C should be undertaken.

Thus in case (*i*), the authority's decision to undertake only project B implies a valuation of a prevented death in the range £10 010 to £18 910. In case (*ii*), the decision to undertake A and C implies a valuation greater than or equal to £30 410. In case (*iii*), the decision to undertake only project C is not consistent with any valuation of prevented deaths.

3. (*i*) This problem involves two parties—the consumers of the treatment and the health authority that supplies this treatment. ('The authority' is a proxy for the taxpayers who finance it.) By choosing the less, rather than the more, accessible site for the hospital, the opportunity cost price of the good 'visits for treatment' is increased from £1·20 per visit to £1·50 per visit. The quantity of this good demanded falls from 10 000 visits per year to 8500 visits per year. The associated loss of consumers' surplus is approximately £2775 per year. The health authority makes financial savings of £3000 per year from being called on to supply treatment for 1500 fewer visits each year. The net effect of choosing the less accessible site is thus a social *benefit* of £225 per year. (This result may seem paradoxical. The explanation lies in the fact that the authority is providing free of charge a good, 'treatment', which is not costless to produce. Whichever site is chosen, the marginal value of the good to its consumers—net of costs of time and travelling—is zero, while the marginal cost of producing it is £2·00. According to the potential Pareto improvement criterion, too much of the good is being produced and consumed. Choosing the less accessible site leads to less being produced and consumed and this, in itself, increases social welfare.)

(*ii*) If the more accessible site is chosen, each year 10 000 visits are made at a total cost to patients of £12 000. This corresponds to a social cost since patients are accepted as the best judges of the value of their own time and travelling costs. The treatment that they receive has a total social value of £38 000 (using the postulated value of £3·80 per visit). The excess of benefits over patient-borne costs is £26 000. If the less accessible site is chosen, patient-borne costs are £12 750, the social value of the treatment received is £32 300, and the excess of the latter over the former is £19 550. As far as these elements of cost and benefit are concerned, choosing the less accessible site imposes a net social loss of £6450 per year. From this net loss must be deducted the savings made by the health authority from supplying fewer treatments. These savings are £3000 per year. In all, the net effect of choosing the less accessible site is to impose a net social loss of £3450 per year.

References

Abelson, P. W. *and* Flowerdew, A. D. J. (1972), 'Roskill's successful recommendation', *Journal of the Royal Statistical Society*, Series A, vol. 135.

Alchian, A. A. (1953), 'The meaning of utility measurement', *American Economic Review*, vol. 43. Reprinted in Breit, W. *and* Hochman, H. M. (eds.) (1968), *Readings in Microeconomics*, Holt, Rinehart & Winston.

Anderson, R. J. *and* Crocker, T. D. (1971), 'Air pollution and property values', *Urban Studies*, vol. 8.

Arrow, K. J. (1966), 'Discounting and public investment criteria', in Kneese, A. V. *and* Smith, S. C. (eds.) (1966), *Water Research*, Resources for the Future, Baltimore.

—— *and* Lind, R. C. (1970), 'Uncertainty and the evaluation of public investment decisions', *American Economic Review*, vol. 60.

Bacha, E. *and* Taylor, L. (1971), 'Foreign exchange shadow prices: a critical review of current theories', *Quarterly Journal of Economics*, vol. 85.

Ball, M. J. (1973), 'Recent empirical work on the determinants of relative house prices', *Urban Studies*, vol. 10.

Baumol, W. J. (1968), 'On the social rate of discount', *American Economic Review*, vol. 58.

—— *and* Quandt, R. E. (1965), 'Investment and discount rates under capital rationing—a programming approach', *Economic Journal*, vol. 75.

Bayes, T. (1763), 'An essay toward solving a problem in the doctrine of chances', *Philosophical Transactions of the Royal Society*, 1763, vol. 53, pp. 370—418.

Beesley, M. E. (1965), 'The value of time spent travelling: some new evidence', *Economica*, vol. 32.

—— *and* Foster, C. D. (1965), 'The Victoria Line: social benefit and finances', *Journal of the Royal Statistical Society*, Series A, vol. 128.

Bergson, A. (1938), 'A reformulation of certain aspects of welfare economics', *Quarterly Journal of Economics*, vol. 52. Reprinted in Bergson, A. (1966), *Essays in Normative Economics*, Harvard University Press.

Bierman, H. *and* Smidt, S. (1975), *The Capital Budgeting Decision*, 4th edn., Macmillan.

Blaug, M. (1967), 'The private and the social returns on investment in education: some results for Great Britain', *Journal of Human Resources*, vol. 2.

—— (1970), *An Introduction to the Economics of Education*, Penguin.

Boadway, R. W. (1974), 'The welfare foundations of cost-benefit analysis', *Economic Journal*, vol. 84.

Bonnen, J. T. (1968), 'The distribution of benefits from cotton price supports', in Chase, S. B. (ed.) (1968), *Problems in Public Expenditure Analysis*, The Brookings Institution, Washington D.C.

Braybrooke, D. *and* Lindblom, C. E. (1963), *A Strategy of Decision: Policy Evaluation as a Social Process*, Free Press of Glencoe.

Breton, A. (1974), *The Economic Theory of Representative Government*, Macmillan.

Buchanan, J. M. (1968), *The Demand and Supply of Public Goods*, Rand McNally.

—— *and* Thirlby, G. F. (eds.) (1973), *L.S.E. Essays on Cost*, Weidenfeld and Nicolson.

—— *and* Tullock, G. (1962), *The Calculus of Consent: Logical Foundations of Constitutional Democracy*, University of Michigan Press.

Burns, M. E. (1973), 'A note on the concept and measure of consumer's surplus', *American Economic Review*, vol. 63.

Charnes, A., Cooper, W. W., *and* Miller, M. H. (1959), 'Application of linear programming to financial budgeting and the costing of funds', *Journal of Business*, vol. 32. Reprinted in Solomon, E. (1959) (ed.), *The Management of Corporate Capital*, Free Press (New York).

Clawson, M. (1959), *Methods of Measuring the Demand for and Value of Outdoor Recreation*, Reprint No. 10, Resources for the Future, Washington D.C.

Coburn, T. M., Beesley, M. E., *and* Reynolds, D. J. (1960), *The London–Birmingham Motorway, Traffic and Economics,* Road Research Technical Paper No. 46, H.M.S.O.

Cooper, M. H. *and* Culyer, A. J. (eds.) (1973), *Health Economics*, Penguin.

Currie, J. M., Murphy, J. A., *and* Schmitz, A. (1971), 'The concept of economic surplus and its use in economic analysis', *Economic Journal*, vol. 81.

Culyer, A. J., Lavers, R., *and* Williams, A. (1971), 'Social indicators: health', *Social Trends*, no. 3.

Dasgupta, P. (1972), 'A comparative analysis of the U.N.I.D.O. guidelines and the O.E.C.D. manual', *Bulletin of the Oxford University Institute of Economics and Statistics*, vol. 34.

—— Marglin, S., *and* Sen, A. K. (1972), *Guidelines for Project Evaluation*, United Nations Industrial Development Organization.

Dawson, R. F. F. (1967), *Cost of Road Accidents in Great Britain*, Road Research Laboratory, Ministry of Transport. Excerpt reprinted in Cooper, M. H., *and* Culyer, A. J. (eds.) (1973), *Health Economics*, Penguin.

Department of the Environment (1976), *Transport Policy: A Consultation Document* (2 vols.), H.M.S.O.

Diamond, P. (1968), 'The opportunity costs of public investment: comment', *Quarterly Journal of Economics*, vol. 82.

—— *and* Mirrlees, J. A. (1971), 'Optimal taxation and public production', *American Economic Review*, vol. 61.

Dorfman, R. (1953), 'Mathematical or "linear" programming: a non-mathematical exposition', *American Economic Review*, vol. 43. Reprinted in Archibald, G. C. (ed.) (1971), *The Theory of the Firm*, Penguin.

—— (1962), 'Basic economic and technological concepts: a general statement', in Maass, A. *et al.* (1962), *Design of Water Resource Systems*, Harvard University Press. Excerpt reprinted in Layard, R. (ed.) (1972), *Cost-Benefit Analysis*, Penguin.

—— Samuelson, P. *and* Solow, R. (1958), *Linear Programming and Economic Analysis*, McGraw-Hill.

Downs, A. (1957), *An Economic Theory of Democracy*, Harper.

Dreze, J. H. (1974), 'Discount rates and public investment: a post-scriptum', *Economica*, vol. 41.

Feldstein, M. S. (1972), 'The inadequacy of weighted discount rates', in Layard, R. (ed.) (1972), *Cost-Benefit Analysis*, Penguin.

Fisher, I. (1930), *The Theory of Interest*, Macmillan.

Flowerdew, A. D. J. (1972), 'Choosing a site for the third London Airport: the Roskill Commission's approach', in Layard, R. (ed.) (1972), *Cost-Benefit Analysis*, Penguin.

Foster, C. D. *and* Beesely, M. E. (1963), 'Estimating the social benefit of constructing an underground railway in London', *Journal of the Royal Statistical Society*, Series A, vol. 126.

Green, H. A. J. (1971), *Consumer Theory*, Penguin.

Gwilliam, K. M. *and* Mackie, P. J. (1975), *Economics and Transport Policy*, George Allen and Unwin.

Harberger, A. C. (1964), 'Taxation, resource allocation and welfare', *The Role of Direct and Indirect Taxes in the Federal Revenue System*, conference report of the National Bureau of Economic Research and the Brookings Institution, Princeton University Press.

—— (1966), 'Efficiency effects of taxes on income and capital', in Krzyzaniak, M. (ed.) (1966), *Effects of Corporation Income Tax*, Wayne State University Press.

—— (1969), 'Professor Arrow on the social discount rate', in Somers, G. G. *and* Wood, W. D. (eds.) (1969), *Cost-Benefit Analysis of Manpower Policies: Proceedings of a North American Conference*, Queens University, Kingston, Ontario. Excerpt reprinted in Layard, R. (ed.) (1972), *Cost-Benefit Analysis*, Penguin.

—— (1971), 'Three basic postulates for applied welfare economics', *Journal of Economic Literature*, vol. 9.

Harrison, A. J. (1974), *The Economics of Transport Appraisal*, Croom Helm.

—— *and* Quarmby, D. A. (1972), 'The value of time in transport planning: a review', in Layard, R. (ed.) (1972), *Cost-Benefit Analysis*, Penguin. (Paper originally presented to a European Conference of Ministers of Transport, Paris, 1969.)

Harsanyi, J. C. (1955), 'Cardinal welfare, individualistic ethics, and interpersonal comparisons of utility', *Journal of Political Economy*, vol. 63.

Hart, H. (1973), *Overhead Costs: Analysis and Control*, Heinemann.

Hey, J. D. (1974), *Statistics in Economics*, Martin Robertson.

Hicks, J. R. (1944), 'The four consumers' surpluses', *Review of Economic Studies*, vol. 12.

—— (1946), 'Quelques applications de la theorie des surplus du consommateur', *Bulletin de l'Institut de Science Economique Appliquee*.

—— (1956), *A Revision of Demand Theory*, Clarendon Press.

Hirshleifer, J. (1958), 'On the theory of the optimal investment decision', *Journal of Political Economy*, vol. 66.

—— (1965), 'Investment decision under uncertainty: choice-theoretic approaches', *Quarterly Journal of Economics*, vol. 79.

—— (1966), 'Investment decision under uncertainty: applications of the state-preference approach', *Quarterly Journal of Economics*, vol. 80.

H.M.S.O. (1967), *Nationalised Industries: A Review of Economic and Financial Objectives*, cmnd. 3437.

—— (1970), *Coal Prices (Second Report)*, Report 153 of the National Board for Prices and Incomes, cmnd. 4455.

Hoinville, G. (1969), 'Evaluating community preferences', in Institute of Municipal Treasurers and Accountants (1969), *Cost-Benefit Analysis in the Public Sector*.

Hughes, J. J. (1970), *Cost-Benefit Aspects of Manpower Retraining*, Department of Employment and Productivity, H.M.S.O.

Jones-Lee, M. W. (1976), *The Value of Life: An Economic Anlaysis*, Martin Robertson and Chicago University Press.

Kane, E. J. (1968), *Economic Statistics and Econometrics*, Harper.

Kay, J. A. (1972), 'Social discount rates', *Journal of Public Economics*, vol. 1.

Klarman, H. E., Francis, J. O'S., *and* Rosenthal, G. D. (1968), 'Cost effectiveness analysis applied to the treatment of chronic renal disease', *Medical Care*, vol.

6. Reprinted in Cooper, J. H. *and* Culyer, A. J. (eds.) (1973), *Health Economics*, Penguin.

Krutilla, J. V., *and* Eckstein, O. (1958), *Multiple Purpose River Development*, Johns Hopkins.

Laidler, D. (1974), *Introduction to Microeconomics*, Philip Allan.

Lavers, R. (1972), 'The implicit valuation of forms of hospital treatment', in Hauser, M. M. (ed.) (1972), *The Economics of Medical Care*, Allen and Unwin.

Layard, R. (1972), 'Introduction', in Layard, R. (ed.) (1972), *Cost-Benefit Analysis*, Penguin.

Lind, R. C. (1964), 'The social rate of discount and the optimal rate of investment: further comment', *Quarterly Journal of Economics*, vol. 78.

Lindblom, C. E. (1959), 'The science of muddling through', *Public Administration Review*, vol. 19.

Lipsey, R. G. *and* Lancaster, K. (1956), 'A general theory of the second best', *Review of Economic Studies*, vol. 24.

Little, I. M. D. (1957), *A Critique of Welfare Economics*, 2nd edn., Clarendon Press.

—— *and* Mirrlees, J. A. (1969), *Manual of Industrial Project Analysis in Developing Countries*, vol. II, O.E.C.D.

—— *and* Mirrlees, J. A. (1972), 'A reply to some criticisms of the O.E.C.D. manual', *Bulletin of the Oxford University Institute of Economics and Statistics*, vol. 34.

—— *and* Mirrlees, J. A. (1974), *Project Appraisal and Planning for Developing Countries*, Heinemann.

Maass, A. (1966), 'Benefit-cost analysis: its relevance to public investment decisions', *Quarterly Journal of Economics*, vol. 80.

McGuire, M. C. *and* Garn, H. A. (1969), 'The integration of equity and efficiency criteria in public project selection', *Economic Journal*, vol. 79.

McKean, R. N. (1968), 'The use of shadow prices', in Chase, S. B. (ed.) (1968), *Problems in Public Expenditure Analysis*, The Brookings Institution, Washington D. C. Also in Layard, R. (1972), op. cit.

Mansfield, N. W. (1971), 'The estimation of benefits from recreation sites', *Regional Studies*, vol. 5.

Marshall, A. (1920), *Principles of Economics*, 8th edn. Macmillan.

Marglin, S. A. (1963a), 'The social rate of discount and the optimal rate of investment', *Quarterly Journal of Economics*, vol. 77.

—— (1963b), 'The opportunity costs of public investment', *Quarterly Journal of Economics*, vol. 77.

Mera, K. (1969), 'Experimental determination of relative marginal utilities', *Quarterly Journal of Economics*, vol. 83.

Merewitz, L. *and* Sosnick, S. H. (1971), *The Budget's New Clothes: a Critique of Planning-Programming-Budgeting and Benefit-Cost Analysis*, Markham.

Merrett, A. J., *and* Sykes, A. (1973), *The Finance and Analysis of Capital Projects*, 2nd edn., Longman.

Millward, R. (1971), *Public Expenditure Economics*, McGraw-Hill.

Ministry of Transport (1969), *The Cambrian Coast Line*, H.M.S.O.

Mishan, E. J. (1960), 'A survey of welfare economics', *Economic Journal*, vol. 70.

—— (1968), 'What is producer's surplus?', *American Economic Review*, vol. 58.

—— (1971a), *Cost-Benefit Analysis*, George Allen and Unwin.

—— (1971b), 'Evaluation of life and limb: a theoretical approach', *Journal of Political Economy*, vol. 79.

—— (1974), 'Flexibility and consistency in project evaluation', *Economica*, vol. 41.

Musgrave, R. A. (1959), *The Theory of Public Finance*, McGraw-Hill.
  —— (1969), 'Cost-benefit analysis and the theory of public finance', *Journal of Economic Literature*, vol. 7. Reprinted in Layard, R. (ed.) (1972), *Cost-Benefit Analysis*.
Nath, S. K. (1969), *A Reappraisal of Welfare Economics*, Routledge and Kegan Paul.
Needleman, L. (1969), 'The comparative economics of improvement and new building', *Urban Studies*, vol. 6.
Niskanen, W. A. (1971), *Bureaucracy and Representative Government*, Aldine.
Olson, M. (1965), *The Logic of Collective Action*, Harvard University Press.
Pearce, D. W. *and* Nash, C. (1973), 'The evaluation of urban motorway schemes: a case study—Southampton', *Urban Studies*, vol. 10.
Raiffa, H. (1968), *Decision Analysis*, Addison-Wesley.
Ramsey, D. D. (1969), 'On the social rate of discount: comment', *American Economic Review*, vol. 59.
Ramsey, F. P. (1931), 'Truth and probability', in *The Foundations of Mathematics, and other Logical Essays*, London.
Rawls, J. (1971), *A Theory of Justice*, Harvard University Press.
Ridker, R. *and* Henning, J. (1967), 'The determination of residential property values with special reference to air pollution', *Review of Economics and Statistics*, vol. 49.
Roskill (1970), *Commission on the Third London Airport, Papers and Proceedings*, vol. 7, H.M.S.O.
Sandmo, A. *and* Dreze, J. H. (1971), 'Discount rates for public investment in open and closed economies', *Economica*, vol. 38.
Schelling, T. C. (1968), 'The life you save may be your own', in Chase, S. B. (ed.), (1968), *Problems in Public Expenditure Analysis*, The Brookings Institution, Washington D. C. Excerpt reprinted in Cooper, M. H. *and* Culyer, A. J. (eds.) (1973), *Health Economics*, Penguin.
Self, P. (1975), *Econocrats and the Policy Process*, Macmillan.
Sen, A. K. (1961), 'On optimizing the rate of saving', *Economic Journal*, vol. 71.
  —— (1967), 'Isolation, assurance and the social rate of discount', *Quarterly Journal of Economics*, vol. 81.
  —— (1972), 'Control areas and accounting prices: an approach to economic evaluation', *Economic Journal*, vol. 82.
Sidgwick, H. (1907), *The Method of Ethics*, 7th edn., Macmillan.
Smith, R. D. (1971), 'The evaluation of recreation benefits: the Clawson model in practice', *Urban Studies*, vol. 8.
Somers, G. G. *and* Wood, W. D. (eds) (1969), *Cost-Benefit Analysis of Manpower Policies: Proceedings of a North American Conference*, Queens University, Kingston, Ontario.
Sugden, R. (1972), 'Cost-benefit analysis and the withdrawal of railway services', *Bulletin of Economic Research*, vol. 24.
  —— (1974), 'On the political economy of social discount rates', in Culyer, A. J. (ed.) (1974), *Economic Policies and Social Goals*, Martin Robertson.
Thomas, J. J. (1973), *An Introduction to Statistical Analysis for Economists*, Weidenfeld and Nicolson.
Tullock, G. (1964), 'The social rate of discount and the optimal rate of investment: comment', *Quarterly Journal of Economics*, vol. 78.
  —— (1976), *The Vote Motive*, Institute of Economic Affairs.
Turvey, R. (1971), *Economic Analysis and Public Enterprises*, George Allen and Unwin.

Usher, D. (1964), 'The social rate of discount and the optimal rate of investment: comment', *Quarterly Journal of Economics*, vol. 78.

—— (1969), 'On the social rate of discount: comment', *American Economic Review*, vol. 59.

von Neumann, J. *and* Morgenstern, O. (1947), *Theory of Games and Economic Behaviour*, 2nd edn., Wiley.

Wabe, J. S. (1971), 'A study of house prices as a means of establishing the value of time, the rate of time preference and the valuation of some aspects of environment in the London Metropolitan Region', *Applied Economics*, vol. 3.

Walters, A. A. (1975), *Noise and Prices*, Clarendon Press.

Weisbrod, B. A. (1968), 'Income redistribution effects and benefit-cost analysis', in Chase, S. B. (ed.) (1968), *Problems in Public Expenditure Analysis*, The Brookings Institution, Washington D.C.

—— (1971), 'Costs and benefits of medical research: a case study of poliomyelitis', *Journal of Political Economy*, vol. 79.

Wildavsky, A. (1966), 'The political economy of efficiency: cost-benefit analysis, systems analysis and program budgeting', *Public Administration Review*, vol. 26.

—— (1969), 'Rescuing policy analysis from PPBS', *Public Administration Review*, vol. 29.

Wildsmith, J. R. (1973), *Managerial Theories of the Firm*, Martin Roberton.

Williams, A. (1972), 'Cost-benefit analysis: bastard science? and/or insidious poison in the body politick?', *Journal of Public Economics*, vol. 1.

—— *and* Anderson, R. (1975), *Efficiency in the Social Services*, Basil Blackwell and Martin Robertson.

Winch, D. M. (1971), *Analytical Welfare Economics*, Penguin.

Ziderman, A. (1969), 'Costs and benefits of adult retraining in the U.K.', *Economica*, vol. 36.

—— (1973), 'Does it pay to take a degree?', *Oxford Economic Papers*, New Series, vol. 25.

—— (1975), 'Costs and benefits of manpower training programmes in Great Britain', *British Journal of Industrial Relations*, vol. 13.

Index